Born in Malta in 1933, Edward de Bono attended
St Edward's College, Malta, during the war, and
then Malta University. Having obtained a degree
in medicine, he then proceeded as a Rhodes Scholar
to Christ Church, Oxford, where he gained an
honours degree in psychology and physiology and
then a D.Phil. in medicine. He also holds a Ph.D.
from Cambridge. He has held appointments at the
universities of Oxford, London, Cambridge and
Harvard.

Dr de Bono has been Assistant Director of Research in the Department of Investigative Medicine
at the University of Cambridge since 1963, and
Director of the Cognitive Research Trust,
Cambridge, since 1971.

Among his publications are *The Use of Lateral
Thinking* (1967), *The Five-Day Course in Thinking*
(1969), *The Mechanism of Mind* (1969), *Lateral
Thinking* (1970), *The Dog-Exercising Machine* (1970),
Technology Today (1971), *Practical Thinking* (1971),
Lateral Thinking for Management (1971), *Po: Beyond
Yes and No* (1972), *Children Solve Problems* (1972),
Eureka!, an illustrated history of inventions from
the wheel to the computer (1974), *Teaching Thinking*
(1976), *The Greatest Thinkers* (1976), *The Happiness
Purpose* (1977) and *The Edward de Bono Science Fiction
Collection* (edited by George Hay, with an intro-
duction by Edward de Bono; 1976). Many of these
have been published in Penguins. Dr de Bono has
also contributed to several journals, including the
Lancet and *Clinical Science*. He is married and has
two sons.

Penguin Books Ltd, Harmondsworth,
Middlesex, England
Penguin Books, 625 Madison Avenue,
New York, New York 10022, U.S.A.
Penguin Books Australia Ltd, Ringwood,
Victoria, Australia
Penguin Books Canada Ltd, 2801 John Street,
Markham, Ontario, Canada L3R 1B4
Penguin Books (N.Z.) Ltd, 182–190 Wairau Road,
Auckland 10, New Zealand

First published by Pierrot Publishing Ltd 1977
Published in Penguin Books 1979
Reprinted 1980

ILLUSTRATED BY GEORGE CRAIG
DESIGNED BY ALEX VINING
IAN LOGAN ASSOCIATES

Made and printed in Great Britain by
Richard Clay (The Chaucer Press) Ltd,
Bungay, Suffolk

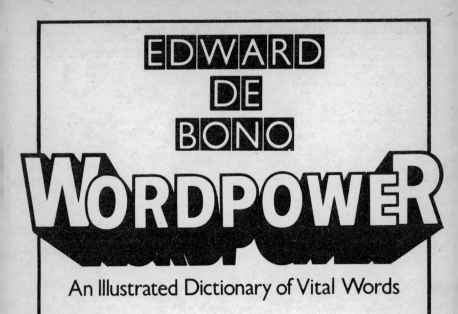

EDWARD DE BONO

WORDPOWER

An Illustrated Dictionary of Vital Words

PENGUIN BOOKS

Wordpower is to the mind what horse-power is to a car.

Just as petrol is the fuel of a car so ideas are the fuel which keeps the mind running. But there has to be a way of turning this fuel into something tangible and real. In a car there is an engine which turns the fuel into motive power. In the mind we have 'words' which take ideas and group them together to make them tangible and usable. Words are convenience packages. With the right word you may express a complicated idea that would be difficult to express without that word. Take the idea of 'trade-off'. This implies that you may want two different things: for example you may want to live in a house near to your work and yet you may want a large house. If you work in a town you may not be able to realise both your wants. You may have to trade-off one against the other, giving up your nearness to work in order to get the house you want. The concept can be explained in a roundabout way but the word 'trade-off' provides a simple way of expressing the whole situation.

The difference between an educated and an uneducated person is not usually a matter of intelligence or even of knowledge. It is simply that the educated person has a bigger stock of concepts with which to express himself. But even the educated person may not have available some of the useful concepts that are continually emerging in language, especially in such fields as management and systems behaviour. Many of these concepts and words are very valuable in ordinary life because they express in a crisp manner an important process. This book is intended to provide a range of such concepts to add to a person's repertoire and so to his education.

The book can help to explain concepts that you may come across in reading, but its main purpose is to put forward concepts that the reader can use in the *expression* of his thoughts. Normally we use a dictionary if we come across a word we do not know, but we do not look through the dictionary to find useful *new* words. This is because the explanation in the dictionary is necessarily much too short to familiarise us with a new concept. It is only in rare cases that you would be able to use a new word having read it merely in the dictionary. But in this book each word is treated at much greater length and especially in terms of the *usable meaning* and context of the word. So a person can read through the book and enrich his supply of concepts and words.

Words often have many meanings. The obvious meanings are not given in this book. For instance the words hedge, peak, field, hunting, muscle and window are all common words with straightforward meanings. What is more interesting is their specialised and useful meanings which are often not given in dictionaries. For example 'hedge' is used in investment terms to mean setting up one risk to balance another. Peak is used in the sense of an athlete or singer who has 'peaked' or passed the summit of performance and is now on the way down; unemployment figures may also have 'peaked'. Field is not just a place with cows and grass but a magnetic field or force field which affects everything within it. The ordinary word 'hunting' is extremely important in control systems since it implies a state of wildly swinging control. 'Muscle' is applied to the power and force of an organisation as in the 'marketing muscle' of a multi-national corporation. 'Window' can refer to the 'launch window' of an Apollo rocket, that is to any short period of time during which something becomes possible.

There are words which a reader may vaguely know but about whose meaning he is not sure enough to be able to use them with ease. Yet these may be powerful and useful words. Such words include: cybernetic, existentialism, transducer, eclectic, hormone, metasystem, rhetoric, sophistry, cloning and chauvinism. Reading about them in this book may make all the difference between understanding such words when one comes across them and being able to use them oneself.

From the world of business and management come many powerful words which have developed to describe the live processes that go on in that world. In contrast to the academic world which is a world of description, the business world is a world of action and special words have developed to describe in a direct way some complicated processes. Such words include: marginal, added value, through-put, cash-cow, know-how, franchise, counter-productive, lagtime, multiplier and downside-risk.

From the world of systems and systems behaviour come a variety of words that can be applied to everyday use and are already part of everyday language: positive and negative feedback, step-function, curve, regulator, modulation, ceiling, trigger, quantum jump, order of magnitude and cycle. Our understanding of systems processes is much greater than it has ever been and it is necessary to capture this understanding with suitable concepts and words. These words have to come from the people who understand systems and are not likely to come from the descriptive or literary world.

Psychology provides another source of new and useful expressions. These are not the specialised words or jargon that are sometimes used in the literature of psychology but words that have originated in psychology usage but have a proper place in ordinary language. Such words include: pecking order, self-fulfilling, peer-group, empathy, interface, lateral thinking, conditioning, behaviourism, subliminal and game-playing.

There are also vivid words and expressions that have arisen in common language (mainly in the United States) which deserve to survive because they describe in a graphic way situations that can otherwise only be inadequately expressed. Words are but concept handles. Some of these are new words and others are new meanings for old words. For example the word 'uptight' describes in a marvellously visual fashion a person who is tense and over-reactive about some issue. 'Ball-game' especially in the phrase 'different ball-game' is a neat way of saying that the rules of behaviour of a particular universe are different or have changed. 'Catch-22' from Joseph Heller's novel of that name defines in an inimitable way a situation which appears fair but which a person cannot possibly win. Even an ordinary word like 'cosmetic' acquires a much wider meaning when it is applied to any situation where a proposed change is merely for appearances; for example, 'That new worker–management committee is just cosmetic.'

From the world of medicine comes another batch of words that have found their way into general use. These include: genes, sensitise, epidemic, therapeutic, homeostasis, digest, immunise, enzymes, carrier and cloning.

In general it seems likely that our biggest source of language enrichment in the future will be the 'systems behaviour' area. This is because an understanding of dynamic and interactive systems means a whole new way of looking at *processes* rather than just at *things*. For this purpose we are only now beginning to build an adequate vocabulary. When we have built this vocabulary and assimilated the related concepts our understanding of the world around will be much improved. This I see as the next quantum step in our cultural development. That is why so many expressions come from those areas such as business, medicine and psychology which deal with complex interacting systems where you have to describe what is going on rather than what it looks like.

This book is not meant to be a book of difficult or rare words. On the contrary it is meant to include those words which are partly familiar because they are already in use. These are the words which we would like to get to know better in order to be able to express our own thoughts through them. The words in this book are 'thinking chunks'.

Edward de Bono

There is a wordlist on the back page.

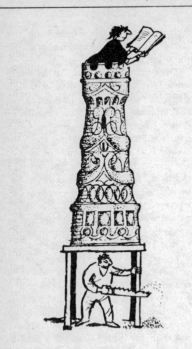

Learning for the sake of learning and knowledge for the sake of knowledge is the characteristic of an academic. Scholarship tends to become the triumph of form over content. A person may spend his life in deep scholarly study of five years in the life of a Persian poet who lived in the thirteenth century. Another person may become the world expert on one type of ladybird.

The habit of knowledge for knowledge's sake was established by the ancient Greek philosophers and especially the mathematicians amongst them. Mathematics seems to carry its own justification. One thing leads to another and now and again there occur synthesising ideas which suddenly pull everything together (for example Descartes' development of analytical geometry). It is supposed that as this knowledge for knowledge's sake progresses certain basic laws of nature will be discovered and then these can be taken over and applied by the practical man or technician.

The opposite point of view holds that too many minds are wasted in academic tail-chasing and that if we devoted our energies to the solving of practical problems then there would be enough spin-off from this to keep basic knowledge expanding. The divide between academic endeavour and practical problem solving certainly seems to be widening. This tends to happen because an academic seeks academic promotion and needs to demonstrate an output rather than a failed attempt to tackle an important but difficult problem. So the academic tailors his problem to suit his talent, and this becomes an end in itself.

Academics are supposed to live in ivory towers and to pursue knowledge for its own sake without regard to practical considerations. It is said that Euclid instructed his servant to give a few coins to a pupil who wanted to know whether the geometry he was studying had any practical use. Knowledge has its own momentum. If something is half known then the academic seeks to complete that knowledge. The practical man may claim that the half that is known is the most important half and that much can be done with it even before the rest is discovered. This has certainly been the case with medicine where doctors know very little about the action of such useful drugs as aspirin and colchicine (for gout).

There are supposed to be a group of people who are 'high achievers' which must mean that there are other people who are low achievers and others who are ordinary achievers. The high achievers work hard at school and in later life. They are driven not by fear of failure or by fear of punishment but by the need to achieve: the need to pass an examination or obtain a qualification; the need to make something happen. For a high achiever there is a pure joy in making something happen (for example setting up one's own business) or in completing some task (for example weeding the garden).

The achievement involved in building a brick wall is definite. The wall stands where there was no wall before. It is difficult to get as strong a sense of achievement from writing a book. Physically the book may be written and published but unless it seems to be appreciated by being bought and read and favourably reviewed the achievement is not there.

Achievement which depends on the judgement of other people is tantalising but elusive.

Does achievement consist in doing something outstanding like climbing Everest or rowing single-handed across the Atlantic, or does it also consist in doing something like growing your own tomatoes or decorating the bedroom? Is it achievement in the eyes of the world that matters, like being a politician or a television interviewer, or is it a contract of achievement between oneself and oneself like a woodcarver who never shows his carvings to anyone or makes any attempt to sell them? It would seem that the psychology of achievement operates just as well at either of these levels. The person who finds achievement in climbing Everest has simply chosen that method of achievement; it is not that more personal and less public methods are too tame for him. Churchill is said to have derived a sense of achievement both from politics and from painting or building brick walls in his garden. The hobbies of famous men provide areas in which they can find a sense of achievement that does not depend on others. It could be said that the more simple one's choice of a sphere of achievement the more likely there is to be a sense of achievement. As in so many areas expectations and the ability to fulfil them are what matter.

Anyone who earns a living must claim that his efforts have added value to some product or service. A corner shop makes a profit on the goods it sells because it has added the value of convenience, choice and short travelling distance. A supermarket would claim to have added a bigger choice and the economies of self-service which allow for lower pricing.

The iron ore that is mined in Western Australia could be exported directly to Japan in bulk carriers. The miners would charge for the value of owning the ore and for the added value of getting it out of the ground. If the ore is converted into steel before shipment then there is the added value of this conversion. If the steel is formed into girders, wires and sheets then there is the added value of this shaping. If the steel is made into specific products like motor cars and refrigerators then there is even more added value. The price at which the final product is sold to Japan would reflect the value that had been added in Australia rather than in Japan. It could happen, of course, that the Japanese would not be interested in paying for this value added in Australia since it would mean that their own producers of refrigerators or cars would be put out of business.

An artist might buy up some plain white dresses at a low price and then hand-paint designs on them. The painted dresses would then be sold at a high price. If the artist had a famous name the disclosure of this name might constitute further added value both in terms of snob appeal and in terms of the dresses becoming collectors' items.

There are times when a purchaser does not want the added value. A young couple might prefer to buy unpainted furniture and paint it themselves. An electronics freak might prefer to build his own hi-fi set from components. The Japanese, in the example above, might prefer to do their own steel processing. What does sometimes seem unfair is that the person who adds value somewhere downstream can make more profit than the original producer (as may happen in the case of farmers and agricultural produce). Transport is an added value which many people ignore; the fact that something you want is available to you in a shop is a value added to its intrinsic value.

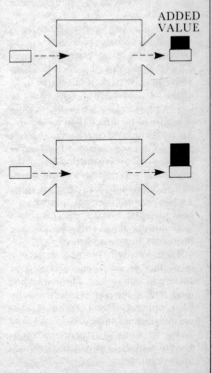

ADDED VALUE

There is a famous Dutch story about the young boy who put his finger into a hole in the dyke so plugging a leak that would otherwise have gone on growing until the whole dyke was breached. There is also the story of a vicar who put out a fire in a church steeple by urinating on it. Both these examples would qualify as ad hoc solutions to a problem.

There may be planned responses to a situation, such as contingency plans for using troops for essential services during a prolonged general strike. There may be packets of routine solutions that can be put into effect to solve a problem, such as a doctor's use of aspirin as the first step in treatment. An ad hoc approach is one that is not planned but which is put together at the moment to solve the problem of the moment. I was once in a country cottage without an iron to press my shirt. The ad hoc solution was to heat up a heavy iron frying pan, insert it into a large brown paper envelope and use the contraption as an iron.

Traditionally ad hoc equipment in a laboratory is supposed to consist of string and sealing wax. The first ad hoc model of a hovercraft made up by Christopher Cockerell consisted of a vacuum cleaner and a cocoa tin. Many ad hoc responses to a situation or problem have subsequently turned into useful inventions.

The advantage of an ad hoc solution is that it does not require planning or foresight. There is also a certain exhilaration in being able to solve the problem at all. The ad hoc solution is likely to be original because it arises from the actual circumstances rather than a repertoire of solutions. For instance in architecture an ad hoc solution to a problem need not be derived from established styles; it is likely to be original – if quite probably ugly.

The political policy of 'drift and cope' relies on the development of problems to the point where they need a solution and then applying an ad hoc solution which solves the problem. If the boat springs a leak put a patch over the leak and drift on. The cure of the leak does not, of course, have any effect on the direction of the boat.

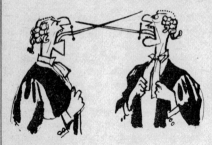

The adversary system has penetrated so deeply into our culture that we could be said to be dependent on it. We translate the heroics of a Horatio on the bridge, the glorious combat of two armies, the enjoyment of a boxing match, the clash between two stags for domination of the herd into a way of thinking. Schoolboys are taught debating skills. Politics is run on the basis that one side is right and the other wrong and that skilled argument can sort out which is which.

The German philosopher Hegel proposed that all development was a matter of thesis which was opposed by antithesis and from the clash emerged a synthesis. In other words there was a situation which grew up in direct opposition to the existing situation and eventually clashed with it. From the clash would emerge a new order. This thinking was directly responsible for the political ideology of Karl Marx and through him Communism. It is not hard to trace the emphasis on clash and opposition as a means of evolution.

But long before Hegel, Western thought had been dominated by the adversary system. The Greek philosophers and in particular Socrates adopted it as the route to wisdom. The Church in the Middle Ages with its heresies and theological disputes relied heavily on adversary argument.

In the adversary system it is supposed that if you prove the other party wrong this somehow proves you right. In reality this is nonsense because both parties may be wrong or both may be right in part. Intellectually the adversary system is childish in the extreme. Both parties spend their time attempting to pick holes in the argument of the other party instead of exploring the matter itself.

Our judicial system is based on the adversary procedure. Only now, in a few areas like divorce, is it being realised that the system may not be the best one.

The overriding limitation of the adversary system is that it is negative. It has no constructive element at all.

The approach to a problem is very different from the solution to that problem.

A town has a race problem. The authorities feel that there are three approaches to this type of problem. The first approach is to encourage separation so that the different communities have little contact with each other. Each is allowed to go its own way. A second approach is that of partnership in which the cultural identity of the two groups is preserved but they are encouraged to work together and to respect each other's culture. Finally there is the integration approach in which an attempt is made to ignore the differences of race.

Almost every economist has a different approach to the problem of inflation. One economist might favour the approach of limiting the money supply by restricting credit. Another economist might insist that once it has started inflation is fuelled by wage demands and he might argue for tight control of wages. A third economist feels that inflation is a psychological process made worse by uncertainty and so he might suggest indexation of wages and pensions in order to remove the uncertainty.

In each case the approach to the problem would set down the broad guide-lines. The actual working out of the solution and the practical steps that would have to be taken to put the solution into effect would follow later. The problem will only be solved by an actual worked out solution but the type of solution is determined by the approach that has been chosen.

The difficulty is that a solution should really be determined by the nature of the problem. An approach is, however, very often determined not by the problem but by some separate philosophical intention or bias. For example there are several approaches to the problem of taxation (direct taxes, indirect taxes, escalating taxes, taxes on property). If the problem was simply one of raising the maximum amount of money for the government a solution would not be difficult. But if the approach is based on a philosophical intention of levelling social differences then the pure solution may not be applicable.

An approach may use existing roads or may take a new path that does not follow these established approaches.

Imagine a long established factory in Lancashire which has been making textiles for many years. With the growth of the textile industry in the Far East the factory is no longer very competitive. In fact the company which owns it is losing money. Another company comes along and buys up the textile business. But it makes no attempt to revitalise the industry. Instead the new company closes down the factory, knocks down the building and sells the land at a high price for building development. In the process the new company makes a large profit. The old company saw its assets as being a textile business that was losing money. The new company recognised the huge property assets that existed. Different perceptions of value are quite legitimate. The process can, however, be called asset-stripping when the new company buys the old one, strips it of its assets and in so doing kills a business that could have revived.

It can even happen that the new company buys the old company with its own money. A man approaches a company that is going bankrupt. He buys it up for a sum which is not paid immediately. The new owner quickly sells off the assets (land, stock, etc) of the company and uses the proceeds from this sale to pay the purchase price of the company. This is now illegal. A company may also buy a company by offering the shareholders stock in the buying company. This stock is thought to be likely to increase when the assets of the new company are added.

Obviously assets depend on who is looking at them and what value can be obtained for them. A lady may consider that her assets are her good looks. Through them she may obtain employment as an actress or chorus girl or she may marry a rich husband and live on alimony for ever. An asset is something that can be turned into practical value or at least be appreciated by others. An eccentric person may consider that his collection of old bottles is an asset but unless a buyer can be found the asset has no real asset value – at least for the moment.

Good health is undoubtedly the most valuable personal asset anyone can have but it is not marketable as such.

At the bottom of any argument there are axioms which are not argued about but are taken for granted. In fact the axioms often cannot be proved. We may take it as axiomatic that every person has a right to live. Thereafter we can build arguments from this about different rights, freedom, the quality of life and so on. In another ideology it may be regarded as an axiom that the good of the state is more important than the good of any particular individual.

From a handful of basic axioms (for instance that parallel lines on a plane surface will never meet) Euclid set out to build an entire system of plane geometry. He was so successful that geometry ever since has been synonymous with his name. Indeed until the beginning of this century his original textbook was still in use in schools throughout the world, more than two thousand years after he wrote it. From his basic axioms he built certain simple theorems using accepted notions such as the idea that the whole was greater than its parts. These theorems then provided the basis for more complicated theorems which in turn gave rise to further theorems until the whole field of plane geometry had been covered.

A system cannot prove its own axioms. This is sometimes known as Gödel's theorem, after the thinker who demonstrated the truth of it. In practice it means that there have to be certain truths that are accepted as axioms. If we set out to prove them we find that we are basing our proof on other axioms. And if we try to prove those in turn . . . It is usually held that an axiom is a self-evident truth; for instance that two things must either

be related or not related to each other. Many such axioms are really circular; truth is what we are searching for when we are searching for the truth.

In addition to logical or mathematical axioms there are moral axioms which have arisen from custom based on centuries of acceptance. We accept as axiomatic that it is wrong to kill but qualify this by excepting war, self-defence and judicial execution. We accept as axiomatic that honesty and truth are important because we cannot conceive how a society would be run if this axiom was abandoned. We accept the concept of impartial justice as axiomatic. Most axioms are arbitrary and self-evident only to those who see things the same way.

ARGUMENT

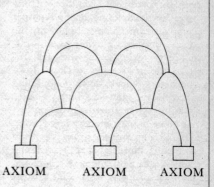

AXIOM   AXIOM   AXIOM

A salesman goes forth to sell a new type of vacuum cleaner. He is a good salesman and he gets orders from a large number of stores. He is very pleased with himself. Then nothing happens. The company for which he is working is unable to make or deliver the vacuum cleaners: there is no back-up to his sales effort. His front-line performance in selling has been marvellous but there is nothing to back him up.

On the Apollo missions to the moon there were times when one or other system failed. As soon as this happened the back-up system came into operation. Behind every front-line system there was a back-up system. And sometimes there was a further back-up system behind this.

A teacher disciplines an unruly boy in her classroom and tells him that she is going to report him to the head-master who will suspend him. But the headmaster fails to back her up and suggests that the boy be given a second chance. Thereafter the teacher's position with the class appears to be weakened.

Back-up is best understood in terms of what happens behind the front line. In the days when generals fought battles with lines of brightly uniformed soldiers it was understood that the purpose of the front line was to get

things started and enable them to develop in a definite direction. The major stage of the battle then followed. This consisted in committing the back-up troops in one place or another. The campaigns of Napoleon and his generals, of Wellington and of Frederick the Great show again and again the tactical importance of the reserves which often turned the tide of battle.

Today it is much less usual to think in terms of back-up as the front-line effort is so difficult in itself. Perhaps the most successful export nation is an exception. The striking feature of the Japanese selling effort is the importance given to back-up.

In the United States a ball-game would be a baseball game, a basketball game or a football game. Each game is different only because the rules are different. The rules call for different playing areas, different numbers of players, different equipment and different characteristics of play. It would not be much use playing baseball according to the rules of cricket. It would not be much use assuming that the rules of table tennis applied to lawn tennis.

An artificial universe such as a game is defined by the set of artificial rules that have been used to set it up in the first place. If the rules change then the ball-game changes. A person who is used to one situation may not realise that the ball-game has changed, that it has become 'a different ball-game'. A change in government regulations may change the investment market to such an extent that it becomes a different ball-game; for example a restriction on the level of dividends, or control of the buying of gold, or the need to pay a premium to invest overseas can all change the ball-game.

Referring to a universe of activity as a 'ball-game' is particularly apt if the rules that define that universe are as artificial and as arbitrary as the rules that define a ball-game. Children are very quick to learn the rules of a game. They are also apt to invent their own games. When they do invent their own games the rules are chosen to give some advantage to the inventor: a short child will insist that a ball must bounce before it is caught whereas a tall child insists that it can be caught in the air. There is the same tendency and motivation to change the rules of the game in the adult world.

A person who has been working for the Ford Motor Company and goes to work for IBM may find that he is in a different ball-game. The old rules and expectations and strategies do not seem to work any more. It takes time to learn the rules of the new ball-game especially as only a few of them are made explicit. It is much easier if one can be an observer at first but in many cases you are forced to play the different ball-game even as you learn how different it is.

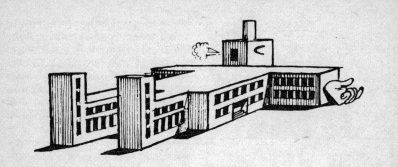

The idea behind a limited company or corporation was that it should acquire an identity separate from the people who had set it up or the people who owned it. The limited company was to be a legal animal or individual which went about its business: buying, selling, organising and attempting to make enough money to ensure its survival. Like an animal a company needs nourishment and the nourishment is the amount of business that is being carried on. But the nourishment has to be of the right type because it has to be absorbed into the body of the company. No one can live entirely on a diet of lettuce. Similarly a great deal of unprofitable activity will not keep a company going. When a company starves to death the input of nourishment is insufficient to provide the energy needed to keep the company active. Without such energy there is no hope of further nourishment and the company dies or goes bankrupt. Bankruptcy is an acknowledged starvation. The starvation may be the fault of the business idea, of the people running it or of the times; the end result is the same.

Idea bankruptcy occurs when an organisation or an individual runs out of the idea energy that is necessary to keep it going. Unfortunately there is nothing which stops an organisation which has run out of ideas from continuing to use variations of old ideas. Architects, entertainers, designers and advertisers often suffer this sort of bankruptcy as do novelists. As in the business situation an attempt is made to keep going at all costs in the hope that business will pick up again.

In business bankruptcies often occur when a bank which has been supporting a company refuses to extend any more credit. The bank's estimate of what may happen in the future turns out to be different from that of the owners of the business. In turn the owners of the business have a different estimate of what can be sold from the public's estimate of what it wants to buy. The difference between these three points of view can be contained for a time on the basis that things may get better. As usual the mere passage of time kills expectations and promises and bankruptcy follows.

When the expectations and promises of a marriage run out then the bankruptcy that follows is called divorce.

Behaviourism is a school of psychology which holds that behaviour can be shaped directly without any help from the processes of understanding or will. The simplest alteration of behaviour is the conditioned reflex which was first described by Pavlov who got his hungry dogs to salivate at the sound of a bell which had for some time been paired with the appearance of meat. Much more recently, Professor Skinner at Harvard University has been shaping behaviour by breaking it up into very small and simple steps and then reinforcing each step by reward. For instance if the desire is to train a rat to press a lever then any chance movement of the rat towards the lever is rewarded with a pellet. Then a movement even closer is also rewarded. If the rat chances to rest a paw on the lever this is also reinforced. So a whole chain of behaviour is built up or shaped.

There is much antagonism to the behaviourist school for two reasons. First the system seems to work and it does seem possible to shape behaviour in this way. Secondly, as a result it is feared that an acceptance of behaviourism would lead to powerful methods of shaping people's behaviour without going through their minds. In effect behaviourism denies the need for will; it does not exclude the possibility of will but denies the need for it in action or choice.

Because the effects produced by behaviourists are undeniable, the emphasis has shifted to arguments about how much of behaviour can really be shaped in this way. Because with a lot of effort certain types of behaviour can be shaped, can this be extended to mean that with appropriate effort all behaviour can be thus shaped? Is behaviourism a phenomenon for laboratories and for animal trainers or should it be part of our upbringing of children and rehabilitation of criminals?

The attraction of behaviourism is that it seems to work and also that it by-passes the mysteries and uncertainties of the mind. Instead of trying to control the mind you control behaviour and forget about the mind. It may turn men into programmed robots but this is better than badly programmed robots, so it is claimed. Why, its advocates continue, leave it to chance to set up the programme?

The main asset of the human mind is its desire to believe. The mind can only function by putting together what it observes as a predictable pattern. This pattern, no matter how wrong it may later prove to be, is used as the basis for any action that has to deal with the future. We have no alternative but to believe in the patterns that our senses put together for us.

Stage magicians provide the most extraordinary examples of belief. A skilled stage magician can fool not just the majority of the audience but every person in it. He does it by cleverly manipulating our expectations and our belief in our expectations. Salesmen are equally clever at manipulating our feelings in order to create a belief in a product.

Astrology is becoming increasingly popular although there has been no evidence at all that the stars affect our behaviour. The strength of this belief is based on a feature unusual in a religion: the ability to measure something. The paths of the planets and stars can be measured with great accuracy. Since the accuracy of this measurement is so impressive and the predictions derived from it are so attractive then surely we must believe in the effect of the celestial bodies on human behaviour?

A newspaper has six racing correspondents. All of them back a different horse in the race. Since there are six horses in the race one of them is bound to win. But to the people who have backed this correspondent his accuracy is uncanny: they pay no attention at all to the unsuccessful correspondents. We can shape our perception to what we want to see and what we then see will reinforce our initial perceptions.

If you believe in a guru then you will elevate his every saying into a profound truth. If you believe in a soothsayer then you will interpret an event to fit his prediction.

Belief is an emotion rather than a reaction to evidence. Possibly it is almost as inbuilt as an instinct. In animals that go about in herds belief is more important than seeing things for yourself since clearly not every member can see the imminent danger or the reason for a move.

There is a black-box on the breakfast table. You pour a pancake mix into the funnel at one end and press a button three times. A few minutes later out come three perfectly cooked pancakes, one after the other. You cannot see what is happening inside the black-box. All you know is what you have put in and what comes out. You cannot see anything of the mechanism or the 'wiring'. Contrast this black-box with a glass box in which you can see all that happens.

A child of four switches on the television set and selects a channel. Her mother pre-sets the washing machine to go through a routine of washing, rinsing and spinning dry. Her father gets into his car and starts up the engine and drives off to work. Neither child, nor mother, nor father need know anything about the actual workings of the television set, washing machine or car. These are black-boxes. All that is necessary is to know how to work them, not how they work.

There are people who do understand the working of television sets and motor cars so in these cases the black-box label is a relative one depending on the user. For some users a car is a black-box but for others it is a glass-box since they can imagine the workings in detail. There are other situations, however, where the mechanism is a mystery to everyone. We know quite a lot about the human body but in general it is still a black-box. We know that some treatments work but we do not know the actual mechanisms responsible.

In a glass-box situation we can see the mechanism and can predict what should happen. In a black-box situation we are unable to see the mechanism but we can find out a lot about it by trying different inputs and seeing what comes out at the other end. For example in the pancake-making black-box we can try putting in only a small amount of pancake mix and still pressing the button three times. What should we expect to come out? Will there be one full-sized pancake and no others or three undersized pancakes? The result will tell us something about the mechanism. To see if any mixing takes place internally we could put in some ordinary mix and some coloured pink and then wait to see whether the pancakes were uniformly pink or not. It is possible to use black-boxes effectively without being able to see inside.

Where is the bottleneck? Any administrator or businessman, or indeed anyone who wants to get anything done, needs to find out where the bottlenecks are. A bottleneck means a constriction in flow. The diagram shows a true bottleneck. Flow through the tube comes to a narrowing of the tube, a constriction or bottleneck, which slows down the volume flow. The actual speed of flow through the bottleneck may go up but the existence of the bottleneck slows down the total flow in the system (unless the pressure can rise to compensate for the constriction). The process is more easily understood with a traffic system. In the diagram we can see several roads which converge on one road. There is a bottleneck. The traffic slows down. For the flow to remain the same the traffic on the exit road would have to move three times as fast as the traffic on the access roads. Traffic piles up before the bottleneck.

When there is part of a system which cannot handle the flow generated by other parts of the system a bottleneck occurs. A particular new product may be selling well in the shops but supplies cannot keep up with demand. The shopkeeper assumes that production is slow. He is surprised therefore to be told that the warehouses are full of the product. It seems that there is a bottleneck in the dispatch department.

It may take many months for someone charged with a crime to be brought to trial. Where is the bottleneck? It may lie in the availability of judges or courtrooms or within the judicial procedure itself. Relieving the congestion at one bottleneck may shift the congestion to another bottleneck further downstream in the process, as in the traffic system.

Essentially a bottleneck is a point which itself generates a disproportionate amount of delay in the system. Quite often bottlenecks are created by government departments. For example getting permission to add to a building may take three or four times as long as the actual building itself.

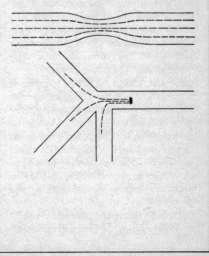

In a steel mill there are a lot of fixed costs that have to be paid no matter how much steel is being produced. The costs do not decrease when less steel is produced. The profits from the sales of steel, however, increase both with the amount produced and with the market price. For the mill to operate at a profit the returns from the sale of steel should be enough to pay for the running costs, the interest on the capital investment and allow for a profit. The break-even point is reached when both profit and loss stand at zero. The same thing applies to a paper mill, which is also a large-scale operation. When it is running at full capacity a profit is made but when it is not running at full capacity there is a break-even point. If the capacity used falls below this point a loss is made; if it rises above a profit can be made.

A couple are setting up a shop to sell antiques. They rent a shop, redecorate it, buy some stock and advertise in the appropriate places. They run for several months before they reach break-even point, the point at which they are no longer making a loss but have not yet started to make a profit.

In any venture there is investment and there are running costs. The ultimate aim of the venture is profit of some sort. This need not be in terms of money but in terms of effectiveness. For example a philanthropist setting up a home for old people may not be interested in making a financial profit but he may be interested in reaching break-even point so that the home can continue to survive. He takes his profit in terms of satisfaction and philanthropy.

It could be argued that all successful enterprises run at break-even point.

When income exceeds outgoings there appears to be a profit but this is really another sort of expense: the expense of investing in tools and research; the expense of rewarding the stockholders so that capital can be obtained again in the future. If profits are looked upon as legitimate business expenses then there is always a break-even position (tax is included too). The trouble is that there is no limit to what could be set aside for investment or stockholders' reward. The fact that the expenses only become payable in a good year does not mean that they are not genuine outgoings. There is nothing to say that outgoings have to be constant.

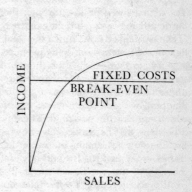

A few weeks before the end of its financial year an education department finds that it has not yet spent several thousand pounds in its budget. A frantic search ensues to find something on which the money can be quickly spent. Finally someone suggests some old army huts. These are gratefully bought but never actually used. This sort of thing happens again and again in government departments and industrial divisions. If the department has not spent its budget for the year then next year that budget will be cut. No one is praised for underspending or being economical. On the contrary they are blamed for having overestimated in the first place. What happens is that everyone overestimates their budget in order to get what they need and to allow for emergencies. Then they add a little bit more to this in case the central finance department knocks a bit off every budget just to justify its existence. Finally, towards the end of the year, the overestimated budget is deliberately justified by spending any money that remains. Salesmen of expensive equipment well know that the time to call on government departments is in the last month of the financial year.

A budget whether in a household, a government department or a film studio is supposed to be an estimate of expenditure. The emphasis is usually put on what is to be achieved and a budget is then planned in order to make this possible. The household situation is somewhat different insofar as the expenditure is fixed first and an examination is then made to see what can be done within this expenditure. It is likely that in the future government department budgets will be set up in a similar manner.

In practice most budgets are used to maintain the status quo. Only a small portion is actually spent on new projects. However inclined a person is to trim a budget he soon finds that the ongoing activities resist trimming because they have become so interlocked with the whole structure that they cannot be changed.

The overriding problem is that there are no natural incentives for cutting budgets or for underspending. Perhaps the underspending in the first year should go directly as salary supplement to all those who have achieved it.

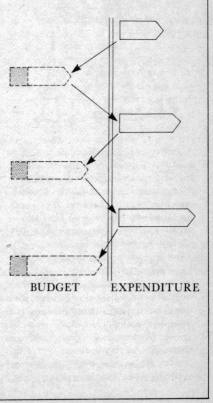

BUDGET   EXPENDITURE

A bureaucrat is a convenient scapegoat or hobgoblin to blame for all the inefficiency and expense of centralised government. A bureaucrat is someone who rules (no matter how small his kingdom) by virtue of his position at a desk. A bureaucrat rules by controlling the flow of information. If some application has to pass through his desk he can hold it up, send it back for resubmission or lose it, thus exercising complete power over anything that requires an application. If a decision is called for then the bureaucrat can make that decision without incurring any responsibility by claiming to be interpreting the law or applying standing instructions.

Bureaucrats are blamed for showering the public with forms and counterforms and applications and reports to such an extent that a farmer often spends more time filling in forms than planning the future of his farm. The besetting sin of bureaucracy is the need to supply itself with work. There is a fear that if the paper flow should slow down then a bureaucrat will become redundant. Just as a farmer produces crops or a manufacturer produces goods so a bureaucrat produces paper, which is not always the same as information. Professor Parkinson's famous law that work expands to fill the time allotted to it applies both to work and to paper-work. Unfortunately the work produced by bureaucracy requires outside form-fillers to play their part. This is always difficult since forms are designed more for the convenience of the bureaucrat than the public.

The many complaints about bureaucracy are directed at the structure more than the people involved. There seems to be no incentive for efficiency, for simplification or for empathy. The overriding consideration seems to be to avoid error and responsibility at all costs. The matter is an important one since the system seems designed to increase costs and decrease consumer satisfaction.

In a complex society control of the communication channels gives control of the system. The term bureaucrat, along with mediacrat, may well come to indicate the true government.

Typhoid Mary was a fit healthy woman who unwittingly gave the serious disease of typhoid to a great number of people. She was a cook and she was a carrier of the salmonella germ that causes typhoid. Now and again the germ would infect the food and give typhoid to the people who ate it. There are many nurses who carry in their noses the staphylococcus bug which before the days of antibiotics could cause serious infection of operation wounds. What would happen if an astronaut coming back from space was found to be a carrier for a new virus which was fatal to some people but did not affect others at all. Would we lock him up for ever? The situation could well happen not with a spaceman but with carriers of the dreaded African disease known as Lassar fever.

It is claimed that the fall of the Romanoff dynasty in Russia was hastened by the fact that the heir to the Czar had haemophilia, the bleeding disease in which there is a fault in the blood-clotting mechanism. The genes for this disease are carried by a female, who herself does not show the disease but passes it on to her offspring in whom it then becomes manifest. The Hapsburgs were known to be carriers of this gene. Two brown-eyed parents can have a blue-eyed child because both parents can be carriers of the gene for blue eyes.

Many religions have been successfully spread by missionaries who had little theological understanding of the message they were carrying. Successful salesmen do not always have to understand what they are selling; it is enough that they are carriers of the message.

In the First World War the army in France used carrier pigeons to send messages back from the front line, or indeed back to England.

With a carrier we separate the communication from the interaction function. The carrier itself takes no part in the interaction. We receive radio and television through 'carrier waves' which are modulated to give us the message. A carrier is a type of communication channel.

There is a saying in business that eighty per cent of the profits come from twenty per cent of the activities and eighty per cent of the activities only provide twenty per cent of the profits. This twenty/eighty rule tends to apply in many situations: twenty per cent of the effort produces eighty per cent of the results. This is why it is so often possible for a new manager to produce quick results by being ruthless enough to chop off much of the unproductive eighty per cent of the activities, so reducing costs while keeping profits intact.

The twenty per cent of the activities that produce most of the profits tend to include several 'cash-cows'. A cash-cow is a product or activity that can be milked for money and profits without much attention. This cash-cow is usually a well-established line of business in which all the development costs have been written off. Just as a cow goes on giving milk, placidly and without causing any problems, so the product goes on producing the profits. The profits are then used for new ventures and development costs in other areas. It is suspected that one day the product will become obsolete and the cash will dry up just as milk from a cow may dry up, but until that day the business is happy to draw profits from this cash-cow. For a publisher the cash-cow might be a line of standard textbooks which go on selling steadily even though they are slightly out of date and of no excitement at all to the publisher. A long-established detergent or brand of cigarette may serve as cash-cows in other businesses. For a motor vehicle manufacturer the cash-cow might turn out to be a line of vans which get little attention from the press and are not at all glamorous.

The advantage of a steady income from the cash-cows is that it enables the corporation to survive and to pay its overheads while it experiments with new products. It might seem to make sense to resist the temptation to experiment and to restrict activities to looking after the profitable cash-cows. The profitability of the company would certainly increase in the short term. But if the cash-cow dried up (for example by someone producing a newer textbook) then there would be nothing with which to replace it. The purpose of the experimenting is to breed the new generation of cash-cows.

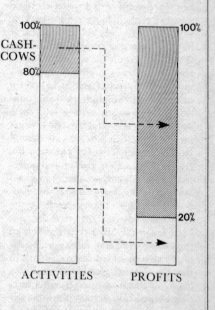

The phrase 'Catch-22' comes from Joseph Heller's famous book of that name. In that book a fighter pilot asked to be excused flying duties on the grounds that he was insane. Since flying under the particular conditions involved in the book was regarded as highly dangerous this request showed signs of sanity, and he was therefore refused permission to be grounded. In other words if a pilot was sane enough not to want to fly then he could not be excused flying on the grounds of insanity.

If one looks around there are any number of catch-22 situations. Television producers are always crying out for new ideas but if the idea is really new they will not be able to tell from past experience whether it will work. So they say: 'Give us a new idea but if it is really new then we shall be unable to use it.' The same thing tends to happen in education. Teachers know that only the simple and direct methods actually work in the classroom. But on the other hand if they come across a method that is direct and simple they are apt to be unimpressed by it because it seems to lack the necessary theoretical and psychological jargon. Their particular catch-22 becomes: 'Give us something which is so complicated that we shall be impressed by it, but unable to use it.' Business corporations suffer from the same problem. Senior executives are always on the lookout for talented juniors but if the junior is really talented then the senior executive fears that the junior might take over his job. So this particular catch-22 becomes: 'We are always on the lookout for promising managers, on condition that we do not find any good enough to

threaten our own jobs.'

In a parallel fashion the catch-22 situation applies to pricing. If the Post Office increases the cost of sending letters then it should get more revenue, except that fewer people will send letters and so revenue may fall. The same applies to rail fares. It may also apply to taxes. If taxes are very high then so much effort is spent on avoiding them that the actual yield to the Revenue department may fall.

The Schools Council in the United Kingdom, reacting to a request for funds in connection with the development of thinking as a school subject, provided a perfect catch-22: 'If the project is successful then it should not need extra funds; if it is not successful then it is not worth supporting.'

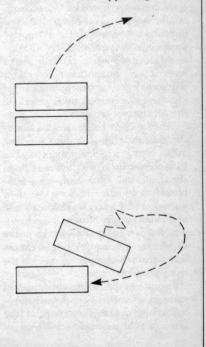

In biology there are said to be two types of mind: the lumpers and the splitters. The lumper looks at a lot of birds and decides that they have definite features in common; he lumps them together into two categories or groups. The splitter looks at the same birds but instead of looking at what they have in common he looks at the differences. As a result he splits the two groups of the lumper into six sub-groups in each case giving twelve categories in all.

There are sixty applicants for a job. In order to simplify the selection process the applicants are divided into the following categories: those with enough experience; those without adequate experience; those with experience that is not quite adequate but could be compensated for by outstanding intelligence. This categorisation is done on the basis of the submitted application forms. Categorisation could also have been carried out on the basis of age, qualifications or salary requirements. Categorisation could also have been mixed, using several of these features together.

Categories are convenient for understanding something, doing something about it or just talking about it. The basis for the categorisation may lie in the thing itself (mammals are warm-blooded animals that suckle their young) or in the way we choose to look at it (the category of formal teachers). The features must always exist in the subject categorised but we can choose which features to make the basis of the categorisation.

In spite of the many advantages of categorisation there are the usual disadvantages of a labelling system. If the labels are appropriate they tend to stick. Someone who has been put into one category tends to stay in that category. A young man may classify his girl-friend as wife-material or mistress-material and thereafter it would be difficult for the unsuspecting girl to switch categories.

The German philosopher Kant believed that the mind had inbuilt categories (such as the cause/effect idea) into which received information was automatically fitted.

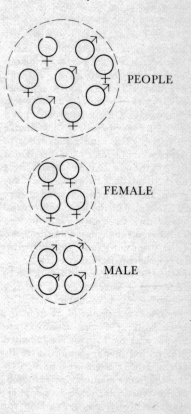

PEOPLE

FEMALE

MALE

The problem with any positive feedback system is that there is no inbuilt ceiling. At an art auction a Rembrandt goes for a high price. When it is next sold the price is higher still. Since much of the buying is on behalf of museums some of the paintings go off the market altogether. This means that the rarity value of the remaining ones increases. So prices rise even further. It could be argued that by raising prices in this competitive manner buyers are only making things more expensive for themselves. If there was a ceiling to prices then with the same amount of money a museum could buy more works of art, including modern ones. The dealer, the seller and the non-museum buyer however are all happy with the rising prices because it means more profits for them.

Society has never really come to terms with the difference between use value and rarity value. If a man produces a certain number of ceramic pots a day and these can be sold at a certain price then clearly it would be impossible to pay him more than his craft had earned. If, however, the ceramic pot is a rare Greek vase then the price is what anyone is willing to pay for it on a competitive basis. No one is obliged to live by Greek vases so this would not seem to matter, until the same process starts to operate on building land or property prices. For example a speculative developer could buy up all the suitable development land in an area and then force people to pay his 'monopoly' price. A monopolist manufacturer could exert the same price pressure and so could a surgeon with special skills. To set a ceiling on this type of price would solve many of these problems since the buyer would only buy at the ceiling price if he really wanted to use the painting or land and not because he could resell at a higher price (since that selling price would be at the same ceiling).

Many countries have found it advisable to set a ceiling of fifty per cent on the maximum amount of income tax that could be demanded from an individual. In most organisations there is an age ceiling for employment. Aeroplanes have a ceiling height above which they cannot operate.

A freely fluctuating system with ceilings and floors is an alternative to a rigidly determined system, its only disadvantage being that values tend to get stuck at either ceiling or floor levels.

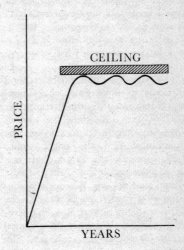

In an atom bomb, neutrons emitted from one radioactive nucleus dislodge neutrons from other nuclei and these in turn serve to dislodge further neutrons in a chain reaction that leads to the explosion. In a nuclear power station this chain reaction is slowed down by the insertion of rods (often of cadmium) which serve to mop up some of these neutrons and so make the process controllable. A similar process may be seen with the spread of an epidemic. One person gets infected. In turn he passes the disease to his comrades each of whom becomes a focus of infection. The resulting chain reaction leads to a rapid spread of the disease. If, however, some of the infected cases are immediately put to bed in an isolation ward then the spread is slowed down.

The so called 'domino effect' is a particular example of a chain reaction. It was felt that if South Vietnam became Communist then this would allow an adjacent country to become Communist and the effect would spread just as a row of dominoes collapses when the first one falls on to the second and so on. Whenever something that is affected becomes in its turn an infector there is a chain reaction. Each link of the chain is formed by the actor and the receiver. The receiver in its turn becomes an actor for the next link. The explosive spread effect occurs when an actor can act upon several receivers (as in the nuclear explosion and the epidemic).

When a major bank fails it can set in train a chain reaction that can bring about the collapse of other banks. The other banks may have lent money to the first bank or they may be partners in projects backed by the collapsing bank. So the effect spreads. In addition there is a chain reaction of failing confidence because clients of other banks will seek to withdraw their funds: since only a proportion of these are covered by liquid assets a crisis develops.

The spread of a rumour is the classic example of a chain reaction. Anyone who hears a juicy rumour is anxious to tell it to as many people as possible. Each person vouches for the validity of the source of the rumour and so it spreads in an explosive fashion. Official denial helps it to spread further on the basis that there must have been some truth in it.

A communication game in which one group has to act out, usually in silent mime, the name of a famous book, film or play whilst another group tries to interpret what is being communicated in this way. To add motivation the actor is chosen from the opposing team, which has then to interpret what he is trying to put across. For example if the title is *Gone with the Wind* the actor might mime a housewife who hangs her washing out on a line. He then mimes a furious gale and the woman coming out to find that all her washing has blown away.

The point about a charade is that it is something elaborately acted out, as a game, and for a communication purpose. A show trial in a totalitarian state is a charade. The guilt, confession and verdict are all known beforehand. The show is intended to frighten other people or to give an appearance of legal process to a regime which makes little regular use of it.

When a gesture is made purely to give an impression it becomes a charade. Machiavelli, the Italian political realist of the Middle Ages, urged princes to make a great show of liberality because this would be popular with the people. He also urged the princes not to put any substance in the show because this would be costly and would mean raising taxes, which would be unpopular with the people. Politicians quickly acquire the habit of saying the right things about the current issue, and even making larger gestures, but never letting this interfere with their actual behaviour.

Pomp, ceremony and ritual are not the same as a charade. Pomp and ceremony have their own value. For instance the ritual of the Catholic Church or of a tribal dance in Africa has an emotional reality and purpose: the involvement of the audience. A charade occurs when the acting is false and is designed to convey a message or cover up something.

In times of crisis many corporations go through a cost-cutting charade involving cutting down on telephone calls and having simpler lunches. These peripheral economies do not make much difference but they give the appearance of being efficiency-conscious and of having cut down to the bone on all other expenditure.

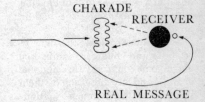

CHARADE RECEIVER

REAL MESSAGE

Two polished metal spheres are placed about six inches apart. Each one is given a higher and higher electrostatic charge. Suddenly a point is reached when a spark leaps across the gap between them like a miniature flash of lightning. The process is actually the same as that of lightning. Water droplets moving upwards in clouds due to warm air currents carry small electrostatic charges. The point is reached when the charge is so high that lightning flashes down to the earth below.

Demolition workers who have to knock down an old building calculate very carefully the exact amount and placement of the explosive charge so as to bring the building gracefully down in a slump instead of blowing it to bits and damaging the buildings around.

Some issues such as abortion, race relations and child care (animal care also in some countries) are emotionally charged and any discussion on them is likely to arouse as much emotion as logic.

It is usually claimed that people are more influenced by emotional charges than by thinking and that trying to improve general thinking levels is unlikely to have much beneficial effect. It is felt that in a practical situation emotion comes first, followed by experience and finally by thinking. Yet it may not be so. The relationship between the emotional charge in a matter and the thinking skill involved in perception (the way someone looks at a situation) is similar to the relationship between the aim of a gun and the explosive charge with which it is loaded. The explosive charge itself does not determine the aim.

In a communication system the charge does not affect the direction in which a message travels nor the content of the message but it does determine the energy attachment of the message. An unimportant message accompanied by a heavy charge is more likely to be effective than an important but weakly charged message. Charge is the energy content. Without sufficient energy content nothing may happen even though everything else is in order for it to happen.

Protests and demonstrations are often successful because they indicate the emotional charge attached to some issue. This adds nothing to the logic of the issue or to the factual content but authorities are more apt to respond to charge than to logic.

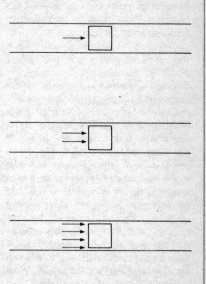

A Napoleonic veteran called Chauvin gave his name to the type of bellicose patriotism that has come to be known as chauvinism: my country, or my cause, right or wrong. The paradox is that the word chauvinist has come to signify reaction when used by members of the women's liberation movement attacking men who seem disinclined to alter the status quo (the male chauvinist pigs). It is a contradiction in terms because the word denotes fervent and bellicose support of a cause and this applies more exactly to the strident supporters of the women's movement than to the conservatives at whom the accusation is levelled.

There are those who feel that in society every member should have a broad and balanced view of things and be able to make up his mind, as an individual, on any matter. But this is only one view of society. There are others who feel that in such a society nothing would ever get done and no grievances would ever be righted because grievances are more apt to be of interest to those suffering from them than to those who are benefiting from them. From this other view arises the notion that society should be a sort of free-for-all made up of special interest groups each of which battles for the survival and advancement of its own interests. There is to be no control on this group selfishness except the good sense of those involved and the abolition of the grievances which fuel the chauvinism.

Just as people 'own' a country by belonging to it, so people own a cause by belonging to it. If a country is threatened then patriotism and chauvinism seem in order. They may also seem in order to those who feel that their group or cause is threatened by the state or by the pressure of others. When defence is involved attitudes and behaviour that would be intolerable in an aggressor suddenly seem to become acceptable. The reason for this change of mind is easy to see: for an aggressor chauvinism is a troublesome luxury; for a defendant it seems to be necessary for survival. Unfortunately groups can sometimes be as paranoid as individuals, so the definition of defence and persecution may be real enough to those involved but less real to those looking on.

Science fiction writers sometimes conceive of a world in which there are many more women than men. It is claimed that from a biological point of view only one man may be necessary for a large number of breeding women. In the cattle world one prize bull may, through artificial insemination techniques, sire over two hundred and fifty thousand calves. In theory there are already techniques available which would make it possible for men to have children without the need for women at all! This is the process of cloning which has already been tried successfully in some animals.

In the normal reproductive process a male cell and a female cell unite to form a zygote which then divides and redivides to form the embryo which in turn develops into the appropriate animal. But this whole process can be by-passed by taking an undifferentiated cell from the animal body and stimulating the nucleus so that it starts to divide on its own, just as if it were a zygote. The process of division goes on until a fully formed animal is created. Since the body contains millions of such cells it is, in theory, possible to create millions of animals as the 'offspring' of a single animal.

What is especially interesting about the cloning process is that the offspring will be *identical* to the solitary parent.

In normal sexual reproduction each parent provides a set of genes and it is the mixing of these genes which determines the characteristics of the offspring. In cloning there is no mixing at all. The full gene set of the single parent is repeated exactly in the offspring. Thus from one Einstein it would be possible to breed a thousand other Einsteins who were exactly the same in their genetic make-up.

It would, of course, be necessary to provide the growing embryo with the right sort of environment. But already it has proved possible to implant the fertilised egg from one species into the womb of another. For example fertilised cattle eggs may be transported by implanting them in the womb of rabbits. So it might become possible to clone human beings and implant the embryo in human wombs or cattle wombs.

Why anyone should want to take advantage of the technical possibilities of cloning is another matter.

CLUSTER

A man has an epileptic fit in the park. People cluster around and watch or try to help. There is no basic relationship between the clustered people except that they are now standing close to each other and have been brought into that position by their curiosity.

A graph may show a cluster of points as in the diagram. This cluster may show that in the population sample used there were many people of a certain age with a certain income.

A personality analysis may show that good salesmen have a cluster of personality characteristics: lack of self-consciousness; sensitivity; liking for people; high achievement drive. The analysis shows that these characteristics seem to cluster together.

A cluster is a coming together in space and time so that the density of whatever is clustered contrasts with the density around. The reason for the cluster may become apparent later. It may be that the cluster is really a group. For example a cluster of people in an airport lounge may really represent a party of people who are all travelling with the same tour organiser. A cluster of people in a room may turn out to be the upholstery class at the technical institute.

A cluster refers to the coming together of people, features, characteristics or attributes. It is noticed that the density in the cluster is greater than the density around it. A cluster in itself says nothing about the reason for the coming together. There may be a very good reason for the cluster and if this is discovered there may be a group instead of a cluster. Alternatively no good reason may be found and the cluster may always be referred to as a cluster, with the emphasis on the coming together rather than the reason behind it.

Sometimes clusters are quite obvious. At other times attempts may be made to discover clusters by taking apparently uniform groups and measuring them in different ways.

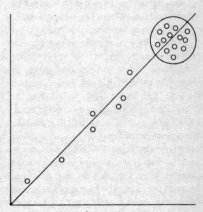

In wartime each side tries its hardest to find out what the other side is doing or about to do. If you know the enemy is going to attack at a certain point you can move up reinforcements. If you know the enemy is short of munitions you can direct your bombing at the munitions factory to increase the shortage. Because war is a highly complicated process there has to be a lot of communication between headquarters and the fighting units. Some of this has to be by radio (for example communication with a submarine or aeroplane). The enemy can listen to this communication as easily as the people for whom it is intended. So elaborate codes are used. A code book or coding machine is used to translate the message into code. The code is then sent and at the other end the message is decoded. It is said that in the Second World War the British had found a way of breaking the German code and so could anticipate much of what was going to happen.

Schoolchildren often develop secret codes with which the members of a group talk to each other to the confusion of outsiders. Such codes usually involve repeating the last syllable of a word or substituting one letter for another.

A code is the opposite of open communication. With an ordinary radio transmission anyone with a set can listen in, receive the message and act upon it if he wishes. If the message is sent in code then only those who understand the code will receive the proper message. A radio broadcast in a foreign language is really in code since only those who understand that language will get the message. Any language is a code because we have to interpret a series of sounds as words with meanings.

In a code situation meaning is supplied by the listener. The listener is supplied with a code book or with experience in recognition. The communicated message is a code that triggers the meaning. For example the message '258' may indicate to the listener that he has to follow the elaborate instructions that are laid out on page 258 of a manual.

Codes lead to privacy of communication or discrimination between listeners. They also lead to great economy of effort since a code indicator can be sent instead of the full message.

Learning, thinking, perceiving, noticing all have in common a distinction from feeling or willing. Increasing attention is now being paid to the cognitive processes. It is at last being recognised in the field of psychology that there is a difference between man and animals. In the traditional days of philosophy there was much metaphysical speculation about man's mind and much introspection regarding how it might work. The early psychologists were determined to make psychology into a science and so they sought for a measurable basis in facts. It was not easy to do this with human beings, so animals were used (rats, cats, octopuses and flatworms). It was possible to rear these creatures in more rigorously controlled conditions and to chop out bits of their brains in a way that was unsuitable for human subjects. It was supposed that the basic mechanisms discovered in animals such as these would apply in general to man since man was but a more sophisticated living creature. Man does, however, have the distinction of possessing considerable cognitive powers and any scaling up of the animal brain had to take these into account; this it could not do. So there is an increasing interest in the study of man's cognitive processes.

From time to time it is also fashionable to discount man's cognitive processes and to ascribe his behaviour to dark forces in the subconscious or to emotions that override his thinking. Thinking is then seen as a sort of rationalisation that works to make sense of whatever man has otherwise decided to do. Freud started this fashion by claiming that sexual tensions in the subconscious mind were responsible for much of the activity in the conscious mind.

In an experiment I carried out, thirty youngsters (aged nine to eleven) were asked if they would like a wage for going to school each day. All of them enthusiastically supported the idea. They were then asked to talk about the points in favour of the idea and those against. After five minutes of such talk twenty-nine out of the thirty had changed their minds. So a purely cognitive procedure had reversed an emotional reaction.

As a result of our neglect we know surprisingly little about man's cognitive processes and what he can do with them. Mathematics are a tool for extending these processes in one direction.

A factory may be very inefficient and never make a profit. A potter may be very careless and produce too many cups that are misshapen. A driver may make a mistake and drive into a wall. A political party may lose the election in a disastrous manner. Inefficiency, mistakes, incompetence, bad steering, poor assessment are all errors in the functioning of a system. But the system itself continues to function. Collapse occurs when the very nature of the system or structure falls apart.

A man collapses in the street from a heart attack. In a visual sense he has collapsed just as a building may collapse: it is no longer upright. In a functional sense he is no longer an upright walking man: that system has collapsed. His health is also collapsing because his heart is not doing what it is supposed to do. It is not unusual for a man to be horizontal rather than vertical but it is unusual if he wants to be vertical but cannot be.

There can be a collapse of confidence, of morale, of credibility and of credit. In each case the particular system involved falls apart and ceases to function. A collapse of law and order means not only that it does not function but that the system responsible for it has collapsed: along any particular street the crime rate may not alter at all – it may even diminish because the usual petty criminals can operate as easily elsewhere – but there may still be a collapse of law and order. There can be a collapse of a financial empire even though there is still a lot of money in the system and it seems to function from moment to moment. This is because the system has collapsed at the centre and is no longer able to survive as a system.

A system or structure depends on the relationship and interaction of the parts. It is the arrangement of the parts in a specific way which creates the structure. A tower is only a specific arrangement of bricks and wood. In a collapse it is this functional arrangement which falls apart. This is quite different from errors in control, behaviour or design. It is quite true that such errors may eventually lead to a collapse but until that moment they may be capable of correction. A system that has collapsed cannot put itself together again any more than Humpty Dumpty could.

The hardest part of the Russian revolution was imposing collectivism upon the Russian peasants. The Marxist revolution should have started not in Russia but in an industrialised society. In Russia the peasants found that instead of the tyranny of their feudal overlords they were to be subjected to the tyranny of collectivism.

From each according to his ability and to each according to his needs sounds a noble sentiment. If a farm or a factory is owned jointly then all efforts will contribute to the common good. This must follow since the efforts are not benefiting any single owner (it is possible that they may not be benefiting anyone). A person who is privileged enough to be talented with brains, brawn or managerial ability exercises that talent in the same way as everyone else exercises their talents, without any claim to privilege or special reward. Conversely a person who has special needs because of ill-health or a large family would draw from the common pool what is required. There is no reason why the system should not work, except that it demands a lot from human nature. The hard worker becomes conscious that his efforts are going to support the person who is not so inclined by nature

to hard work. Furthermore, what belongs to everyone is not especially cared for by anyone.

Basically collectivism is negative because it attacks the greed and selfishness of individual ownership and the neglect of the disadvantaged rather than constructing a system for the development of human potential. To attack faults is not necessarily to develop virtues. The Protestant religion with its work ethic seeks to make a virtue both of hard work and of the sharing of the fruits of this hard work with others less fortunate. Again the system only works when fervour is running high. The ordinary tax system in most countries is a tolerably good attempt to solve the problem provided its use does not become counter-productive and actually discourage effort.

Perhaps the ideal system would involve collective ownership of land and the means of production but individual use of these. The common ownership would prevent the abuses of speculation and inefficiency and the individual usage would encourage effort and achievement.

Jesus Christ is reputed to have said that those who were not with him were against him. This is a polarisation of commitment. Those who were unable to commit themselves to his side were, by default, committed to the other side. Commitment means decision and on this decision action can be based. If a person is going to act he must be committed. Before acting he may entertain alternative possibilities; he may even have a scale of priorities and preferences. But when the point of action is reached he has to decide upon a definite course of conduct. Doing something half-heartedly is not avoiding commitment; it is making a commitment and following it through in a sloppy fashion. If you decide to drive to Bristol rather than to Edinburgh the fact that you may be driving slowly, badly and without enthusiasm does not put you on the road to Edinburgh or on both roads at once.

There are times when commitment becomes fashionable. At such times commitment to a cause (equality of women, ecology, urban renewal, religion) is regarded almost as an end in itself, no matter what the cause may be or how much consideration has been given to the commitment. As the opposite of apathy and indifference commitment certainly has a value. Commitment suggests action rather than drift. It suggests a willingness to express an opinion and to control events instead of feeling impotent in the face of them.

Yet there are dangers to commitment. Commitment often excludes the ability to see other points of view. It often leads to polarisation and clash by making adjustment and com-

promise impossible. In order to exhibit or reinforce their commitment those involved take up extreme positions. If you are seen to be in an extreme position then it must follow that you are more committed than those in less extreme positions or anywhere near the centre.

Political parties thrive on commitment because they have to be certain of their votes. The result is that the country is in practice governed by the three or four per cent of floating voters who are not committed and are therefore able to switch their votes according to party promises and results. By switching their votes these uncommitted voters are able to change governments.

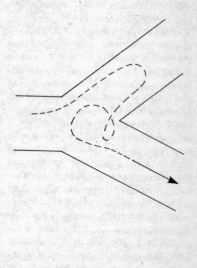

In its technical sense a commodity is any substance that is traded on the commodity market, for example cocoa, tin, copper and wool. In a general sense a commodity is something which is used as a substance rather than an item. There are huge differences between types of wheat yet wheat, like rice, can be treated as a single commodity. The price is set, and fluctuates, for a commodity as a whole. Commodities are something like water: they may be an essential part of life but at some stage they have to be bought in bulk.

A commodity is part of the background to living. It is taken for granted unless something goes wrong and the supply is interrupted or the price rises sharply. People can live without cars or television sets but not without grain. The absolute necessity for a commodity can be very different from the perceived necessity. Many people would consider beef an essential commodity but others would argue that in the absence of beef protein can be obtained from other meats, fish or from vegetable sources. Cattle are inefficient converters of grain into protein. Far more people could obtain protein if the grain was fed to them directly instead of passing through cattle in order to provide the traditional taste. It is claimed that in the great potato famine in Ireland people continued to starve even when they were provided with corn because they were not used to corn and did not know how to cook it. Similarly when corn is brought to a famine area the people may feed it to their animals as they consider corn to be animal food.

An interesting study could be made of the commodity base in different cultures. What items are seen as basic needs: housing, clothing, food, entertainment, transport, fuel? It is easy enough to put down everything but if a restriction had to be made different priorities might emerge. It may be wrong to think of commodities as supplying the basic necessities of existence. Perhaps we ought to think of them as supplying the necessities for a satisfactory existence. In that case some sort of belief system could be considered a commodity.

In general commodities are given too little attention. They are taken for granted because we feel secure in their supply and want to occupy ourselves with more interesting matters.

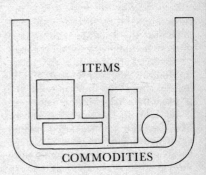

ITEMS

COMMODITIES

A community is the local environment of people. It is small enough to have interests in common. It is small enough to be agreed about matters that affect it. Monastic communities were tightly defined by their uniform and the physical boundaries of the monastery in addition to the rules and beliefs. Modern Californian-style communes are equally tightly defined. A village is a geographically defined community since there are a limited number of houses and people in the village. By contrast people living in cities may lack this sense of community. A person may have more to do with friends who live in a different part of town than with his immediate neighbours. Devices like the car and the telephone separate a person from his neighbours by allowing him to make communication neighbours of people at a distance. So one of the chief problems of modern planning is that of creating real communities in cities and yet not creating ghettoes.

A community is the next unit of organisation after the family. Beyond it are formed tribes, states and nations. A community is supposed to be small enough for everyone in it to have an identity and a life-space. Each individual has his status and his importance. Relationships between people are fairly stable and community pressure can be brought to bear on anyone who does not play the game. A community can encompass quarrels, hatred and even vendettas provided these are formalised and recognised. Instead of equality there is acceptance in a community. Status and pecking orders are much more firmly established than elsewhere.

In many people's eyes the community is a convenient device requiring a centralisation that goes beyond individual self-gratification but does not reach the impersonal centralisation of totalitarianism. Somewhere between 'the individual matters' and 'the state is supreme' there is a trend to say 'communities are what count'. A person is to derive his individuality and his life-supporting organisation from the community rather than from his own efforts or from the state.

There may be bases other than geography for a community: for instance economics or science.

A concept is an object in the world of the mind. We can focus our attention on the objects in the world around us. We can pick up a cup and drink from it. We can walk around a table or bump into a chair. We can hitch a tractor to a plough and use the combination to do useful work. All these physical objects are described by concepts in the world of the mind. The concept includes not only an acknowledgement of the physical object but also of its use and perhaps a parcel of associations that are usually attached to it. The whole package has a code word or name which we use when we try to communicate the concept to someone else. Concepts are both personal and universal just as faces are personal but have enough that is universal to make them recognisable as a face. So each person's concept of a tractor will be partly personal and partly universal.

But what about things which do not exist as physical foci of attention in the outer world? What about government, justice, profit, inflation, ego and so on? What tends to happen is that constant referral to a type of situation or a type of dynamic event soon leads to a name for that situation or event. The concept, as a focus of perception, has come first but the convenience of using a name soon takes over: the concept becomes attached to the name. There are many concepts which do not yet have a single convenient name: for example the-way-we-look-at-something is not adequately covered by the concept 'perception'. I invented the term 'lateral thinking' to describe the concept that involved changes in concepts or approaches to a problem. We need a new concept for the person who

is governed by the ethic of 'what you can get away with' since words like opportunist, selfish and exploiter are too inexact.

Concepts are recognisable bits of the external world, or of the internal world of our thinking, around which we draw an imaginary red circle so that we can treat them on their own. We could generate an infinite number of concepts if we so wished. For example we could generate a specific concept to cover the situation where a person who is intensely thirsty has a first sip of water. We can describe this adequately with words like deprivation and pleasure but they do not convey the full flavour of the situation, of the speed with which intense satisfaction is succeeded by satiety.

We also need a graveyard for concepts that should be buried.

PERCEPTION

CONCEPT

THE WORLD

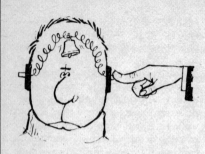

Pavlov was a thoroughgoing materialist. He had no time for the soul or mysterious processes that made up the psyche of an individual. For him the brain was something like a telephone exchange in which an incoming call was connected up to an outgoing line. The incoming call was the stimulus coming from the environment. The outgoing line was the action which followed. In his famous experiments he showed that if a bell was rung at the moment when meat was being offered to hungry dogs there would develop a conditioned reflex in which after a time the mere sound of the bell, with no meat present, would cause the dog to salivate. He called it a conditioned reflex because at that time physiologists were concerned with describing natural or inbuilt reflexes (reflexes such as that which causes the leg to jerk when the tendon below the kneecap is tapped). A reflex was something which connected up an input and an output without the intervention of consciousness. In Pavlov's reflex the dogs became conditioned to respond in a reflex manner to the sound of the bell.

The importance of conditioning is that the brain can be made to give a response without any intention or willing on the part of its owner. Consciousness, self and will are all by-passed. The advertising of cigarettes tries to condition the smoker to associate a certain brand with a certain life-style so that when he comes to buy the brand he will feel that he is buying the life-style. Brainwashing is regarded as an extreme form of conditioning in which a whole set of beliefs and attitudes are put into the mind to replace those already there.

Conditioning may be deliberate. For example pigeons can be trained by conditioning to stand by a conveyor belt and pick out the deformed pills from amongst the normal pills that are moving past in front of them. By the use of aversion therapy attempts are made to discourage alcoholics or criminals by playing a film of what they have hitherto enjoyed and accompanying it by an injection to make the person violently ill. After a while what had seemed pleasurable will cause a revulsion. Conditioning can also be accidental. A person brought up in a welfare state may feel that he has a right to education, health, housing and so on, without any effort being required on his part.

Recession and boom are based largely on business confidence. If an industrialist is willing to borrow and to invest, this will create employment and in turn will create a market. If one person alone has this confidence the effect will not occur but if most industrialists have the same confidence then a boom will follow. Conversely a loss of confidence means cutting back in investment and in marketing with a consequent fall in employment and a fall in the market. The wise industrialist is reacting to market indicators when his confidence moves one way or the other but the final link is that of confidence. In a mood of optimism bad news is explained away but in a mood of pessimism it is built upon to worsen the mood.

In itself confidence is an emotional state. As an emotional state it is the true opposite of anxiety and fear. It is not the same as courage because this involves overcoming fear. Nor is it mere calmness. It is something much more positive. A confidence trickster has confidence; so does a good salesman. Quite often a psychopath has confidence because in psychopaths the chemical basis for the fear mechanism may be deficient.

False confidence is confidence based on a false prediction as to how things will work out, or on incomplete information or even stupidity. The interesting thing is that very often the positive feedback effect is so strong that confidence alone will create the situation that justifies the confidence in the first place. For example a salesman who is confident of making a sale will increase his chances of doing so.

The borderline between confidence and arrogance is as indistinct as that between apathy and calmness or complacency and contentment. Arrogance dismisses the possibility of failure whereas confidence never even notices it.

Perhaps one day we shall have a confidence pill alongside our tranquillisers and anti-depressants. It would be more useful than either. Pills that are stimulants are not the same thing since confidence is not the same as stimulation or euphoria.

If you want to be sure that your metre rule is accurate you can refer to the standard metre length that is kept in France. If you want to be sure that a picture is by Rembrandt you can refer to art experts even though they are by no means infallible. But if you want to show that a course of action you propose is right there is little you can refer to apart from consensus. Consensus means the general agreement of the people concerned. Since morals and ethics are created by the people for the good of the people it seems appropriate that judgements of this sort should be referred back to the people. For instance a politician might claim that it is the general consensus that pornography should not be on display where children can see it.

But how large is a consensus? Does it mean the majority of people, and if so, a fifty-one per cent or a ninety-nine per cent majority? A person might refer to a consensus without ever actually making an effort to see what consensus exists (apart perhaps from asking the garage mechanic, the lift attendant and his secretary). Opinion polls properly carried out do provide a more accurate picture of consensus views than has been possible before but the results depend very much on how the questions are phrased and what alternatives are given.

The major drawback to consensus is that it tends to give the lowest common denominator amongst the population rather than the highest common factor. If politics relied on consensus at every step there could be no leadership and probably no change. It is unlikely that the majority of the population will suddenly and simultaneously wish to change their views.

Any poll to assess the consensus on capital punishment would very likely show a consensus in favour of having it. Yet politicians, quite rightly, take it upon themselves to lead opinion in such matters, responding to the more enlightened sections of the population (a consensus of an imagined elite). As always the dilemma is whether to lead from behind or in front. Leading from behind involves doing those things which exactly reflect consensus. Leading from in front means doing things which change rather than conform to consensus.

Claimed consensus is always a good excuse for anything.

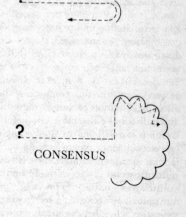

CONSENSUS

Each star is identifiable on its own but it is also part of an identifiable constellation. A constellation implies a fixed and definite series of relationships that has an identity of its own. A group contains members that have something in common. A cluster is a collection of things that have temporarily come together for some purpose, which may be hidden. A constellation is a fixed and permanent relationship between things which are separately recognisable.

We recognise a chair because it has a constellation of features which always occur in a chair: four legs, a seat, a sitting-down height above the floor, a back. Not all chairs have these features but when these features occur as a constellation we can recognise a chair. It is the fixity and predictability of a constellation that matters most.

A system or a structure is also a fixed relationship between separate parts but here the emphasis is on the relationship between the parts for this is what forms the system or structure. In a constellation the emphasis is on the individual elements and the relationship is restricted to the fact that 'they occur together in a definite way'. There is no special functional significance in the different shapes of the constellations in the night sky.

Many of our abstract concepts such as justice, humanity or truth depend on a constellation of features rather than a specific definition. If any feature is missing then the constellation is broken. For example if we start talking about a truth which is not permanent (and most human truths are not) we seem to be talking about something else. (The point is that even if truths are not permanent we must treat them as if they were.) Constellations are unalterable. If something is missing or lacking then the constellation no longer exists.

A constellation is probably the strongest word for a permanent and definite collection of items.

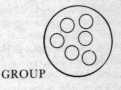

CONSTELLATION

GROUP

CLUSTER

Creative people are supposed to sit around sparking off creative ideas in all directions. It is supposed that any restraint on their creativity will kill it. Like a fragile flower it is only to be cosseted and admired. In the practical world, however, freedom of action is often limited by many constraints.

There are constraints of cost. A wonderful idea may be impractical because the object would have to be sold at a price no one could afford. The qualities of the material often provide another constraint: it is not possible to give concrete the colour of mellow brickwork. In designing for the space programme there were constraints of weight.

A designer may be set the problem of designing a personal transport device that would have the following constraints: it should be four times as fast as walking; it should not weigh more than one pound; it must fold and fit into a briefcase; it must be cheap. Some of these are more design objectives than constraints.

The behaviour of most organisations is constrained by budgets; quality of people available; considerations of public image; the law. Sometimes the constraints are given too much importance and are even used as an excuse for inaction. Sometimes constraints are purely imaginary: for instance it was claimed that shops in the main shopping street of London could not open on Saturdays because there would be no staff (in fact staff proved easy to find).

There tend to be two different styles of design. The first designer keeps the constraints in mind all the time and actually builds around them in order to develop his idea. The second type of designer ignores the constraints and develops the idea as he wishes. Once the idea is complete the designer then sees whether it can be modified or tailored to fit the constraints.

Many constraints are practical considerations. Others may be imposed by law in order to ensure that the more agile do not take advantage of the less agile. Freedom to play your transistor radio in the park denies someone else the right to peace and quiet there. So many constraints form the boundary between freedom and licence.

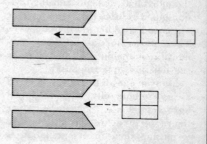

In our explanation of how things work we may have to invent in our imagination mechanisms for which there is no objective evidence. As an example theologians invented the concept of 'soul' in order to tie together man's humanity and reason and his relationship with God. Such concepts are 'constructed' by philosophers and theologians. The numbers we use in arithmetic are similar constructs. The number system is an artificial one which has been put together to serve a useful purpose.

A construct may be put forward as a sort of hypothesis. For example the ancient Greeks believed that moods were secreted as a liquid by the liver; hence 'melancholia', meaning black bile. Such hypotheses or constructs of convenience may be proved correct or they may be overtaken by fresher constructs. Today we believe that mood is probably a matter of different secretions in that part of the brain called the hypothalamus (not very different from the Greek idea). In between these two hypotheses there were others concerning stars and spirits and possession by the devil.

It was Voltaire who said that if God did not exist 'it would have been necessary to invent him'. This would be the supreme philosophical construct. The nirvana state sought by many Eastern religions is a parallel construct.

The human mind is forced into a position of constructing entities by its ability to ask questions. We assume that if a question can be asked then it must have an answer. If we ask, 'What is the purpose of life?' then we assume that there must be an answer and we spend much time looking for it. It is possible, however, that life just happened through the self-organising characteristic of certain chemicals and through such processes as evolution: there is no purpose, only history. But that is emotionally unsatisfactory so we construct a theology to answer the question.

Today the masters of construction are the sociologists. In order to explain the behaviour of people and societies they construct a variety of concepts such as 'pecking order' and 'peer group' in order to make concrete vague processes and relationships.

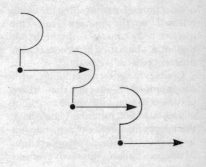

Contact is quite possibly the most important characteristic of any system. Without contact there could be no system. Two things may be in contact directly or contact may be effected through a communication channel. The brain is in contact with the ovaries through a controlling hormone released from the pituitary gland. This in turn is in contact with the hypothalamus which itself is in contact with different parts of the brain.

Contact is almost synonymous with communication except that there may be a communication channel but no contact. For instance I may have the telephone number of someone but have so far been unable to contact him. Messages, signals, interactive effects all presuppose contact.

A large amount of business is based on contacts. A person with the right contacts knows what is happening, he becomes aware of needs and opportunities and can often put the two together. One contact can lead to another contact and the net spreads. A person without the contacts only hears things long afterwards when the news has become common knowledge.

A newspaper reporter with the right contacts can uncover stories that cannot be reached by other reporters. The Watergate investigation depended on an important contact. A spy without the right contacts would not gain much

information and would not be able to pass it on.

In some countries or in certain jobs, success is supposed to depend on having the right contacts.

In the animal kingdom animals have to make contact in order to mate. Elaborate signalling systems are used to bring about this contact. A female moth releases a tiny amount of scent which attracts male moths from miles away.

When there is contact there is interaction in the system and energy can flow through it. Organisation and especially self-organisation of a system depend entirely on contact.

In a family quarrel a wife tells her husband to control his temper. A nuclear power plant uses the same energy processes as does an atom bomb but the process is controlled and slowed down so that the release of energy is gradual instead of being explosive. If the speed of the chain reaction increases cadmium rods are inserted into the pile and by mopping up neutrons they slow it down: they control it. In the early days steam engines were apt to run faster and faster until the 'governor' was invented. This was a device which responded to the speed of the engine and controlled this speed by shutting off the steam. A governor in a tape recorder controls the speed and so prevents recorded speech from sounding like Mickey Mouse. Speed controls on the highway are intended to keep the speed of vehicles below a defined limit.

The type of control described above suggests a damping down or restraint which is designed to keep something within limits. The control which a driver exerts over the speed of his own car by means of pressure on the accelerator is very different from the speed control sign he passes on the road. The driver has the power to bring about whatever speed he wishes. The puppeteer has complete control over every movement of the puppet. Each jerk or step the puppet takes is controlled by the puppeteer. The man in the control box in a crane controls the whole activity of that crane: he raises or lowers the jib; he swings it around; he raises or lowers the load.

A train driver controls the speed of the train and the starting and stopping. But he does not control the direction which is set by the rails and the switching of points. In turn the train driver is controlled by the signals which are operated by the signalman.

Control implies the ability to steer an effect in a particular direction, to increase or diminish the effect. It is always implied that the effect is independent of the control and exists in its own right. The car driver is not the engine, the train driver is not the train, the puppeteer is not the puppet. But the effectiveness and achievement of the activity depends on the control. The control may simply set limits or may exert a tight control of every movement. The control may be coarse or fine.

A young juggler is practising. He picks up one ball after another until he has four bobbing about in the air. He picks up a fifth ball but finds he cannot cope with so many and the balls tumble to the ground. He tries again and again but it is obvious that at the moment he can only cope with four balls.

A shepherd has a large flock of sheep which he is trying to move from one field to another. To help him he has a Welsh border collie which responds instantly to his whistles and commands: running round the sheep, crouching down, then springing up to head off a breakaway group. Together, the shepherd and his dog cope very well.

There is a train derailment and the injured people are rushed to the nearest hospital. Another hospital in the area telephones to see if the first hospital can cope or whether they would like to send some of the casualties on to the second hospital.

A sales manager finds that he could cope very well when he was dealing with a country sales district but that he cannot cope with the new metropolitan district.

A mother who is suffering from depression finds that she can no longer cope with her four children.

Coping implies managing and keeping on top of things. It implies just enough competence to stop things from developing into a crisis. Coping does not imply brilliance or the solution of problems, nor does it indicate in itself whether or not the coping is done with ease or with difficulty. It is enough that the situation is being managed or contained.

A manager may be able to cope with the day to day problems that arise in the running of a business but unable to cope with long-term planning. He can react to what is there but is unable to create a picture of the future and plan to meet it. The problem often arises of deciding how well a person is coping. If there are no visible signs of the situation getting out of hand then it is assumed that he is coping. It may only be later when the person has moved on to another job that it is discovered that problems were being hidden rather than solved.

Make-up has a long history extending back to the ancient Egyptians. When smallpox was prevalent make-up had a practical value in covering over and hiding the scars but otherwise the purpose has been that of beautifying. Clowns wear clown make-up to make them into clowns. Tribes in Africa, New Guinea and the North American continent wear elaborate face and body paint as part of their rituals and to make themselves look fiercer in wartime.

Make-up or war paint is always on the surface: it alters the surface appearance of things. Since we can only look at surface appearances this is usually enough: someone who looks beautiful is thought beautiful; someone who looks fierce is thought fierce.

A corporation that has been plagued by poor labour relations decides to set up a special committee of inquiry made up from management and the unions. The committee is set up but things continue just as before. The purpose of the committee is simply cosmetic: to give the surface appearance of action. Another corporation appoints a few union members to its board. But they have no real power and are soon disowned by their own unions as 'having gone over to the other side'. Again the action is purely cosmetic.

An important visitor is coming to a school. Everything is tidied up, a fresh coat of white paint is applied over the graffiti and the rowdiest pupils are taken on a nature walk. The visitor is impressed by the cosmetic effect. An ambitious young teacher appears to take a great interest in the new subject area of 'General Thinking Skills'. He talks a lot about it but never actually gets round to teaching it. The effect is cosmetic.

Cosmetics are effective. Many people would look far less attractive without them. Cosmetics are a communicating device and as such are useful. It is their function as a camouflage that is more dubious. If a gesture and a symbol are enough to show that one's intentions are well directed, is there any need to follow up such intentions with action? If reality can give no better an impression than cosmetics why bother with reality?

If you set out to achieve something but the measures you take lead to the opposite result then they are counter-productive or operating counter to the effect you intend.

The Post Office is losing money so it puts up the charge on the mail service. This makes it too expensive for advertisers to use for mail-shot so the revenue actually falls. The charges are increased still further. Again this cuts down usage. In effect the price increase tends to be counter-productive: it fails to increase revenue.

There is a campus demonstration and in an attempt to control it the authorities charge some of the students with damaging property. This enrages the other students who now have a definite grievance. So the demonstration gets worse instead of better. The measures prove to be counter-productive.

An airline has an enviable safety record because it has never lost a passenger. Someone suggests that this record should be included in their advertising. The effect is counter-productive because some people feel the airline must be due for an accident and others are frightened off air travel by being reminded of the possibility of a crash.

An advertising campaign is designed to discourage smoking. It pictures men who have died from lung cancer. The effect is counter-productive. The fate is so awful that people assume it could never happen to them and so the campaign has no effect. In contrast a campaign that claims that smokers are unpleasant to kiss is more effective because it is more credible.

A doctor sets out to be entirely honest with his patients. The policy turns out to be counter-productive because the patients prefer him to be definite and decisive rather than to admit to hesitation and indecision.

A lowering of the interest rate in order to encourage industrial investment may at first be counter-productive as industrialists hold back to await a further fall.

Rent control can be counter-productive if it results in the disappearance from the market of properties for rent.

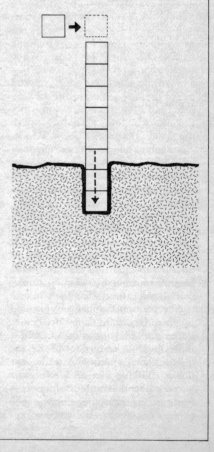

It is nice to think that if you are honest, objective and sincere people will believe what you have to say. Unfortunately, credibility and honesty are two different things. Credibility is the likelihood of people believing in what you have to say.

A motor car manufacturer comes up with a design of engine that uses only half as much fuel per mile as any other comparable engine. He wishes to advertise this advantage.

'Our new car uses half as much fuel as any other.'
'A series of tests have proved that our new car uses half as much fuel as these other cars.'
'The *Journal of Motoring* has carried out its own tests and shown that fuel consumption is only half that of other engines.'
'Our new engine uses twenty per cent less fuel than other engines.'

An honest statement of the fact may have little impact since readers have now come to expect that claims are exaggerated by advertising. An attempt may be made to shift the emphasis from statement or opinion to 'scientific tests' which are more believable. If an outside authority which is not especially concerned in selling the car carries out the test the results are even more credible. Finally it may be dishonest to say that the car uses twenty per cent less fuel but this may be more credible than the honest statement which suggests too big a difference.

The famous Avis advertisement slogan: 'We are number 2 so we try harder' is entirely credible because trying harder is a credible consequence of being number 2 in the field.

Credibility is the readiness of the listener to believe and this depends on his assessment of the communicator. The listener naturally discounts advertising claims, even when they are true. Internal credibility is to do with the message in itself, quite apart from who is sending it. An advertising message which points out faults in a credible way may enjoy some of this credibility for the advantages of the product.

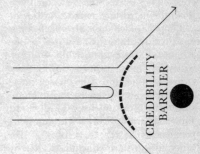

CREDIBILITY BARRIER

There is a suspicion that outside a newspaper office there is no such thing as a crisis. Every other newspaper headline indicates a crisis of one sort or another. There is a leadership crisis in the current election. There is a political crisis in some foreign country. There is a crisis of confidence. There is an economic crisis. There is a labour relations crisis in the form of a strike. There is a crisis in education. There is a crisis when there is no news which can plausibly be called a crisis.

People love things to happen. They love to be brought to the point of drama: what will happen next? When planes were being hijacked the drama was intense because it was long drawn out and there were so many stages at which something could happen. The pleasure and excitement of expectation are quite separate from the content. So newspaper, television and radio coverage, ever mindful of human needs, create moments of drama and calls them crises. A crisis is simply a point at which you expect something to happen next.

A crisis is a point for decision or action. If you do nothing then the situation deteriorates rapidly to the point of disaster or catastrophe. If you

do something then the action itself becomes the development.

A crisis is a sort of vertical crossroads, as shown in the diagram. This is not a normal crossroads since one arm goes upwards and another downwards. The ball is rolling along on the level. The crossroads, crisis or decision point is reached. If no action is taken the ball falls down to disaster. If the right action is taken the ball bridges the gap and rolls along. If, however, advantage is taken of the crisis the ball may find itself moving upwards.

There is always a possibility that the crisis is not so serious as is claimed and that no action is the best action. This also is suggested in the diagram showing the ball rolling over a channel that is not wide enough to swallow it up.

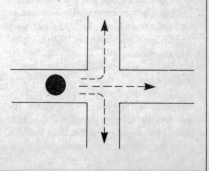

A government like an individual can survive for a considerable period by borrowing money to meet its debts. The time will come, however, when no one will be willing to lend it money and when in any case most of the money it borrows will have to be used to pay the interest on the money borrowed earlier. The crunch will have come. This happened to the city of New York in 1975 and for a while it looked as if the city would be allowed to go bankrupt. In the end a new package of taxes, expenditure cuts, new borrowings and the use of pension funds saved the situation.

An organisation like a person can go on putting off the crisis by delaying tactics but the day comes when the crisis can be put off no longer. This is the crunch. In an Irish story a man jumps from the top of a skyscraper. As he passes the third floor window he is heard to mutter, 'So far so good.' The crunch lies ahead of him.

A crunch is more than a crisis. A crisis is the acute presentation of a problem that has to be solved. The crunch is what happens when it is not solved. A crisis is an impending attack or impending bankruptcy. The crunch is the actual attack or the actual bankruptcy. Because we use the word crisis to mean something that can still be avoided we have to use the word crunch to indicate something that is happening. The time for avoidance is past. One can picture the closing jaws of disaster. Up until the last minute there is always, in theory, a chance of avoiding the jaws. But suddenly this chance is gone and the jaws are crunching together.

When it comes to the crunch things that are flimsy collapse; people who are full of bravado turn out to be full of air; luxuries have to be abandoned; true values come to the fore. The crunch is regarded as a testing and even as a purifying process. In a curious way many people actually welcome the crunch because the days of fear and anticipation and desperate problem solving are over. When it comes to the crunch, day to day survival is all that matters and that concentrates the mind wonderfully.

A crunch is usually fairly sudden but it is possible for a slow squeeze to reach a point where it finally becomes a crunch.

The characteristics of a crystal are that it is small, crystal clear and, with its sharp edges and geometrical faces, as definite as can be. A crystal is the antithesis of anything that is vague and amorphous.

With the gelling process we wait for something intangible to gel into something more definite. The crystallisation process goes much further. To obtain crystals one boils and boils the fluid in which the chemical is suspended until at last the crystals emerge when all else has been boiled away. So crystallisation is a reduction process: boiling something down to its sharp-edged essence. Simplification, clarification, condensation all come into crystallisation.

Chemically speaking, crystals are pure. They always consist of one chemical compound. You can have crystals of sodium chloride (common table salt) or of copper sulphate but you cannot have a crystal that is a mixture of the two compounds together. When we crystallise something we have to decide what constitutes the pure essence of the matter. A crystallisation should never be confused or ambiguous.

Since confusion and ambiguity are so unpleasant a state for the human mind there is a strong drive towards crystallisation. This can go wrong and end up with a slogan which is taken to be the crystallisation of a whole argument or attitude. The slogan is then bandied about and comes to have a life of its own. People who use and believe in the slogan may have little idea of its background. For true crystallisation to occur the individual himself should go through the process rather than accept the end-product second-hand.

It is not always useful to crystallise attitudes or feelings because it may give them a definiteness which they do not really have. It may also remove useful ambiguity.

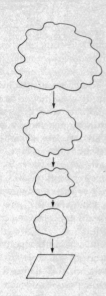

Cultural is a very convenient word because it allows someone to say that two people are very different even though at the same time it is admitted that they are the same. In other words the two people are equal as human beings but different in terms of their cultural background.

In Japan women tend not to go out to work. They stay at home to look after their homes, children and husbands. A Japanese woman will walk a few paces behind her husband and will obey him at all times. In the United States husbands rush forward to open doors for their wives, women feel unfulfilled unless they also have a career outside their homes, obedience to a husband is replaced by give and take or dominance over the man. In Africa and New Guinea there are tribes which are famous for the beauty and delicacy of their wood carvings. Yet nearby tribes have no tradition of wood carving whatsoever.

Culture primarily refers to the habits, beliefs, customs, relationships and general way of behaving of any group of people who have a culture in common. If any group of people, be it a tribe or a nation, behave in a uniform manner then there is a definite culture. Some cultures may have a lot in common but others may be totally different. In general the older the culture the more likely it is to be distinct.

In New Guinea there are seven hundred separate languages and to some extent each language represents a different culture. The country is very mountainous and people live in isolated valleys without much contact with each other. Each tribe develops its own culture and language. Better communications mean a spread of culture so that today's youth culture is fairly uniform across the world, having everywhere the same dress, the same music and the same problems.

Culture also denotes the arts and those interested in them. Since artists are driven by critics and buyers to be distinct from each other there is an inevitable escalation which takes the works out of the range of appreciation of ordinary people. So culture tends to become an in-game or a sort of club without any relevance to the mass of people. There are few opportunities (such as those provided by Church art) for contact.

The king of Lydia is supposed to have been the first to use coins as currency in about 700 BC. But there have been all sorts of other currencies. The Aztecs used cocoa beans or gold-filled quills. Many seafaring civilisations used shells.

Currency is as much a communicating device as a telephone or a letter. Currency has the advantage that the communication can be stored. As a communicating device currency has the immense value that it can relate things which are otherwise dissimilar. There is no obvious connection between a gramophone disc and an apple but by means of currency one can be exchanged for a quantity of the other.

In any communication system a message is exchanged for an effect. A commander sends an order for his troops to advance. This message is exchanged for the advance of the troops. A doctor telephones to tell a man that his wife has recovered from an operation. The message is exchanged for his joy and relief. Similarly the communication of currency involves the exchange of some goods or service for the currency. The only difference is that the currency itself has had to be obtained through work or other expenditure of energy. But the telephone has had to be set up by payment of some kind and so has any other type of communicating system.

The currency may differ from one system to another. In an electrical circuit the currency is electric current. In a political election the currency is charisma and promises. In a snobbish society the currency might be a title or suitable ancestry. A currency is any form of communication energy that makes a difference. A strong currency makes a lot of difference whereas a weak currency makes little. Individuals have little currency apart from an occasional vote for changing government action: perhaps their only currency is a protest that is publicised by the media. The currency of a government is tax and the law. The currency of the Church is comfort and reassurance (it used to be a sense of purpose and virtue). The currency of the human mind is an idea.

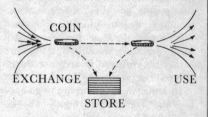

In the world of functions and relationships a curve may be a straight line. The word 'curve' is used to describe a relationship between one thing and another. It comes directly from the curve that is drawn on a graph to show the relationship between the two things which are related in the graph. Suppose we are looking at a company that makes refrigerators. The first graph in the diagram shows a 'straight line curve' between salesman and sales of refrigerators. This means that if the company increases the number of salesmen then the sales of refrigerators will rise proportionately. In the second graph there is a relationship between advertising and sales. The curve can be said to 'flatten off'. This means that at first an increase in advertising leads to a great increase in sales. This continues for some time but a point is reached when increasing advertising only leads to a slight increase in sales. We may imagine that by now most people know about the refrigerators but are not buying because the price is not right (or the market is saturated). The final graph shows what is called an 'S-shaped curve'. This relates expenditure on research to sales. At first there is not much effect. A small amount of money spent on research is almost useless. But when significant amounts are being spent on research the investment pays off in better products and the sales rise. There comes a point, however, when the curve 'flattens off' and increasing expenditure on research does not result in better sales.

When we talk about the curve of a relationship we picture a graph in our minds and hope the listener does so too. We then describe the curve. For example we may talk about an 'S-shaped curve' relating exercise to health. This means that a little exercise does not make much difference. Moderate exercise is more beneficial the more one takes. Excessive exercise adds very little more.

The description of the 'curve' of a relationship is a direct and simple way of describing the relationship.

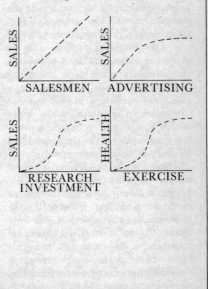

We know that the cost of developing the pilot's seat for the Concorde supersonic airliner was £356,000. In development costs the airliner itself cost about £900 million. Once money had been committed to the project it was difficult to operate a cut-off for political and other reasons: there was the co-operation with the French, there were the number of jobs involved, the existing investment that would be wasted, the chance of technical success.

Cut-offs are always difficult to operate because by definition they involve a decision to waste the money that has already been spent on a project. Du Pont spent $100 million trying to launch as a substitute for leather a new type of plastic that looked like leather and allowed air to pass through it for ventilation. Both RCA and Xerox invested heavily in computers before they reached a cut-off point and decided to drop out of the computer field. The decision is between losing the money already invested or investing further with no guarantee of success. Many individual entrepreneurs have gone bankrupt precisely because as individuals they could not operate a cut-off but felt compelled to invest more and more money in order to overcome a problem; as individuals their problem solving pride was challenged.

There are also times when a cut-off is operated too soon and a promising project is killed. After extensive work everyone had lost interest in the chemical dopamine and it was only chance that led a Greek scientist to use much larger doses and show the great effectiveness of the drug in treating Parkinsonism (a state characterised by rigidity and tremor). Early work on the possibility of making plate glass by floating it on a bed of molten metal came to nothing. It was many years before the project was taken up again by the Pilkington company and turned into a huge success.

A young man is hopelessly in love with a girl who spurns his attentions. Ultimately his persistence triumphs over the attractions of rival suitors. Another young man in a similar position operates a cut-off and marries someone who is more responsive.

Knowing when to persist and when to give up and cut one's losses is probably the most difficult of all decisions because there is everything to lose and little to gain.

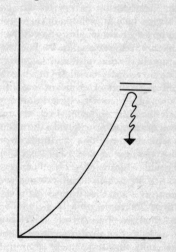

Norbert Wiener is credited with the discovery of cybernetics. In fact he gave it the name and worked out some of the basic mathematics of feedback loops and control systems. The name comes from the Greek for governor or steersman since cybernetics is the study of control. The original impetus for the work came from the need to keep the aim of an anti-aircraft gun locked on to the aircraft even when the pilot was taking evasive action.

Although some of the principles of control and feedback and homeostasis had existed for some time before Wiener coined the term cybernetics, it is fair to credit him with establishing this field. In its way the development of cybernetics is one of the most significant intellectual steps of all time. Traditionally systems had been seen in terms of cause and effect linked together in linear chains. With cybernetics there was a feedback loop from the effect to the cause. If you shoot a gun at the target your vision of the extent of the 'miss' feeds back to alter your aim. In a chemical process the temperature of the chemical in the vat is fed back through a thermometer to alter the heating system so as to keep the temperature constant. This is as true of the central heating system in a house as it is of the temperature of the human body.

Although cybernetics was developed as a study of control systems the same principles apply in self-organising systems. So in effect cybernetics is the study of systems and especially of dynamic systems. Through cybernetics we can begin to look at the complex organising systems that make up living matter. We can also look at the complex interacting systems that make up economics.

The Wright brothers were among the first to apply practical cybernetics. Unlike their rivals in Europe they designed an aircraft which could *not* fly by itself. Instead they built in controls which allowed the pilot to control any tendency to tilt or dip. The pilot's eyesight (and seat of his pants) completed the feedback loop.

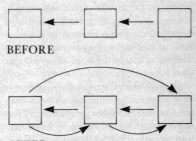

BEFORE

AFTER

A steam engine would not work if there was a constant pressure of steam on the piston. Because the flow of steam is periodically interrupted by the valve the piston is able to move backwards and forwards and so generate motion and useful power. The power of a permanent magnet cannot be turned into a useful engine because there is no way of switching it on or off, so once the pull has been exerted the attracted metal remains stuck to the magnet. If we could switch this magnetic attraction on and off in a cycle then we should have a useful engine. This is what is done in the electric motor.

On/off cycles seem to be a characteristic of nature because they provide the simplest form of a dynamic system. The electromagnetic waves that form the basis of radio, light or X-rays can all be described in terms of cycles of energy or a wave motion. The ordinary waves in the sea transmit energy over long distances although we have not yet succeeded in harnessing this. A cork or buoy floating in a harbour goes up and down as each wave passes. There is a cycle of movement: up to a peak height then down to a trough. The leg that turns the pedal on a bicycle goes through the same sort of up and down cyclical motion. The rotation of a wheel is also a cycle insofar as a point on the rim moves to a point as far distant as possible on the other side of the wheel and then comes back to the original point.

There are cycles in fashion: skirts get longer and then shorter and then longer again. There are cycles in morals from Victorian to permissive and then back again. In any system where there is change and yet the direction of change is strictly limited there is likely to be a cycle. This follows because people are bored with what exists or react against it. People who are bored with short skirts can only make them longer and when they have reached the ground they can only be made shorter again.

Business and economic cycles arise for two reasons. The first is the operation of greed and confidence. People buy property because it is doing well so it does better and better until a point is reached when the increase in price slows down and the second part of the cycle (decline) takes over. The second reason is the mismatch between supply and need. Whenever things are out of phase a cycle results: investment followed by overcapacity, followed by a fall in investment and eventual undercapacity and so on.

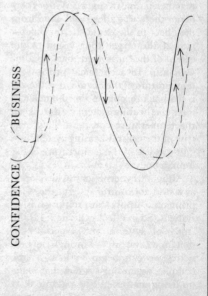

Car springs have dampers attached to them. Were it not for these dampers the car would bounce up and down like a yo-yo for a long time after it hit a bump in the road. The dampers do nothing to reduce the effectiveness of the springs in absorbing the impact of the bump but they act to prevent the springs continuing to oscillate. Without these dampers or shock absorbers the springs would oscillate until all the energy of the bump had been dissipated as heat through the friction in the spring itself. The diagram shows a damped oscillation of a spring compared to an undamped one. In practice the dampers are friction or viscosity devices.

There are times when oscillations can be inconvenient. Many people have large swings of mood from being elated to being depressed. Some of those who read books on psychiatry even consider themselves to be manic-depressives. In fact many of these mood swings are comparatively normal for people living in the stress of modern society. They can, however, be an indication of depression. It seems that the increasing stress of life produces chemical changes in the brain that lead to those mood swings. We do not know exactly what is happening but it may be that the system is forced into a hunting state (see under 'Hunting'). As regards treatment it might seem logical to try to retain the upswings and get rid of the downswings. In practice it is easier to try to damp down the swings altogether and to try to restore the person to a 'normal' mood (if there is such a thing). If, however, the damping down is overdone then all mood fluctuations may be lost: but treat-

ment is rarely that effective.

The price of many commodities such as cocoa, wool, beef, grain and copper fluctuates wildly. This may seem hard to understand since the world's consumption of these items does not fluctuate to the same degree. It is true that poor harvests can cause shortages but many people suspect that the wild fluctuations are caused by the structure of the market. People buy commodity futures ahead and hope that at the time of delivery the price will have risen so that they make a profit. Conversely they promise to sell at a certain price and hope that when called upon to do so the buying price will have fallen. There is a growing feeling that these artificial fluctuations need damping down.

There is a growing fashion for collecting data of any description. This is because the dinosaurs of the electronic age are the computers which need to be fed with prodigious amounts of data. Anyone with access to a computer feels a compulsion to feed it with as much data as possible. Fortunately there is no danger of anyone running out of data. It is always possible to generate as much data as one wants. Imagine that you are measuring a potato. You could measure its longest length or its widest width. But you could also choose to measure its circumference at an infinite number of points and so have an infinite source of data. You could do the same for any number of potatoes.

The diagram shows the outline of a shape cut out of cardboard. It is possible to measure lengths at any point and in any direction so generating limitless data. There would have to be a reason for doing this but, too often, the possibility of measuring something is so appealing that the reason is only found afterwards, as a sort of excuse.

The data that can be obtained from people is limitless in the same way: height, weight, colouring, racial background, protein chemistry, smoking habits, food habits, food preferences, buying habits, income levels, attitudes to work, political attitudes, sleeping patterns, psychological hang-ups, sexual performance and so on. In most cases science has now become a matter of measuring everything in sight, feeding it all into a computer, asking the computer to sort out which things relate to which, and then sitting back and waiting for a significant idea to emerge.

Francis Bacon who is credited with being the father of modern science was a Lord Chancellor of England in Elizabethan times. His basic notion was that instead of thinking how things ought to be (as was fashionable at the time) scientists should carefully observe nature and list down the features they saw. There would then be a general comparison of the items which had certain features and those which did not. For a long time his ideas were regarded as impractical until, suddenly, the computer made them possible. Unfortunately, data only becomes information when it is looked at through the spectacles of an idea; the idea has to come first.

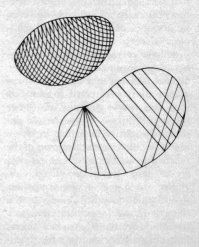

I want you to design a building to provide fifty thousand square feet of office space, to fit in this corner site and to blend with the buildings around.

I want you to design a wage-paying system that will be simple to operate and yet very flexible.

I want you to design a new set of cutlery that will be both attractive and distinctive.

I want you to design a stage set for a new production of *Macbeth*.

It is said that at one time in Japan the design of every article in the house (tables, teapots, flower vases) was prescribed according to the social status of the household. Although this allowed little free choice it did mean that everyone grew up in surroundings of good design, which has become a cultural characteristic of the Japanese.

A designer is a problem solver who has to shape something to meet some need. A designer may design for use if all his effort is directed to ensuring that the object, whether bicycle or typewriter, works properly. A designer may design for selling in which case he would pay full attention to the visual appearance of the object and also to its selling price: there is no reason why a functioning typewriter should not be beautiful as well; there is no reason why a pocket calculator should not be attractive to look at and to feel. Finally a designer may design

for production: the design can be put together quickly and easily by unskilled workers and the chance of error or breakage is low. In practice a designer usually keeps all three things in mind but it is the different priorities that matter.

A designer may design for beauty, for cost or for durability. The designer's aim creates his problem: he sets up his different targets (function, cost, appearance) and then tries to find a way of reaching them all at once.

Designs tend to move in a saw-tooth fashion. A trend starts and then develops by steps (more chrome and more fins were added to 1950 cars) until someone makes a radical change and it all starts again.

Determinism is the opposite of free will. The concept of free will has arisen for two reasons. The first is that we are conscious of the difference between doing something because we are told to do it and doing something 'of our own free will'. The difference is very real, so since the situation of being told or forced to do something is clearly not free the other situation must be free. Whether the 'free' situation is really free or simply an illusion does not matter. It is possible to hypnotise someone and to tell her that after she has come out of the hypnotic trance she will respond to the code word 'rain' by getting up and pouring herself a glass of water. Some time later the word 'rain' is introduced into the conversation and the person gets up and pours a glass of water. If she is asked why she has done this she would maintain that it is because she 'wanted' to. The hypnotised subject feels that she is free to act in this way but observers know that the action is determined.

In practice it is our sensation of freedom which gives us our sense of ego and individualism. If all our actions were determined by orders or conditioning then we would seem to be driving on a railway track rather than on the road. Of course if we did not know or feel that our actions were determined then we should still feel as free as ever.

Religion has provided the second, and most powerful, reason for the concept of free will. If people were to be encouraged to get to heaven then they had to be virtuous and do the right things. This could best be achieved by punishing them if they did wrong. So there were created the concepts of sin and guilt and hell-fire and damnation. Now this would have been most unjust if a person was not 'free' to choose to do good or evil. If his actions were predetermined towards evil then punishment would be directly predetermined. Moreover reward and punishment would have no meaning if decisions could not be made freely. Finally no one would deserve to get to heaven if the actions that got him there were predetermined without his having any choice in the matter.

In fact if we include within a person's ego all his experiences and consciousness of customs and habits then his ego seems to be free to do what it has been conditioned to do. If we leave all these things outside our definition of the ego then its behaviour is determined by them.

Socrates was the first to place emphasis on dialectic, that is the art of logical argument. In essence the process takes the form of a statement countered by an opposing statement with an ensuing debate between the two points of view. A more precise meaning was given to the term by Hegel, the German philosopher of the nineteenth century, and by Marx with his concept of dialectical materialism. The notion is that there is a thesis which is opposed by an antithesis and finally the two resolve into a synthesis. Then the whole process starts again. This process is supposed to underlie the evolution of history and the social condition of man. Progress is seen as arising from the necessary clash between the thesis and antithesis. It is for this reason that Marx and Lenin put such great emphasis on the transition stage from capitalism to Communism. This transition stage was the state of struggle. By concentrating on this conflict rather than the utopia that was to result at the end, the founders of Communism gave a sense of mission and purpose to their followers: opposition and struggle are easier and more tangible than constructive evolution.

In society as a whole we pay a great deal of attention to the dialectic model. We run many of our systems on an adversary basis. The legal system is run on the basis that one side holds one point of view and the other side attacks this. The political system is run on the basis that the government has a policy and that this is necessarily opposed by the opposition. Schools put a lot of emphasis on debating skills. Negotiations in business and between employees and employers are also conducted on an adversary or dialectical basis. We rarely challenge the system and yet from the point of view of increasing understanding it has several outstanding deficiencies.

In the dialectic process more time is spent trying to destroy the opposite case than exploring the matter itself. Proving the other side wrong is taken as evidence for the rightness of your case, and yet both may be right or wrong. Polarisation is encouraged to the extent that political parties must try to disagree even on matters where there is obvious agreement. In short the force of thinking is directed towards debating skills rather than problem solving skills.

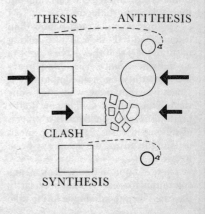

THESIS   ANTITHESIS

CLASH

SYNTHESIS

When two sides are speaking to each other there is a dialogue. When one side is giving orders and the other side is obeying, or disobeying them, there is no dialogue. When one side is talking and the other side is not listening there is a monologue. Usually requests for a dialogue are based on the notion that one side has listened long enough and feels it is time for the other side to do some listening. In the days of student disorders the main battle slogan was the need for a dialogue between students and university authorities. In many cases as soon as the structure for a dialogue was set up the students lost interest in carrying out their side of the dialogue.

Talking is much more fun than listening and those who like talking naturally feel that they have a right to an audience. Since it is unfair to inflict this duty on non-combatants it seems just that those who have done the talking hitherto should now do the listening. Hence dialogue is a process of talking in turns. It can also mean listening in turns but this is apt to be forgotten.

There is a notion that talking means communication. This is not necessarily the case when the dialogue has to take place in public because much that is said is by way of gesture and is directed towards the listeners on one's own side rather than towards those on the other side. As a result public dialogue can confuse an issue more than clarify it. There should be a formalised method whereby a public speaker could indicate to which side he was addressing his remarks at the moment. Lack of such a formal indicator has led to much misunderstanding in the past. Since we are today sophisticated enough to make the distinction a politician is in the happy position of being able to say anything he wants and afterwards claiming that it was directed towards one side or the other.

In fact there is extremely little dialogue in society between the government and the governed. Most of the communication is very one-sided and is processed by media mechanisms that are almost the opposite of dialogue. The opinion poll is almost the only effective step towards a social dialogue and even that is limited in its usefulness. The vote is no part of a dialogue since there may be disagreement with both sides or a mixture of agreement and disagreement with one or other side.

Diffusion is a gentle process of mixture or spread. When two gases meet the molecules of one gas move slowly in amongst the molecules of the other until eventually there is a mixture of the two gases.

The diagram shows some different ways in which something can spread. In the first instance there is a hard-edged spread which swamps anything which gets in the way. In the second instance fingers spread out and intrude into the surroundings. Each finger itself becomes a point of spread with further fingerlings spreading out from it. In the third instance there is a more gentle spread with a diffusion out from the centre and a mixing of the new with the old. The processes can be likened to a spread of a religion or ideology: by conquest, by colonisation or missionary work, or by cultural diffusion.

Diffusion is the opposite of clash and confrontation. It is a soft rather than hard sell and though more powerful in its consequences, is much more difficult to effect. We know what a diffusing molecule is in a gas but what corresponds to this molecule in other situations? Is it a person with a set of ideas and attitudes? Is it a book which carries some message? Is it a number of apparently separate ideas, slogans and attitudes that spread independently but actually add up to something coherent? The diffusion of American culture in Japan is taking place through the language with importation of American words and concepts (*shokku* for shock), and through such items as golf, Coca Cola and American business attitudes (for example towards executive mobility: the Japanese habit was for an executive to

stay with the same firm for life).

In modern society pop records, films, television programmes, magazines and to a lesser extent books have provided very powerful diffusion devices, with the result that youth culture at least is now almost universal. Throughout the world everyone wears jeans and listens to the same music.

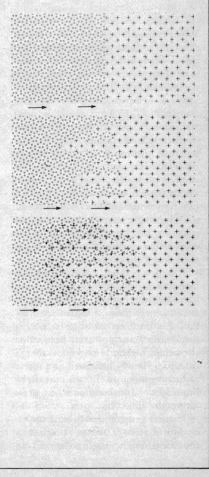

The digestion system sets to work on the food we eat almost as soon as it enters the mouth. There are enzymes in the saliva that start the process of breaking the food down into chemicals that can be absorbed by the body. The process continues in the stomach with further enzymes and strong hydrochloric acid. The main process of digestion takes place in the small intestine. The purpose of digestion is to change the food into sugars, amino-acids and fats that can be absorbed into the blood stream. The blood from the gut all goes to the liver first and here much of the material is removed and stored.

We can talk about digesting an experience. We can talk about digesting information. In both cases we mean taking in the experience and information and then breaking it down so that we can assimilate it. This is quite different from reacting to the information or storing it. Nor is it the same as analysing the information for in analysis we break things down in order to understand them whereas in digestion we absorb rather than understand: we can absorb a mood or feeling without really understanding it.

The process of digestion is not unlike the process of putting everything into the melting pot so that it can be stewed into something nourishing. Digestion is different from the normal pick-and-choose process of perception. Perception tends to choose what confirms an already held idea and rejects what does not fit in with available knowledge. Digestion seeks to break down the individual perceptions and to extract nourishment from them.

The digestive system is active in digestion: what is being digested has little effect on this system. It could presumably cause indigestion which in functional terms might mean a surfeit of information leading to confusion. In general digestion is an absorbing process rather than a communicating one. The diagram illustrates the difference between reaction, analysis and digestion.

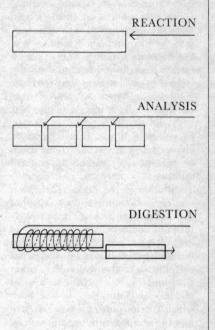

REACTION

ANALYSIS

DIGESTION

Traditionally dignity was based on what was due to a person because of the office he held. The respect which that person could claim was the measure of his dignity. The office or ritual was all-important and the person holding that office could claim the dignity of the office no matter how unworthy he might be. In a particular ceremony the individuals taking part in that ceremony, whether religious or civil, acquire a temporary dignity by virtue of their office. Today we are less inclined to give respect to an office independently of the person occupying it. Yet instead of degrading the concept of dignity we have freed it from the attachment to office and generalised it to mean 'worthy of respect'.

By dignity we seem to imply a person who has a proper sense of his own value as a human being. This sense of value is internally generated and does not depend on the acclaim of others. The difficulty is that a person who has an internally generated sense of value can be insensitive to others, callous or arrogant. Clearly this has nothing to do with dignity. Similarly a person who has an exaggerated sense of his own value might appear to be conceited or pompous. It would seem that the sense of value has to be fitting. Everyone is ready to acclaim the

dignity of a peasant or farmer as he tills his land or rides a donkey into the sunset. There is something timeless and romantic about this. But would everyone accord the same dignity to a mechanic repairing a combine harvester for use in the wheatfields of Kansas?

There is something about dignity which requires it to be quiet. There must be no clamouring for attention. Worth must be internally generated even if not noticed or appreciated. Perhaps it is the simplest way of saying that a man is fulfilling his role as a human being and his role in society. But this fulfilling of roles must be part of the man's nature. It must not seem to be a matter of striving or effort. That too will merit praise but is not the same thing as dignity.

A government knows that if it relaxes credit control, investment will increase, there will be more jobs and unemployment will decrease. At the same time there is a danger of increased inflation. On the other hand tighter credit control will reduce inflation but will probably keep unemployment at the same level or increase it. There is a dilemma. Whichever way the government moves seems to be dangerous.

There is a sudden epidemic of a new virus disease. The disease is quite serious. A scientist has developed a new treatment for the disease. If he uses the treatment on all the cases and they recover he will never know how good it is. If he uses the treatment on only half the cases this will show him how good it is but will also mean that many of the untreated cases might die unnecessarily. There is a dilemma.

Following the thalidomide tragedy much stricter controls have been imposed on new drugs. It is said that the tests are so exacting that penicillin itself would not have been passed had they been in force when penicillin was being developed. There is a dilemma. If the controls are not strict enough then dangerous drugs may be introduced. If the controls are too strict then valuable new drugs may never be used or even developed.

A manufacturer of furniture wishes to improve the design of his furniture. But he knows that the cost will go up. This will probably mean that his sales will go down since other people will be selling at a cheaper price. But if he does not change his design he might lose sales anyway. He is caught in a dilemma. He would probably solve it by deciding where his likeliest market was and by trying to improve design without raising the price.

If a kidnap ransom is paid this may encourage other kidnappers. If it is not paid the victim might be killed to show that the threat is serious and to encourage payment in future.

A dislocation of the shoulder joint occurs when the head of the upper arm bone (the humerus) comes out of its socket. It is very painful but it is always possible to replace the bone, although a tendency to further dislocation may follow.

A dislocation implies something out of place in time or space. For instance a tight schedule may be dislocated because one of the meetings takes ten minutes longer than it should or because traffic density extends the travelling time longer than anticipated. If the next appointment can be cancelled the schedule may be restored. But if none of the appointments can be cancelled the dislocation will run right through the programme.

Dislocation is different from disintegration or destruction because the parts are still intact. They may, however, be in the wrong relationship to each other in time or space.

Building a large office block is a carefully scheduled operation. Everything is worked out in detail. The materials must be there when needed, but *only* when needed or else they will get in the way. The work force has to be tailored exactly to the job. It is not much use having people standing around because they cannot get on with the second part of a job until the first part is finished. Overtime is expensive and should be used as little as possible. This whole tightly knit programme can be dislocated by a strike at one of the suppliers or by an unsuspected design fault in the plans. A delay causes everything to get out of phase.

A new person appointed to a department may dislocate the work pattern that has been built up. The resignation of a key person may dislocate a project.

Because complex systems depend on each part interacting with each other part, time and space positions matter a great deal. Any upset in these is a dislocation. It is a dislocation when something does not happen when it should. It is also a dislocation when something is taken out of its proper place.

We are usually concerned with passing on energy in a useful form. We are concerned with action and with bringing things about. We are concerned with communication and the flow of communication energy. But with 'dissipate' the emphasis is on waste-disposal. For some reason there has been a build-up of energy at some point and we now want to get rid of this energy. It is immaterial to us where it goes to: the intention is simply to dispose of it.

The purpose of a car radiator is to dissipate the heat that builds up in the engine.

The purpose of the heat shield in a space capsule is to protect the capsule and its occupants from the fierce heat of re-entry caused by air friction and to dissipate this heat.

It is said that football matches provide a means for dissipating the energy and aggression that would otherwise build up and be released elsewhere (it can also be said that they are a training ground for aggressive behaviour).

A mob works itself up into a state of anger. Efforts are directed towards dissipating this anger. Tension builds up in a meeting. This is dissipated by someone making a joke.

The basic point in these examples is that energy is building up to a dangerous level and efforts are directed towards dissipating it.

Dissipation is the opposite of head-on clash or containment. In the mob example head-on clash would mean a show of opposing force. Containment would mean an effort to hold in the energy. Dissipation is a structure, device or action that allows the energy to leak away.

Dissipation can occur in a different context, when the build-up of energy is useful but where the energy is carelessly dissipated so that no useful effect remains. It is said that Peron dissipated the great wealth that had built up in Argentina after the Second World War. Heirs are said to dissipate the fortunes left to them.

The government of a country may wish to take over its shipbuilding industry because it is badly run and inefficient. This would be a pragmatic decision designed to guarantee the jobs of the workers and to maintain the industry. Alternatively the takeover might have been on the grounds that the industry was making huge profits and the government coveted these. This would be another pragmatic decision whether or not one agreed with the morality of it. In the third alternative the takeover decision may simply be based on the socialist doctrine of nationalisation of major industries, irrespective of the actual conditions in the industry. In practice the case is rarely clear-cut but it is often felt that certain actions and decisions are propelled by a sense of doctrine rather than actual need or a desire to do good.

A boy involved in an accident is taken to hospital. He has been severely injured and has lost a lot of blood. The doctors are about to give him a blood transfusion when his father objects on religious grounds: blood transfusions are not allowed according to the doctrine he follows. In the end a legal decision is made to overrule the father and to give the boy the transfusion.

In many Catholic countries a number of women take contraceptive pills even though this is directly against Catholic doctrine. Their behaviour is pragmatic: they cannot afford to support any more children. In contrast the attitude of the Catholic Church towards contraception is doctrinaire. It is based on adherence to a strict doctrine regarding interference with the natural purpose of life. Many people cannot understand why this doctrine is not changed to meet the demands of the modern world with its concern about overpopulation and the availability of effective contraceptive methods. The Church's reply would be that if doctrine was forever being altered to suit immediate convenience then there would be no doctrine at all.

The adherence to doctrine as a basis for decision, action and judgement makes life easier. Doctrine is not a substitute for thinking but a definite reference framework to which all thinking is referred. Being doctrinaire means being propelled by doctrine first and by the circumstances second.

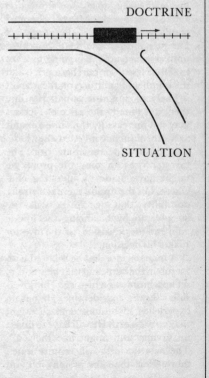

DOCTRINE

SITUATION

It is very easy to assume that risks are symmetrical. If you put your money on the red colour at roulette you will either lose all your money or gain an amount equal to all your money. Few risk situations are as exactly symmetrical as this. In a risk situation we can look at what might be gained and we can compare this with what might be lost. What might be lost we call the downside risk.

An investor puts his money into a Picasso painting. What are the downside risks? Possibly the painting will be shown to be a forgery, but this can be covered by guarantees from the dealer. The painting could be destroyed by fire or flood or stolen, but protection against these risks can be obtained through insurance. The price of Picasso paintings might fall, but this is unlikely since no one is going to want to sell at less than purchase price and the number of paintings on the market is likely to diminish as galleries buy them up. Finally the price of Picassos may not increase by the same amount as a sum of money invested elsewhere. This is the true downside risk. The investor risks forgoing the profits he might have made by investing elsewhere. On the upside there is a strong possibility that art prices will rise steeply. So by balancing the upside gain and the downside risk the investor makes his decision.

A man decides that he is bored with his job in the bank and that he wants to set up a business on his own. The downside risks are considerable. He has no experience in business and so might make a mess of it. He will have to invest his savings and might lose them all. The new business will require much more effort than the present job and

there are no inbuilt promotion benefits. Against this considerable downside risk the man can only put his boredom with the present job and his emotional need to be independent. This may well be enough since such decisions have to be emotional in the end.

A kidnapper demands ransom. The downside risks of refusing to pay it are greater than the possible gain, so ransom tends to be paid. A politician decides to switch parties after having calculated the downside risk of losing his supporters.

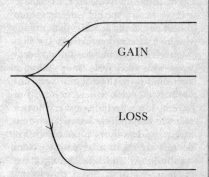

GAIN

LOSS

It is fashionable to be polarised. It is fashionable to be committed. It is fashionable to look only at one philosophy and to reject others. A person who makes an eclectic choice demonstrates an opposite attitude: he chooses something from one philosophy and something else from another. He does his philosophical shopping much as he might do his weekend shopping in a supermarket. He likes variety in his intellectual diet and sees no reason why he should not pick the best from any source. Such eclecticism infuriates a zealot or a bigot who is totally committed to one point of view.

It is easier to be eclectic about philosophy and politics than about people. You can hardly take the best characteristics from several different people (humility from one, brilliance from another, wit from a third) and put them together as a new person. But you can do it with philosophy. You can take the free enterprise and personal incentive idea from capitalism; you can take the centralised planning from Communism; and you can take the community system from developing countries to give a political philosophy that combines an acknowledgement of human nature with a need for effectiveness.

But being eclectic requires a good deal of self-confidence. The eclectic person is confident enough of himself to see himself making a choice. The committed person derives his confidence from the philosophic sense of mission that he has found: he has abdicated his ego to his philosophy. It is also easy to make a choice by being violently opposed to some other philosophy. Hatred of capitalist exploitation is more responsible for left-wing fervour than the coherence of a left-wing philosophy. Unfortunately this momentum derived from hatred is not available to an eclectic person because he can be found turning over the garbage of even the most worthless philosophy in the hope of finding something of value.

The polarisation of politics and the polarisation of argument both operate against the gentler philosophy of eclecticism. You cannot vote for parts of different political figures. You cannot switch sides too often in an argument without infuriating everybody.

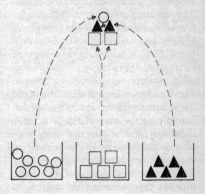

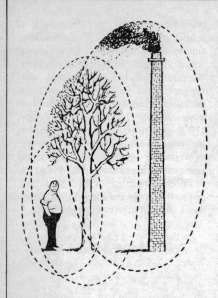

This has come to mean the study of the living environment with all its plant, animal and bacterial life. In a more general sense it means the interaction of something with its surroundings. Ecological considerations delayed for several years the building of the Alaska pipeline that was intended to carry oil southwards from the rich Alaskan oil fields. The interest in ecology has been explosive. Most schoolchildren in industrialised countries know all about pollution and ecology as a result of their teachers' enthusiasm. Ecology has no enemies. At worst someone will protest that there may be higher priorities in a few cases: like flooding a valley to provide irrigation and power for thousands of people.

The main theme of ecology is the balance of nature. If man upsets this balance in some way then things get out of hand. The introduction of a new species for some practical reason (rabbits into Australia, catfish into Florida) has usually had unfortunate results. The introduction of powerful insecticides such as DDT has had even more unfortunate results since the substance becomes concentrated more and more strongly as the food chain is ascended (birds eat insects killed by DDT, bigger birds eat smaller birds).

The relationship between man and his world has suddenly altered in recent years. Until recently man seemed so insignificant in relationship to the world that he felt that nothing he did would make any difference to the natural order of things. It was probably the development of the atom bomb and the realisation that he had in his power a means of contaminating the whole world that awoke man to his responsibilities. Already a sea like the Mediterranean is measurably polluted by mercury and other substances. Already the carbon dioxide concentration in the atmosphere is measurably increased by man's consumption of energy through burning fuels.

Ecology has gradually come to embrace the whole of man's relationship with the world: his pollution, his consumption, his interference. Now the problem is whether the developing countries are going to hold back their development to satisfy this new concern of the developed countries.

Two cars leaving a car park are approaching the exit. Neither wants to give way to the other. One car gets its nose in front and the other car is forced to pause. The difference is slight but sufficient. Two well matched boxers are slugging it out. Looked at in terms of their records and their ability both seem equal. But when they are seen fighting each other one of them seems to have the edge over the other. Similarly two athletes may be outstanding but whenever they meet to run a mile one of them always seems to have the edge over the other. It is not a matter of speed because both of them have on occasion run faster than the winning times of their meetings. It could be a matter of psychology or of tactics but the same athlete always has the edge.

When two things are nearly equal then a small difference may matter a great deal. All airlines offer the same type of plane and the same schedules over the Atlantic but for an individual passenger one airline may seem to have the edge over its rivals because it offers a choice of meal in economy class. Attention can focus on this edge or small perceptible difference to the exclusion of all else that matters.

In matters of decision if two alternatives seem equal it should not matter whether one tosses a coin or takes either alternative by the exercise of whim. But in such finely balanced situations the usual reaction is to analyse the alternatives even more thoroughly in the hope of finding that one has the edge over the other. The human mind seems to need a definite basis for decision. If a slight edge is found then that is gradually blown up until one alternative seems very much preferable to the other. The process known as 'cognitive dissonance' also ensures that if the alternative is chosen then in hindsight it will seem to be even more attractive.

Advertisers of cigarettes, soap, cars and television sets spend a great deal of time trying to show that their product has a distinct edge over rival products. It can be well worth while because the demonstration of even a tiny edge can have a marked effect on sales. No one wants to buy the second best even if the very best is only fractionally better.

If we always had enough information we should never have to make a decision. We could simply put all the information into a computer and ask the computer to sort it out into a decision. If our models of society and of human behaviour were good enough we could simply feed in any change and see what would happen. A good result would mean that the suggested change was worthwhile and a positive decision could be made.

But we do not have sufficiently good models of society or of people. Nor do we usually have all the information that would be required for making a decision. So we often have to guess.

A man placing a bet on a horse at the races believes that he is making an educated bet. He believes he has studied the breeding and present form of the horse sufficiently and that his guess is based on information. His wife at home who backs the horse because she likes the sound of its name calls it intuition.

An antique dealer is asked to place a value on a set of Regency chairs. He gives a value which is based on his knowledge of the market and the demand for such chairs. His valuation is an estimate or educated guess. The same dealer is asked to give a value for the chairs in two years' time. He does so but it is no longer an educated guess. The value in two years' time is more likely to be affected by the economic situation than the state of the antiques market, and since he is no economist his guess cannot be educated in that regard. If he assumes that economic conditions are going to be stable then his guess once again becomes an educated guess, as long as he adds this proviso.

The difference between an educated guess and an estimate is that an estimate pretends to be true within certain limits. An educated guess merely claims that it is a guess based on expertise within a field and currently available knowledge. In other words it may be the best possible guess but nevertheless it is a guess and may still be a wild one. There is, however, a difference between an educated guess and a random guess.

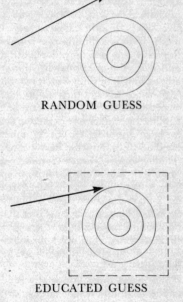

RANDOM GUESS

EDUCATED GUESS

An elastic band has a definite form but it can be stretched and stretched so that it encircles objects of different sizes. In contrast a loop of string would only fit one object and new pieces of string would have to be added if the required object was larger. It is the combination of a definite form and the ability to alter to fit circumstances that gives rise to the concept of 'elastic'.

It may be said that the demand for spectacles is inelastic. This suggests that the number of people buying spectacles will not be altered by changes in price or production. A person who needs spectacles will have to have them irrespective of the price. Similarly a person who does not need spectacles will not buy some just because they are cheap. It could also be said that the price of cigarettes was inelastic. This implies that an increase in price would lead to a fall in sales. Conversely a decrease in price would simply lead to a price war with other manufacturers and no profits would be made. It may also happen that with some items a fall in price would have to be accompanied by a fall in quality which would kill sales. The demand for confectionery is much more elastic, depending on price, presentation, advertising and so on. The pricing of confectionery is also more elastic than that of cigarettes owing to the lower level of purchase tax and the greater opportunities for variation in the product.

In a negotiating situation the demands made by one side or the other may be elastic. This is not to say that they are not definite but that they can be altered to fit in with the general bargaining position. The difficulty is for the negotiator to indicate that the demand is definite and serious but at the same time that it contains this elasticity. The skill of the negotiator on the other side is to discover the limits of the elasticity. No demand will be treated seriously if it is offered as being elastic in the first place.

A person whose needs are elastic will be able to restrict his life-style when simplicity is demanded or expand it when opportunity offers more income.

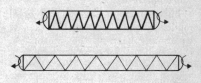

Sympathy and sensitivity are communication processes whereby the receiver picks up signals which indicate to him the situation or state of mind of the sender. The sender is making no deliberate effort to send this message. Empathy is the ability of someone to put themselves into the situation and feelings of someone else. The result may be sympathy or it may not. You may understand someone else's feelings but not agree with them. You may dislike someone and yet still be able to empathise with him. A good salesman has empathy for his sales victim but probably little sympathy. A salesman may well have enough sensitivity to know when he is not wanted but enough sense not to act upon this knowledge. A salesman may well know when he is disliked but does not feel a need to be liked all the time.

A person issuing an order may well empathise with the reluctance of others to obey that order. This empathy may affect the way the order is issued but does not necessarily change it. A good politician will have a feel for a situation and empathy with the people involved. A father who is trying to persuade his playboy son to settle down and do some work may have a great deal of empathy with him be-cause he can put himself in the boy's position. The son, in turn, may have no empathy with the father because he feels that the older generation cannot understand the mood of the younger. The relationship between the police and juvenile delinquents is more likely to be based on antipathy than empathy, yet there is a partial empathy insofar as each side recognises that the other side has a stereotyped role to play.

Do-gooders often claim to have a great deal of empathy with those who are being done good but understanding is not the same as empathy. Empathy involves being able to experience the feelings of another person, not merely to describe or understand them. A person from a happy home background may never achieve empathy with someone from an unhappy background no matter how well-intentioned he may be.

In practical terms it must seem obvious that empathy is better than lack of empathy but what follows next is what really matters. How does empathy affect decisions?

An empiricist is one who observes how things work and is prepared to try things out. As a scientist he would prefer to work from observation than from preconceived theory. An empiricist is usually contrasted with a rationalist who believes that the mind can work out relationships which are then found to occur in nature. The empiricist looks first and thinks later: the rationalist thinks first and looks later. Francis Bacon is supposed to be the father of modern science because he favoured observation rather than the customary metaphysical speculation about the nature of the universe.

In practice there is less difference between the two approaches than might be supposed from the history of philosophy. Observation sooner or later leads to ideas and these ideas then take on a life of their own and lead to further observations which are used to support or confirm the theory. In pure rationalism the original idea may have arisen from a concept of mathematics or of theology. The world would then be looked at to see if this concept fitted or not. The danger is that material can often be found to fit the predetermined theory. The danger with empiricism is

that only the most obvious relationships will be revealed by simple observation.

In fields other than science the empiricist is inclined to use his own experience, and that of history, to cope with a situation. The rationalist is inclined to analyse it and try to understand it before applying a solution. Traditionally doctors have been forced to be empiricists because their need to treat patients has always run ahead of their understanding of disease. This lack of understanding has not always bothered them and they have been quick to generate theories to support such odd practices as bloodletting. Psychology is a constant battle between the empiricists and the rationalists; so also is economics. Astrology is a clear example of a rationalist belief trying hard to find empirical evidence.

The biggest danger arises when rationalism becomes mere rationalisation, an attempt to provide a rational structure to support a few observations and much prejudice.

Every few years there are major flu epidemics. The new variety of flu virus spreads rapidly and the number of people affected may be very high. The process has an explosive quality. But there are other diseases which are always active and which do not occur in this epidemic form. Such diseases which are regularly found in a country are termed endemic. This means that they are present all the time.

In many countries the childhood disease of measles is endemic. This means that most people have had it or been exposed to it and built up some immunity. But when measles is introduced to a country which has not had any previous contact there can be an explosive and fatal epidemic. This happened when the Spaniards discovered the New World. Far more people were killed off by the measles epidemic than by the soldiers. The same thing happened with the missionaries in the Polynesian islands. The diagram shows how in a country where measles has been present for a long time an infected person has only a limited effect on his contacts since many have already had the illness, so the process never develops into an explosive chain reaction. The process is similar to the difference between a nuclear bomb and a nuclear power station. In the bomb an explosive chain reaction takes place but in the power station a steady state is achieved because the cadmium rods mop up the 'infective' neutrons.

Some characteristic or feature which is regularly to be found in an area or amongst a people is said to be endemic. Corruption, laziness, violence may all be said to be endemic. These tend to be negative qualities and it is some-times suggested that they are 'infectious' rather than an intrinsic part of the culture.

It is easier to control an epidemic infection than an endemic one. Isolation or 'fire breaks' can control epidemics but this strategy cannot be applied with endemic infections which yield only to complete immunisation.

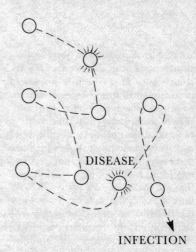

DISEASE

INFECTION

A woman goes to work for a large corporation like IBM. She is intelligent, ambitious and hard-working. She is also good at solving problems. She likes the security of a definite salary and the security of knowing that there will always be a defined job to be done, a definite direction in which to exert her abilities. Perhaps the consciousness that ability will be rewarded is also important. A man goes to work for the government service. He is competent and hard-working but he is not ambitious. He does not like to work under pressure or in a competitive environment. His real interests lie outside work in his love of music. A brash young man who wants only to work for himself proceeds to set up his own business, starting with a ham-

burger franchise for which he borrows money. His satisfaction is to see things happen. He wants to be able to make things happen. He wants to look at the accounts at the end of the month and see what has happened. He wants the maximum responsibility and the maximum reward; he does not mind the risk.

It is the urge to bring something about that defines the entrepreneur. This urge is not unlike that of the painter or writer. There is an urge to make something happen, something that was not there before. The medium chosen by the entrepreneur is action or operation. The aesthetic satisfaction is that of seeing something happening effectively, of seeing decisions correctly made. This satisfaction is made concrete by money. Money is the indicator of success but not necessarily the driving factor. The test would be simple: if an entrepreneur was suddenly given as much money as he wanted would he stop his activities or use the money to develop new ones? History is very much on the side of the new activities.

The entrepreneur seeks out opportunities; he tries things out; he makes decisions based as much on hunch as on analysis. Quite often he starts up a successful business which grows to such a size that his entrepreneurial style of management is no longer the best and he has to resign if the company is to survive.

Entrepreneurs are the risk element in society, the evolutionary element that brings about change as distinct from the operating element that keeps things ticking over. In too many countries they are discouraged as being greedy and selfish.

It costs money to build a factory and after it is built it has to be supplied with fuel and labour to be kept going. In future we shall be using a lot of factories that build themselves and provide their own fuel and labour. These factories will be the small packets of different enzymes that we call micro-organisms. Already there are ways of producing almost pure petrol from sunlight and sea-water by means of a specially chosen micro-organism. In the future a great deal of our materials, food and energy will be produced by micro-organisms which are roughly a thousand times as efficient as our existing productive processes.

Yeast is a micro-organism which converts sugar into alcohol. The human body is full of separate enzymes each of which performs a specific function. Some enzymes convert one thing into another, for example starch into sugar. Others act to destroy some chemical as soon as it has served its purpose. Others allow separate substances to combine into a new substance. Others alter substances by knocking bits off, adding bits or swopping bits around. Each enzyme is a highly skilled 'craftsman' who has a specific job to do and never tires of doing it.

Enzymes do not use themselves up in their work. They are more like special work situations. They hold different chemicals in such a position that they can interact with each other. The diagram shows separate chemicals that eventually combine to form a more structured chemical. This combination could take place by chance but this would be a long process. The enzyme provides certain positions into which the chemicals fit. Suddenly they find themselves next to each other and the 'marriage' takes place.

Some illnesses such as colds, influenza and measles are spread by direct human contact. If a person has such an illness he is likely to infect those around him unless the infectivity is low (as in mumps) or the people in contact have some immunity to the illness (such as a previous attack of measles or of that winter's flu). If a highly infectious illness springs up to which a population has no immunity then an epidemic is the result. This could happen for instance with a new variant of the influenza virus, repeating the pattern of 1918 when a new strain of swine influenza caused the death of millions in what was probably the largest epidemic ever (at least in terms of numbers involved).

The diagram shows how each person infects all those in contact with him. The more contacts a person has the higher the spread of the infection. Each infected person in turn becomes an infector for his contacts and so the explosive chain reaction proceeds. If a person is struck down and goes to bed as soon as he gets the infection then his contacts are likely to be more limited. Unfortunately with many illnesses there is an initial phase in which the person feels perfectly healthy although actually infectious to those around.

Eventually the situation is reached when most people have had the infection so it dies down as the contacts of any infected person are likely to have become immune. This process can be speeded up by isolating infected communities until the epidemic has burned itself out. This works for infections spread directly by human contact. But if, as in plague, infected fleas live on rats then there is a permanent reservoir of infection, and a halt in the

person to person transmission does not end the disease. It is interesting to note that smallpox (possibly the greatest scourge of all in the past) may have disappeared completely from the world following the successful WHO vaccination campaign since it depends on person to person spread.

Ideas, ideologies and fashion can also spread in an epidemic manner. It is not clear whether the excellence of modern communication media helps this process or actually inoculates the population against person to person spread.

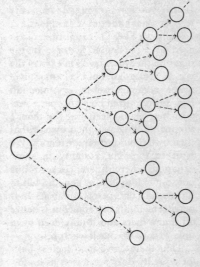

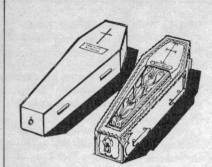

If the Church had not turned envy into one of the deadly sins there would have been little need of the concept of equality as a political driving force. If two things are equal in every respect then they must be identical. Usually we look for equality with regard to a particular feature. In the diagram the water levels in each of the vessels are equal but the amount of water in each vessel is very unequal. Few people attending an opera performance would feel that the tenor's singing should equal their own or that their own should equal the tenor's. We tend to look for equality in those situations where differences seem due not so much to luck or genetics but to the useful concept of 'unfairness'. It may seem unfair that someone is better off than others and it may even seem unfair that someone is worse off.

That there can be no logical basis for equality does not lessen its usefulness as a political tool and as a general tool with which to improve society. The beauty of equality as a notion is that it provides an easily discernible point of focus and opposition and an accompanying emotion with which to fuel the dissatisfaction. Equality should always be treated emotionally rather than logically.

Providing extra jobs for blacks in American organisations sometimes meant that a black applicant came to be preferred over a white applicant who was equally qualified, which meant that in order to achieve equal employment for blacks and whites individual people had to be treated unequally. Backward children should be given the best teachers and most attention, which means that teaching resources should be used unequally in order to give an equal opportunity to all at some later stage.

In a way equality has become a kind of religion with the expected amount of inequality amongst its high priests. As a principle it has served society well.

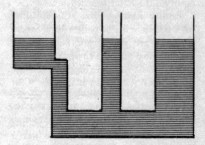

The primary meaning of equity implies justice and fairness. The more usual meaning nowadays implies a share in the ownership of an enterprise.

Three people are leaving their present agencies to set up a new advertising agency of their own. They approach a fourth person who is needed as an art director. They ask him whether he prefers to work on a straight salary basis or on the basis of a lower salary together with an equity interest. They offer him one quarter of the equity. The man turns down the offer on the basis that the initial risk should be borne by the original three, so he suggests a straight salary to begin with but an option to take up an equity if the enterprise thrives.

Equity implies risk, responsibility and the benefits of ownership. Stockmarkets are equity markets. Shareholders buy and sell their share of the equity of the quoted companies. If the company does well or is thought to be doing well by others then the equity holders prosper either through payments of dividend or through selling their equity holdings at a price higher than that at which they were purchased.

There are those who argue that workers should have a direct equity holding in the corporation in which they work. It is suggested that this would give them a sense of responsibility and also an appreciation of the actual trading situation. There might also be more incentive to increase productivity if the increased profits were going to benefit the workers directly. For the advantages to accrue, however, the equity holding would have to be substantial. Otherwise the benefits would be too diluted by the interests of the outside stockholders who, with no extra effort, were benefiting from the extra effort on the part of the workers.

According to Marx capital was continuously being increased by the surplus value created by the workers over and above the wage they received. In other words workers were the creators but not the owners of equity since the new equity created was imperceptibly added to that which already existed, and was owned by the capitalists.

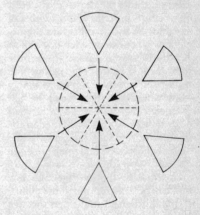

Erratic should imply erring or making errors. In practice, behaving in an erratic way means behaving in a way that is neither random nor predictable. Random behaviour has no pattern. Predictable behaviour has a pattern even if we do not know that pattern. Erratic behaviour may be predictable up to a point but there are many errors or differences from what should take place.

The diagram shows three types of behaviour. A salesman is selling encyclopaedias from door to door. The diagram shows the day to day success of his efforts in terms of the number of sets sold. In the first diagram the behaviour is consistent: each day almost exactly the same number of sets are sold. It could be that the salesman has set himself an easy target and simply stops work each day when he has reached that target. The second diagram shows a wider scatter in the number of sets sold each day. Some days are good days and some are more difficult. Nevertheless the results are quite close to the average-sales line that can be drawn through the points. In the third diagram the performance is much wilder. There are extraordinary peaks of success and there are days when nothing happens at all. It may be that the salesman is very temperamental or that he drinks too much or goes fishing on nice days and tries to compensate for it by working very hard on the other days.

It would seem natural to prefer consistent behaviour but this is not always appropriate. In art, athletics or mountain climbing erratic behaviour may be better inasmuch as it produces the occasional high peak. Once an athletic record is established (on a peak day) it stays there.

The disadvantage of erratic behaviour is that it cannot be predicted or relied upon and for most purposes we feel this is important. An aircraft trying to avoid anti-aircraft fire will try to weave an erratic course to make things more difficult for the gunners. A poker player will try to be erratic to make things more difficult for his opponents.

Unfortunately it is often said that a person is erratic if he has peaks of brilliance arising from a level of general high competence.

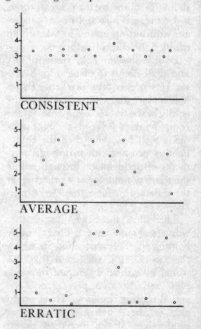

CONSISTENT

AVERAGE

ERRATIC

A protest march is stopped by the police. The demonstrators taunt the police who try to make an arrest. Some stones are thrown. The police charge. More stones are thrown and a car is set on fire. A crowd isolates and surrounds two policemen who are attacked. In defence they open fire. A full-scale riot develops. What started out as a peaceful protest march has escalated into a riot.

A husband is later home from work than usual. His wife suspects he has been drinking. Next day she retaliates by neglecting to prepare any dinner. He cooks his own dinner and the following evening retaliates by eating out and not returning home until much later. In retaliation his wife arranges to spend the evening with some friends. He books into a hotel and stays out all night. She goes to stay with her mother. Eventually there is a divorce.

A man is rude to the foreman at work. The foreman puts him on a harder job. He refuses to change jobs. The company back the foreman and threaten to sack the man. The man is told by his union to stand fast. The man is sacked. The union calls a strike. The men on strike in that department are suspended. The strike enlarges to include the whole company. A simple dispute has escalated into a prolonged work stoppage for thousands of men.

Escalation is almost bound to happen in any action–reaction situation. The first action is met by a reaction which is just sufficient to control it. This reaction is then treated as an action and is itself met by a reaction which must necessarily be larger than the first action. And so the process escalates. If there are reserves of power, threats or sanctions it is unlikely that these will be left out of the action. It is unlikely that the first actor will permit his action to be squashed by the first reaction.

One company promoting cosmetics offers a free gift. The rival company offers a more expensive gift. An escalation of gifts results until neither company is selling more cosmetics or making any profit at all. Cigarette and detergent manufacturers are forced by each other to escalate their advertising expenditure knowing that it is merely defensive and does not increase sales. A price-cutting war is also an escalation. One price cut is exceeded by another in an escalation to and fro.

All jargon tends to be esoteric, that is designed for those who belong to the club and are in the know. It is not difficult to become an expert in something (butterflies, baseball, Baroque architecture, Bach) because there are so many possible areas of expertise that a little knowledge in any one of them must appear esoteric to most people. The problem that concerns some people is how, in the future, anyone is going to be able to communicate with anyone else. There is so much knowledge to be had that to ignore this knowledge in order to remain intelligible to everybody may become an impossible task. The result will be that specialists will talk only to fellow specialists and the rest of us will look at television.

Witch covens and occult groups develop their own special esoteric rituals in order to give shape to their sense of importance. Esoteric initiation rites take place both in African tribes and in boys' schools. Cultural patterns that are taken for granted by an insider are esoteric to an outsider.

In an argument it is a common strategy for one of the arguers to steer the argument round to an area in which he can release some esoteric knowledge, thereby winning the argument since the opponent can do nothing except listen. The process known as 'snowing' is similar inasmuch as someone defends a position by releasing a stream of esoteric information which seems to constitute a defence because the attacker cannot understand what it is about.

The time may come when society will need internal translators whose job it will be to interpret for one group the esoteric communications produced by another. A few journalists already do this job well. The esoteric processes of heart transplantation and space travel were well explained by such journalists when these matters were current news. The trick in such translations is to move one step upwards in terms of 'generality'. For example lymphocytes become the cells that handle the body's reaction to foreign materials. The next stage of generality is simply to talk about 'defence mechanisms'.

We can choose to look at differences or at similarities. In biology there are said to be 'lumpers' and 'splitters'. A lumper will look at apparently different species of birds and will decide that in spite of superficial differences they are really part of one species: he lumps them all together in a single category. The splitter comes along and finding an apparently single species of bird will make intense observations and careful measurements and decide that the single species ought to be split up into several different categories on the basis of length of beak and slight differences in markings. The lumpers and splitters choose to focus and concentrate on different aspects of the same thing.

Ethnic means to do with race and, in a more general sense, with cultures provided these are sufficiently different. Lumpers prefer to see a common humanity beneath the racial differences, and splitters see the differences rather than the similarities. The dilemma has always been to keep the richness that is associated with varieties of race and culture and yet to preserve an equality of opportunity and consideration. The easy answer is to opt for a notional middle stage but this does not really exist. Americans from a wide variety of backgrounds are primarily Americans whether their ancestors came from Ireland, Ger-

many or Sweden. A few customs remain and eating styles may be different but that is all. Ethnologists may prefer the American Indian to retain his own culture because this seems valuable. But the Indian himself may wish to enjoy the advantages of assimilation into the American culture.

It seems very difficult for the human mind to notice differences and yet not to ascribe values to them. Different tribes in Africa, New Guinea and originally in North America all seemed to hold other tribes in respect or in contempt. Brazil is possibly the most successful multi-racial society and there it seems that racial differences are simply not noticed.

The main problem with ethnic questions is that of separating ethnic from economic distinguishing features. A class question becomes a race question if the colour of skin or type of religious belief is also different.

Existentialism is a philosophical movement originating with Kierkegaard, a
Dane, in the middle of the last century
but operating mainly through the
mind and pen of Jean-Paul Sartre in
this century.

For centuries philosophers had been
at pains to analyse and understand the
nature and purpose of human existence. Using the Greek model of intellectual examination they tried to
find the basis of human existence by
analysis. Who was God? What was
His nature? Why was there human
suffering? What was man? What was
the essence of man? What was the
destiny of man? Many answers were
given and many theologies were constructed specifically to provide answers
to such questions.

When a child keeps on asking 'why?'
he is seeking to fit what he has just
been told into the rest of his experience.
'Mummy, why are fire engines painted
red?' 'So that other people can see
them coming.' 'Why?' 'So that they
can get out of the way.' 'Why?' 'So
that the firemen can get quickly to the
fire.' These were the sort of questions
which philosophers had been asking
about human existence. In order to
provide answers they had created a
whole network of concepts like truth,
goodness, god, nature and so on.

In contrast to this the existential
attitude is to face man and reality
directly. Instead of an attempt at
analysis and understanding there is a
willingness to confront life in all its
contradiction and complexity. There
are to be no underlying divine motives
and concepts but instead the direct
reality of existence. An existentialist
should be able to find philosophy in a
pot of marmalade: in a confrontation
with its sheer existence.

Once man has the courage to
realise that he is caught up in a
meaningless web of existence which
goes on and on from moment to
moment without special plan or purpose, he needs to define his own
humanity. This he can only do by
rebelling. Every conscious decision he
makes confirms his humanity because
by a decision he steps outside the ongoing flow of existence and refuses to
be passively carried along with it. It is
at the moment of decision that man
exists as man.

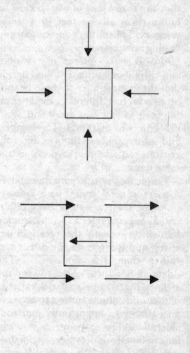

This is one of the beloved words of disapproval, and much used in the political sense. As Marx concluded in the last century capitalists are supposed to exploit workers, and there is little doubt that they did and in some cases still do. It is questionable, however, whether capitalism as such is an exploitative system or whether greedy and unscrupulous people exploit the system in order to exploit others. Marxists argue that because the surplus value created by labour finds its way through profits and reinvestment back into the pockets of capitalists the system as such is exploitative. Capitalists argue that in a free enterprise system capital is necessary in order to provide factories for employment and that union vigilance and government regulations prevent exploitation.

It is often claimed that women who work at home making lace or hand painting toy soldiers are exploited by the manufacturers who pay low wages since the women cannot leave home to find other work. Exploitation is usually to be found in a monopolistic situation where the same body determines both work and wages. If wages were to exceed work output then bankruptcy would result, except in the case of a government organisation subsidised by taxation. If work output exceeds wages that is automatically suspect as exploitation. If the gap is considerable the exploitation may be real.

Women exploit men and men exploit women. A woman charms a man into marrying her and supporting her. She may be inclined to give very little in return and feel that the privilege of being married to her is sufficient reward. Conversely a man may feel that a woman is an inferior creature who can be treated as an unpaid servant.

Exploitation means that the balance between give and take is upset in favour of the 'take' element. Any person or organisation in a position to demand a 'take' without regard to what it is giving is in an exploitative position. The fact that a government may waste its tax-take in inefficiency does not mean that it is not exploiting the governed.

Exploitation is a convenient word of attack because any estimation of the balance between give and take tends to be subjective.

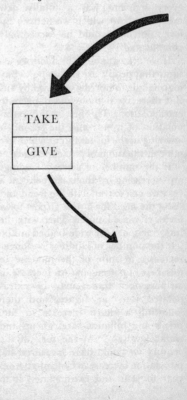

We have no choice but to make assumptions and to extrapolate the whole time. We assume that what has happened in the past is going to continue to happen in the future. We assume that the buses, trains and aeroplanes that have been running yesterday are going to be running today. We assume that the same people are going to be at the office today as were there yesterday. We assume that our family are going to behave much the same next week as they did last week and the week before. Extrapolation means carrying the past forward in order to be able to deal with the future. If every moment was a totally new moment about which we had no information life would be exceedingly complicated.

If we are running a business we assume that people are still going to buy marmalade tomorrow or travel by air. But there are two obvious dangers to extrapolation. The first is the extrapolation of trends and the second is ignoring in the future things which are not continuations of past experience.

If the number of aircraft landings are increasing by about ten per cent a year we can extrapolate the trend and show the need for a new airport for a major city like London. Then with the introduction of the wide-bodied jumbo jets the number of landings no longer increases in spite of the increase in numbers of passengers. An increase in air-passenger traffic may be extrapolated into the future, and then following a sharp increase in fuel prices and inflation fares go up and traffic levels off. At the turn of the century we could have measured the population increase in Cincinnati from year to year and extrapolated it to

show that by mid-century it would be by far the biggest city in the world. Trends have a habit of not being continuous. A special occurrence may have set off the trend and then passed. Another event may occur which kills the trend. The trend may be self-limiting: if many people move into a pleasant small village it becomes large and no longer village-like and so the trend stops. Yet often we have no choice but to extrapolate trends if we are to make plans at all.

The other danger is to base all our plans on extrapolations from the past and to ignore the possibility of new developments.

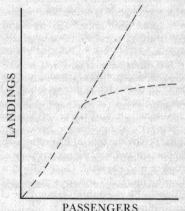

LANDINGS

PASSENGERS

It is widely believed that orientals are more concerned with saving face than are westerners. It is assumed that rank, position and above all respect must be preserved. In the West we rely more on open aggression, pushiness and force of character to establish natural hierarchies. Where a hierarchy is established on more subtle intellectual grounds the aggression may be lacking. That is why the official hierarchy is so important and why the preservation of respect is so essential. Once respect is lost the hierarchy collapses and is unlikely to be re-established by natural aggression.

In Western negotiations we are inclined to think in terms of win–lose situations: one side wins and the other side loses. We are also inclined to think in terms of conflict, polemics, dialectic and debate. There is no great tradition encouraging mutual exploration of a subject in order to extract something of benefit to all. There are times when the substance of winning may be separable from the appearance of win-

ning. In such cases the winner may agree to forgo the appearance of winning in order to save the face of the loser, who does not appear to have lost although in fact having done so. At other times, however, as in politics, the appearance of winning is the actual substance of winning. In such cases face-saving is very much more difficult. Yet it can be managed by the loser shifting his ground so that he appears to agree on the lost issue but maintains that he was fighting on other grounds altogether. For instance a politician who opposes government spending cuts may, when these are announced, claim a victory by maintaining that they were not as large as feared, that they were going to be delayed or that they were not going to lead to unemployment.

In many situations appearance is so closely tied up with reality that face-saving is much more than a cosmetic operation to preserve pride. Confidence depends on appearance and on confidence depends our belief in a person's ability and promises.

Fashion is a dynamic process that tends to follow the basic grammar of dynamic processes as shown in biological systems: there is a wave pattern of energy; the system tends to be self-organising. At each moment there are those who are pushing ahead propelled by the need to keep ahead of the fashion. Step by step the increments are added, by the need to be different and by the way the fashion crystallises as it develops, becoming stronger and more definite. Then there are those who try hard to keep up especially if doing so separates them from those who are not so successful. It is very like selling commodities where those who deal in commodities delight in a fluctuating market because they can then buy and sell slightly ahead of everyone else (no matter which way the market is going) and so make a profit. There is a sort of hierarchy of ignorance in which the few leaders only are knowledgeable and the ignorance of the rest supports them.

There was a time when it was fashionable for men to shave their heads and wear elaborate wigs. There was a time when men wore make-up and applied beauty spots to their faces. There was a time when men were as interested in furs, velvets and satins as their womenfolk. Just before the heavily dressed Victorian era there was a brief period when it was fashionable for women to wear only light shifts of muslin and to wet the muslin so that their naked bodies could be seen more easily through the clinging garment.

Within the general trend of fashion, group fashions arise to distinguish one group from another. Long hair separates the trendies from the squares.

Denim culture used to separate teenagers from adults but does so no longer. Any fashion that acquires a group identity tends to last much longer because the group is unwilling to let go of its uniform.

The cycle of fashion used to be spread over years and even decades. Today the process has speeded up. Television and mass circulation magazines spread the fashion at once. Off the peg mass production of clothes means that everyone can get in on the fashion. Although mini-skirts and hot pants come and go, the present trend seems to be towards the fashion of no-fashion or a general jean uniform. It is supposed that fashions always tend towards the practical but history has often shown otherwise.

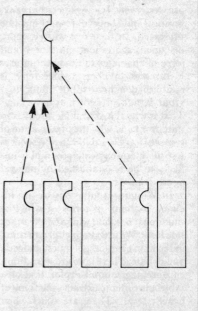

You are throwing darts but the light is bad and you can only just see the outline of the board. You cannot tell where each dart has landed and since you cannot tell this you cannot adjust your aim. For all you know the dart you have just thrown may have landed in the bull's-eye or on the rim of the board. The result of your action is not being fed back to you. Some information may be fed back to you by the sound of the dart hitting the board. But if the light was better and the actual position of the dart on the board was fed back then you could adjust your aim when throwing the next dart.

You are driving a car and you turn the steering wheel anti-clockwise. You can see the car turning to the left. The degree of turn is fed back to you so that you can adjust your movement of the steering wheel in order to obtain the effect you want. Your hand is on the tiller of a boat. You move the tiller one way hoping the boat will turn the other way. But the boat is slow to respond so you push the tiller further over. Then the boat starts to turn and as it turns too much you push the tiller the other way. The boat swings wildly from side to side because you cannot adjust your movement of the tiller to give the right amount of turn. This is because there is a delay in the effect of your action being fed back to you. The same thing happens in a shower bath. You open the hot tap but the shower still seems cold, so you open the hot tap further. Suddenly the shower scalds you so you open the cold tap and shut down the hot tap. Nothing happens for a moment and then the shower becomes cold. Because there is a delay in the feedback it is difficult to get the temperature right. Ideally you should turn the taps a little at a time and wait for the result of your action to be fed back to you.

The diagram shows a lavatory cistern. The water pours in through the pipe but as the water level rises the ball floats upwards until eventually the attached stopper closes off the inflow. The effect of the action (of the water flowing in) has been fed back to alter that action (by stopping it). The essence of feedback is that the effect of an action is fed back to alter that action.

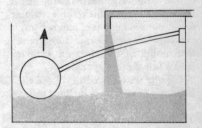

Faraday mapped out the lines of force in a magnetic field by using a small compass and seeing which way the needle pointed at each spot. Science fiction writers are fond of talking about a force field in which some strange force (not unlike that of magnetism) is exerted at each point, just as a mine-field is full of mines or an ordinary field is full of crops of grass.

Usually we think of how A affects B because our minds are inclined to focus on A as the cause and B as the effect. This concentrates on the linear relationship between A and B. Instead of focusing on A and B in this way we can look at the whole field in which both A and B lie, and at the influences surrounding them both (this might be called the ecological outlook). Rather than look for individual causes we look for interacting effects.

Hitherto in mathematics, geometry and language we have tended to isolate points and then to determine the relationship between these points. In dealing with fields, however, it is more a matter of looking at the contours of the field than at individual spots. It is true that the contours may be mapped by making measurements at different spots but the end result is a contour map not a collection of spots. For example if we wanted to see whether something was likely to happen or not we could look at the field of the situation and see whether the contours favoured a flow in the direction of it happening or whether there were basic barriers. In a negotiating situation it would often be more helpful to map out the field of influences and objectives than to argue in the usual dialectical fashion.

It is difficult for the human mind to deal with fields because we need to look at one thing at a time. Furthermore our symbol system is more suited to dealing with isolated features. It may be that we shall have to develop a whole new idiom for dealing with field effects. Certainly the computer would be able to handle it for us. In the so-called 'iterative' process a computer can be programmed to show how each part of a field acts on every other part to produce an overall process.

At every moment we are part of a field even when we choose to ignore it.

At first it would seem that there is a close similarity between a filter and a screen. In a chemical laboratory a mixture in which there has been a cloudy precipitate is poured through a funnel holding a piece of filter paper. The precipitate is filtered out and a clear fluid emerges. Mud and other particles can be filtered out of water; so too can bacteria if the filter is fine enough. In this sense a filter would seem to act to remove matter that was not wanted. In the chemical process, however, it may actually be the precipitate collected on the filter paper that is required.

Filters on the whole are not selective. Their function is to remove material, often as part of a cleansing process (as in air filters, etc). By contrast the purpose of a screen is to aid in the selection of material.

The filtering process is slow and the liquid being filtered trickles slowly through the filter. This slow trickle gives rise to the concept of something that 'filters through'. This means that it passes through but does so slowly. There is no block or obstruction but merely a slowing down of the process.

News may be said to filter through if there is no direct communication line and it follows a roundabout path. The traffic signal which invites motorists to 'filter' through indicates a slow movement with the filtering cars merging when they can with another traffic stream.

It is sometimes suggested that our minds are like filters because they reject things we do not recognise and allow in only familiar objects and experiences. This is the classic rejecting function of a filter. On the other hand we can screen our experiences in order to select those that might be relevant to some matter we have to decide upon.

A drinking glass is stable in only two positions. When you push against the side the glass tilts as shown in the diagram. You take your finger away and the glass returns to its original stable position. You push harder and harder. Finally a point is reached when the glass no longer seeks to return to the original stable position but moves forward to another stable position: in other words it topples over on to its side. One position of the glass could be called the flip position and the other the flop position.

A flip-flop originally referred to a switch which was stable in only two positions. Wherever it was positioned it would move to either one of these positions. Movement from one position to another, say from 'on' to 'off', required some effort at first and then a position would be reached when the switch would 'flip' and 'flop' into the new position.

Inflation is sometimes regarded as a flip-flop situation. Inflation is stable and so is recession. When efforts are made to fight inflation then the whole system can easily flip over into recession. Conversely when efforts are made to cure recession the whole system can flip back into inflation.

In unstable personalities depression and elation are often flip-flop in character. Elation escalates to a peak but once depression sets in it also descends to a trough. There seems to be no stable situation in between. Love and hate can also be a flip-flop situation, stable positions existing in love or hate but not in between; an in-between position moves quickly to one or other extreme.

In an interesting study Dr Sargant, an English psychiatrist, showed that those who were most against a religion were in fact nearest to a sudden conversion. When emotion runs high then conversion seems easier. If this is so it is a striking example of a flip-flop condition.

The essence of a flip-flop system is not the existence of two opposite poles or positions but the possibility of a sudden 'flip' from one stable state to the other: after a little effort at first things then move with a rush.

FLIP   FLOP

The ability to focus is possibly the most important ability of the human mind. Focus implies focusing attention. If we were not able to focus attention then we should be unable to divide up the confusion of the external world into chunks convenient enough to handle. We would never have been able to develop language or the use of symbols. In fact we should have been like an amoeba which can react only to the totality of the environment around it.

It is remarkable that we can look at a building as a whole and admire its setting and proportions, and then be able to focus on the shape of the windows and then on any one particular window we wish. We can look at a map and decide to focus on a particular town, or the line of a river or railway. We can focus on the distance between two towns. We can focus on the space in a Chinese painting.

The development of philosophy has depended on man's ability to focus on his thinking in as acute a manner as he focuses on the external world. By focusing on words and the gaps between words; by focusing on relationships; by focusing on amorphous feelings and on implications philosophers have equipped us with an introspective view of ourselves. We can talk about guilt and soul and motivation and justice.

The ability to focus is simply the ability to separate one thing from another. Once things are separated then they can be recombined by means of defined relationships. From our ability to focus has come our habit of analysis. An analysis is a catalogue of focusing achievement.

The difference in reaction between an art expert and a novice is that the expert can focus on many more aspects of a painting than the novice. The expert focuses on the colour, the composition, the brushwork, the use of light and shade, the skin textures, the treatment of the fingers, the treatment of the background and a variety of different things. The novice reacts to the painting as a whole without being able to direct his attention. Everything that anyone can focus on must be there in the first place but we cannot see it unless we focus on it. In order to be able to focus we have to build up patterns of acceptance for what we see.

The best intentions in the world are useless without any follow-through. A politician makes a speech in which much is promised in the way of improving educational standards. But nothing happens; there is no follow-through. A businessman talks to another businessman who happens to be sitting next to him on the plane and promises to send him samples of his new product. When he leaves the plane he forgets to do anything about it and the other man is not impressed by the lack of follow-through. A horse which jumps the first fence excellently and then pauses to nibble the grass is unlikely to win the race. A tennis player who is so pleased with his first serve that he stands back to admire it is unlikely to win the match. A researcher who sets up an elaborate questionnaire and then fails to find anyone to answer it is unlikely to achieve any results.

Follow-through is a more tedious and demanding activity than taking an initiative. And yet it must be obvious that without follow-through the most exciting initiative will come to nothing. Many brilliant people are far more capable of initiatives than of following-through. There is an implied hope that the initiative will trigger action on the part of the person to whom it is directed; follow-through would then be unnecessary. But no one's idea is as interesting to someone else as it is to oneself so this triggering effect rarely occurs.

A general may make a brilliant attack in a certain sector of the field but then there is no follow-through and the advantage is lost. A chess player is very often in the same position. To open up an opportunity and then not follow-through is by no means uncommon in advertising or marketing. In this respect the Japanese have acquired a reputation for making sure that the follow-through is in order before the initiative is taken.

A political campaign opens with promise but there is no follow-through and it soon fizzles out. A flirt makes a great show of interest but there is no follow-through. An advertisement for a resort promises much but there is no follow-through. An executive threatens to resign but there is no follow-through. A protest meeting makes a lot of noises about the proposed new road but there is no follow-through and the road gets built without demur.

Schoolboys are used to working out the various formulas that relate distance, speed and acceleration: 'If you drop a stone from the top of a building one hundred feet high, with what velocity does the stone hit the ground?' There are formulas for calculating the resistance of the water round the hull of a ship. There are formulas for calculating the energy required to heat a building or drive a motor car.

A formula is a pre-packaged guide. Just as a potato chip-making machine goes through all the stages of washing, peeling, cutting and slicing the potatoes so a formula is a machine for processing information. Instead of working certain things out each time, you put the facts into the formula machine and out comes the finished product. A manufacturer of television sets may give bonuses to the production workers based on a complicated formula which takes into account age, seniority, previous work record and other factors.

A formula can also be a set of instructions which are linked together to form a whole. The distinction is between setting out instructions each time and using the ready-made package. A formula makes life very much simpler because it provides a standard response. The person who has set up the formula may have gone to a lot of trouble to get it right but once the formula is there the user has none of this trouble. Today, with computers, the use of formulas is even easier: you put the formula into the computer and then you put in the data. The computer does all the work.

The only trouble with a formula is that it assumes that the current situation is identical to previous ones. For example a government may use an established formula for controlling public expenditure but the new situation may be different from those on which the formula was based. It is rather like a general having a battle-winning formula. This can work, as was shown by the successful Nazi blitzkrieg tactics in the Second World War. But it can also mean that we are forever tackling the last problem, not the present one. This tends to be the trouble in economics, where there is no better way of proceeding.

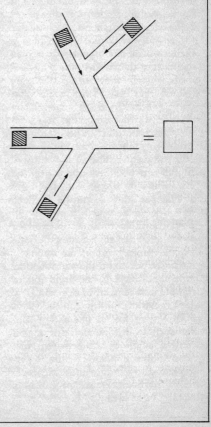

A man with a bright idea sets up a fast food shop that sells hamburgers. The shop is a great success. The man wants to expand the business but does not have the capital to buy up other shops. So he decides to franchise the business. Other individuals like himself put up their own money to open their own hamburger shops. An arrangement is made whereby they can use the name 'Hamburger-Ins'. This means that they benefit from the advertising attached to this name and also from the reputation that has been built up. The decor of the shops is laid down and also the menus. The equipment and supplies are obtained from the central store which means that bulk buying at a cheaper rate is possible. Each franchise owner pays a royalty or proportion of his turnover to the owner of the name. In this way the business expands rapidly without the originator having to put up the money. What the individual buys is the franchise or right to use the name in a certain area.

Franchising arrangements have been set up for all manner of convenience foods, launderettes, copier centres, employment agencies, dancing schools and other activities. A person may also purchase the franchise to sell a particular make of car in a country or an area.

When the business becomes very successful the owners often try to buy the franchises back. They claim that there is not enough control over the standards of the franchised shops, or that a shop owned by the central corporation and managed by a manager is more profitable than one run by the franchisee.

A franchise is an exclusive right to do something in a certain area. This is similar to a monopoly except that a franchise is usually obtained from someone else. There are people who claim to have a franchise on the truth or on honesty or moral concern.

In most franchising situations the person acquiring the franchise is expected to put up a good operating performance or else the rights may be lost. A failing franchise operator gives a bad name to the whole group. It might be interesting to consider what would happen if churches were run on a franchise basis.

One man's freak is another man's connoisseur. An eco-freak is someone who is obsessional about ecological problems. A computer freak is someone who is obsessional, and usually very talented, in computer matters. A chess freak has chess as his area of obsessional interest, activity and talent. A freak is anyone who is abnormal. A person whose interest in any one subject is abnormal becomes a freak. If the area of interest happens to be eighteenth-century watercolour artists or Georgian silver or quarter-horses then we tend to think in terms of 'expert' or 'specialist' or 'connoisseur'. This is not quite as unfair as it seems. With a connoisseur the interest is based on specialised knowledge. With a freak the interest may be obsessional and not based on any specialised knowledge.

Originally a freak was something natural but unnatural, like a lamb with five legs or a freak storm. The drought in the summer of 1976 in the United Kingdom was a freak drought inasmuch as it was the worst drought for more than five hundred years. It is not simply the unexpectedness of something that makes it freaky. A motor accident is always unexpected but it can still be a normal accident. But if a motorcycle rider was thrown from his cycle and managed to land in a truckload of hay travelling in the same direction then there would be a freak element involved.

The attraction of freaks in circuses is that the onlooker can look at them and say to himself, 'It cannot be true, but it is.' There is a consolatory use for the term freak, as when it is applied to a situation that could have been anticipated or taken into account but was not. In such cases the application of the label 'freak' to a rise in raw material prices or weather conditions or a baby boom is a way of saying that it could not have been anticipated. A yachtsman who fails to moor his boat safely and finds it smashed on the beach in the morning might well blame a freak overnight storm.

In dress, behaviour and hair care there seems to be a fine borderline between genuine disdain for social expectations and deliberate group-belonging freakishness.

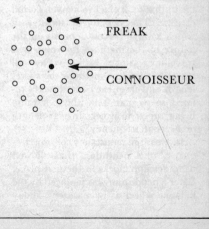

A weight at the end of a short piece of string swings back and forth more rapidly than the same weight at the end of a longer piece of string. The frequency of oscillation is determined by the length of the string in this simple pendulum. Everyone knows how the great Galileo, instead of attending to the ceremony, watched the lamp in the cathedral at Pisa swinging backwards and forwards. He observed that the time taken for a complete swing was always the same. If the swing was a wide one then it was also fast. If the swing was only a small one then it was very slow.

Frequency, wavelength and cycle are all related. The diagram shows a typical illustration of a wave form. A cycle represents a complete wave: starting at one point and eventually stopping at the equivalent point. A wavelength is the distance covered by a complete wave or cycle. Frequency refers to the number of waves or cycles that take place in a given space of time: for example the frequency may be twenty cycles per second. The frequency of the pendulum would be the number of complete swings (there and back) that took place in a given period of time. The velocity or speed with which a wave travels depends on the nature of the medium in which it is travelling. Since radio waves all travel in the same medium the wavelength and frequency are directly related so we can talk about a radio being tuned to a certain wavelength or a certain frequency.

It was the constancy of the frequency of a pendulum that allowed us to develop clocks in the first place. Later a pendulum was replaced by the balance wheel as in a watch. Today the high frequency of electrical oscillations in a quartz crystal gives even more accuracy in clocks. In these cases the natural frequency of the system remains constant. In other cases the frequency may follow or be driven by some outside fluctuation and may tend to follow this rather than its own natural frequency. For example jet pilots find that the natural frequency of their bodies is altered by their flights through different time zones.

If the frequency speeds up then the rate of rise of the curve becomes much steeper and we often talk of a high-frequency response when there is a quick reaction to something. High or low frequency refers to the apparent origin of a sung note.

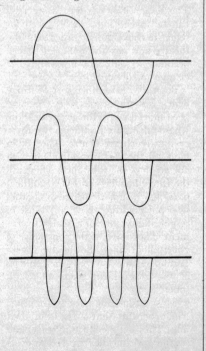

A very successful theatrical production called *Beyond the Fringe* was launched at the Edinburgh Festival which has established a reputation for offering new and unusual material. *Beyond the Fringe* started off as fringe theatre but, paradoxically, became so successful, that it became mainstream establishment. The established theatre in New York lies along Broadway so fringe theatre is off-Broadway. But this in turn establishes a fringe type of establishment so the new fringe is off-off-Broadway and so on to an infinite regression. Just as an ice floe grows, so what was fringe becomes established and a new fringe develops.

It is considered that most new and exciting activity occurs on the fringe. The responsibility is less. More risks can be taken. There is less need for refuge in convention in order to fill the theatre and pay the bills. The fringe becomes a source of innovation, of change and of influence.

But there is another sort of fringe which is made up of those who have been moved out of the centre or those whose talents are insufficient for them ever to reach the centre. They often have all the disguises of talent with not much of the substance. These are the fringe hangers-on. Every political party has its lunatic fringe of fanatics who put doctrine above any sense of responsibility or practical government. They serve as the conscience of government and also as the background against which the policies of the government seem mild and sober.

Most businessmen are aware of the fringe benefits that arise from their jobs. They get a chance to travel and see the world on sales trips, conferences or liaison with foreign suppliers. They may be given the use of a car and even the help of a secretary for matters that arise in the course of business but do not contribute directly to company profits. There may be a special pension scheme. All these benefits are only on the fringe of the main conditions of employment: salary, status and place of work.

Too much energy may be wasted on fringe activities. For instance a marketing drive may concentrate on such fringe activities as special discounts, trading stamps, posters and so on instead of the main problems of pricing and distribution. Fringe activities are usually more fun than central activities but are not always easy to recognise for what they are.

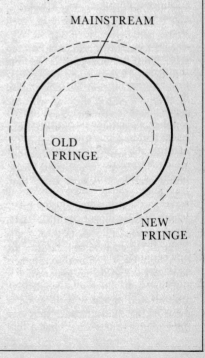

MAINSTREAM

OLD FRINGE

NEW FRINGE

The front-line troops were the ones who drew the enemy's fire. It is true that they did most of the firing back as well but some firing could be done from behind the lines. The function of the front-line troops became well established in the First World War when for years two armies faced each other across no man's land in two lines of trenches. In the Second World War there was no actual front line until towards the end of the war with the invasion of Germany and of the Japanese-held islands. It could be said that civilians were just as much in the front line since they were bombed directly. Indeed in the Second World War more civilians were killed than soldiers.

In the management context the front-line managers are those who actually come face to face with the 'enemy'. The enemy in this case may be the shop-floor worker or the customer. The worker and the customer are not regarded as hostile but as people with interests that may not be the same as those of the management. It is one thing to give orders, direct policy and assess the effects of the policy but it is another thing to be at the 'sharp end' and actually put the policy into operation. The term 'sharp end' comes from the idea of a spade, hoe or other tool where the work is actually done by the sharp end. A lot of effort and aim may be put in elsewhere but the contact point, the sharp end, is where the work is carried out.

What is often forgotten is that the image of an organisation depends entirely on the front-line image. If a bureaucracy has the reputation of being soulless this is because the front-line bureaucrats appear to be soulless. It does not matter how unrepresentative these people may be of the whole system. The front-line troops are always only a small fraction of the total involved.

Too often planners and policy makers forget that to be put into effect any plan has to be carried out at the front line. Attention to general policy directions without any attention to moment to moment action at the front line can lead to disaster. Attention to front-line requirements usually carries with it attention to overall policy decisions.

'What is the function of a screwdriver?' 'We need something with a gripping function.' 'Whose function is it to look for errors?'

A function is a specific type of action. In geometry there are specific shapes that can be defined. A function is a specific shape of action. The purpose of a screwdriver is to unscrew screws but the function of a screwdriver is to lock on to the screw and to rotate it. A gripping function could be provided by a variety of devices ranging from a pair of pliers to a bulldog clip or a couple of fingers. The specific action of looking for errors in a report is a function that may need to be assigned to a particular person.

In mathematics when one thing is said to be a function of another it means that a specific action performed on the latter will produce the former. For example if water consumption is a function of weather and hygiene standards then we should be able to calculate water consumption from a formula that adds or multiplies weather and hygiene standards (expressed in some convenient way). If intelligence is a function of age then there should be a standard table which relates age and intelligence and by applying this table we should be able to calculate the intelligence average from a given age.

We expect dishwashers and microwave ovens to function properly. We expect a television set to function as a television set. In other words we expect something which is designed to give a specific type of action to provide that type of action. The designed function of a frying pan is to fry food. But the pan could also function as a container for growing seeds. Enclosed in a brown paper envelope the pan could also be used for ironing a shirt. An elastic band is not designed to function as a catapult but it can be put to that use.

In considering functions it is important to work at a level which is neither too specific nor too general. The function of a hammer is to provide an accelerating mass which can be aimed conveniently.

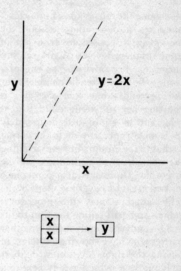

In a game the moves are set up beforehand. In a non-game situation the moves are supposed to arise out of events as these develop. A girl wants to encourage her boyfriend so she pretends to be busy when he phones her or she pretends that someone else is courting her. A young child who is reluctant to go to bed deliberately spills milk from a cup on to the carpet so that in the ensuing fuss and scolding the immediacy of his bedtime will be forgotten. Diplomats at a conference make a great fuss over the shape of the table as they play the procedural game. An agent selling the film rights in a first novel casually mentions other parties who have shown an interest in buying the rights. A hostess deliberately places a seductive lady next to a husband with a jealous wife. Union negotiators go through a ritual of complaints before settling down to discuss the current issue.

The characteristic of a game is that a sequence of moves are recognisable as part of the game. The game may be played very seriously; it may also be played for a purpose rather than as an end in itself. Nevertheless each move in the sequence is determined by the requirements of the game rather than the realities of the situation itself.

Someone who is aware that a game is being played sits back and waits for the game to be played out. Someone who is not aware that it is a game gets involved and manipulated by the games player who knows the moves of the game better. It is this expertise in the moves of the game which makes it worth playing. If the player knows, from long experience, the moves, reactions and counter-moves then he only has to entice the other person to play the game to achieve success. If the situation works itself out naturally neither side has an advantage. But if one side sets up a game with which only he is familiar then that side immediately acquires the advantage of skill and foreknowledge.

A good games player not only knows how to make the next move, he can think one, two or three moves ahead. This is extremely difficult for an inexperienced player. Thus the player who sets up a familiar game can lay traps several moves ahead with very little chance of the opponent noticing what is being done.

Just as a philosopher will always try to run an argument according to his own definitions so a games player will always try to make an opponent play his special game.

In the old penny-farthing bicycle the driving wheel was very large because there could only be one turn of this wheel for every turn of the pedal and so a large wheel allowed a higher speed. The development of the bicycle chain allowed two gears to be linked so that one turn of the pedal would lead to many turns of the driving wheel. When a gear wheel with many teeth on its circumference meshes with a smaller wheel with fewer teeth then one turn of the larger wheel will lead to several turns of the smaller wheel (the actual ratio of turns is the same as the ratio of the teeth on the wheels). The principle of gearing is that a small effort should have a disproportionately large effect.

You could invest a large sum of money in buying industrial shares. If the shares rose by ten per cent in value you could sell them and make a ten per cent profit (from which commission would have to be deducted). So your profit would be one tenth of what you had had to invest. Alternatively you could purchase an option to buy the shares in the future at today's price. For this you might have to pay one twentieth of the total value. If the shares rose by ten per cent you would buy them and immediately sell them

or you could sell the option. So for a small investment you have obtained the full price rise of the shares. In fact instead of ten per cent you have made a profit of two hundred per cent. This is an example of gearing.

A bank is allowed to lend out between ten and twenty times the money that is actually deposited with it. It does this by creating credits. Clients are given overdrafts on which they pay the bank interest. Money then moves backwards and forwards from one overdraft to another as a paper transaction. So on a relatively small amount of money deposited with it a bank is able to earn very much more interest through this process of gearing.

The two major political parties are balanced. A small party with less than one tenth the representation of the larger parties holds the balance of power and so can get its policies adopted in return for its support. This is an example of gearing since the influence of the representatives is out of proportion to their number.

It is as difficult to deal with vague intuitions, ideas, notions and feelings as it is to deal with fog or light. In both cases there is no doubt as to the reality of the experience: a fog is just as real as a brick wall. It is simply that formlessness and amorphousness are meant to be experienced rather than used. Liquid is also formless but can acquire form under two conditions. The first condition is that of freezing. The second is that of 'gelling' when some gelling substance such as gelatine has been stirred in.

At first the jelly (or jell-O) that is made for a children's party is like any other liquid. There comes a point, however, when the jelly sets or 'gels'. Once this point is reached the jelly can be removed from the mould, cut with a knife, balanced on a spoon and generally dealt with more decisively. Similarly if someone is waiting for something to gel he is waiting for an indefinite state of affairs to take on a distinct form which will enable him to act.

A film producer may talk of a deal 'gelling'. A lot of people have expressed interest in the project and some vague promises of finance have been made but as yet there is nothing definite. The whole prospect may disappear like a cloud of steam, or alternatively the vague intentions may gel into definite contracts and percentages.

An inventor may have a vague feeling as to how something can be done. But he is unable to describe an actual mechanism, much less to sketch the design. Similarly an architect may have a general feeling about a new building that is projected but no concrete ideas as yet. In both cases it is a matter of waiting until the feelings gel into something more tangible. Both inventor and architect may try to hasten this gelling process by sketching almost at random, but they are conscious that they are not actually sketching their vague idea but hoping it will suddenly gel and assume a definite form.

For something to gel is for it to mature or to come together or evolve into a definite form.

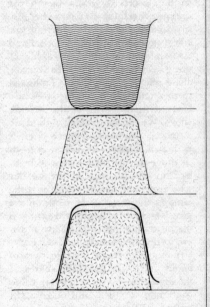

In the process known as cloning you can take a cell from a frog and stimulate the nucleus in a way that will make it divide. The nucleus goes on dividing and from this individual cell eventually develops a whole frog. From one frog, using cloning, you can develop thousands of other identical frogs. The frogs are identical because they have the same genetic material. Applied to humans you could produce a race of warriors, geniuses or slaves as you wished.

The genes are carried on the chromosomes in the nuclei of cells. Every cell in the body carries these chromosomes. The genes are packets of organising instructions. It is the control and interaction of these instructions that allow the development of the body. A cell divides and multiplies to give a fish, cat, cow or dog according to the intrinsic genetic material. A mule is produced by a cross between a horse and donkey but usually such crosses do not work as the genetic material of one species cannot cooperate with that from another.

Suppose we took the cells from a genius like Einstein and cloned them to produce a hundred other beings with exactly the same genetic material. What would happen? Would each new Einstein have to go through exactly the same upbringing, experience, emotions and sequence of living as the original Einstein in order to become capable of similar conceptions or would this happen anyhow? If Einstein had not been turned down for an academic post and had not been bored with his work in the patent office would he have bothered with the considerations that led to his great work? The great question is whether intelligence is a matter of heredity or environment and genes, with ensigned to distinguish the two by testing the IQ of identical twins who have the same genetic material (since they come from one fertilised egg) but have been brought up in different environments. The answer seems to be that intelligence is the combined effect of environment and genes, with environmental factors probably acting either to enhance or hinder the genetic effect.

Selections of genes is used for breeding special cattle, for designing new plants resistant to disease, for developing racehorses but not yet for breeding people because we are not sure that we know what we want.

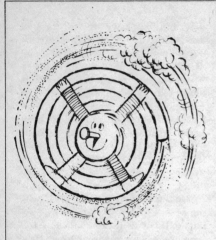

A go-go girl dancing on the counter in a bar is all action. There is stamping and twisting and shivering and shaking in movements that are sinuous or staccato. In the heady days of the stockmarket boom there were go-go fund managers who were always outperforming the market through being exceptionally active. A favourite strategy was to back a stock that seemed to be moving. A stock noticed this way moved a lot more. The price rose dramatically. The fund that had bought in early got out just before the peak and collected the profits. The stock then collapsed and the latecomers were left with the losses. It did not matter whether the stock was really worth anything. All it had to have was promise and the certainty that once its value started to rise someone somewhere would buy it off your hands at more than you paid for it.

'Go' is the term for action, energy, dynamism. At certain times, and with certain people, this desire for action comes first and then a direction has to be found for it. The discovery of the go-go people was that 'go' could itself be the direction of 'go' and action be an end in itself. Once there was action something was bound to develop.

When a whizz-kid whizzes into a staid establishment there is much the whizzer can do because he sees things from a new viewpoint and realises that many of the traditions and unwritten rules are really there to protect the inept. There is a sort of club of mutual protection. When the whizz-kid is all go-go things do happen fast but the very speed of action is its own undoing because one thing tends to depend on another and if one project misfires the whole enterprise can collapse. There also builds up an expectation of ever greater success and since this is impossible any slackening off in pace (which may still be greater than that of the competitors) is taken as a sign of failure. The more profit a person has made by backing the whizz-kid the more anxious that person is to unload and keep the profit.

Energy for the sake of energy, like a catherine wheel sparking as it whirls round, needs a direction. But energy can become a sort of drug that generates its own high. In psychiatric terms the condition is one of mania. In everyday terms the condition is more likely to be one of self-fulfilling opportunism.

Guide-lines are not laws or rules that have to be obeyed. They are more in the nature of policy made concrete and practical by being set out in terms of specific recommendations. The difference between a recommendation and an instruction lies only in the authority of the person who is issuing them. A guide-line is really an instruction that is not an order.

Wellington, in New Zealand, is a very windy city. There are times when ropes have to be slung along the streets to prevent old ladies from being blown across the road. The ropes serve as guide-lines insofar as they provide something to hold on to at difficult times. Theseus found his way out of the labyrinth by unwinding a thread behind him as he went in and following the thread on the way out. This sort of guide-line provided direction. In addition to their frictional advantages railway tracks provide guide-lines which relieve the train driver of the necessity of steering.

Guide-lines may be intended to set a firm direction in order to prevent other directions from being taken. A government's guide-lines on credit control are designed to restrict free use of credit. Guide-lines may also be offered as an aid in a situation where a considerable amount of time might be spent searching for ways of proceeding. For example a book may give guide-lines on the home growing of vegetables. Guide-lines may also be designed to prevent drift. A marriage guidance counsellor may suggest certain guide-lines in order to prevent the marriage drifting towards another crisis.

In general guide-lines may be used for help or for compulsion. The dotted lines in a child's schoolbook are helpful guide-lines by following which he learns to form his letters. The guide-lines set down for the Agricultural Policy of the European Common Market are more in the nature of directives that are to be obeyed. Sometimes such guide-lines call to mind Henry Ford's famous comment that his customers could have any colour of car they wished, provided it was black. So in a tightly regulated society a person may be free to do whatever he chooses, provided he chooses to follow the guide-lines set out for his behaviour.

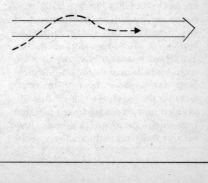

Society runs on a mixture of apathy and fear. People act as they do out of habit and a lack of initiative, and also from a fear of breaking the law and thus losing the approval of fellow citizens. In contrast to society, families run on guilt. Certain expectations of behaviour are made clear but the rules governing the exchange of love and respect are never made clear so that at any moment a person may be made to feel guilty that he is not up to scratch in these respects. A smouldering background of low key guilt overcomes the apathy or detachment that would make family communities unworkable. There is a story of a New York Jewish mother who gave her son a red and a blue shirt for his birthday. Next day he came down to breakfast wearing the red shirt so his mother upbraided him: 'I see you don't like that blue shirt I gave you!' Catholic, Jewish and Protestant ethics all rely, quite sensibly, on guilt as a lubricating aid for behaviour.

Much of psychoanalysis and psychotherapy is designed to alleviate the pressures of guilt in those who are excessively burdened by it through circumstance or temperament. A young woman may feel excessively guilty because she left her mother in order to marry. A parent may feel guilty because his son committed suicide at college. Freud's original investigations of Viennese society ladies suggested that many of their symptoms were caused by guilt about repressed sexual desires and fantasies. The purpose of psychoanalysis was to delve into the subconscious and to make clear the source of the guilt and so alleviate it.

As a motivating system guilt is much more powerful than fear. Fear peaks and then passes away as the contemplated action is performed or avoided. Guilt, however, is continuous. A young man who visited a prostitute once in his youth may feel guilty about it for the rest of his life. What is more, guilt is not only connected to an act that has been committed. It can apply just as powerfully to a 'desire' to carry out the action. A young man may feel guilt that he does not love his mother enough. A mother may feel guilty about moments when she feels like battering her baby. It is said that there are some people so prone to guilt that they even feel guilty about not having anything to feel guilty about.

One method of de-sensitising a person who is allergic to something is to give repeated small doses of the offending substance until the body becomes used to it. This is an habituation procedure. A stimulus which at one time caused an arousal of interest with time comes to be accepted as a matter of course: there has been habituation to the stimulus.

When prices are rising continuously, month after month, people become habituated to this rise and no longer notice or object. If, however, price rises are held back until they can be held back no longer and are then released as one massive increase the resentment is much stronger.

Experienced nannies who wish to overcome a child's dislike of spinach do not make a confrontation of the issue but gradually introduce it a little at a time over a long period until habituation has occurred.

Habituation can be likened to the steady drip of water that smooths a stone. It is natural for organisms to react but it is not natural for organisms to go on reacting in exactly the same way. Sometimes, as in the case of allergies, the reaction can get fiercer and fiercer. This can also occur with phobias. At other times the reaction grows less and less with time. Children are excited by new toys but after a while they become blasé. The excite-ment of a new romance gives way to habituation.

It could be said that the process of perception is a continuous slide into habituation. What was exciting and interesting at one time becomes familiar and boring. The purpose of art, and the purpose of some religions, is to try to revive this interest in the world by providing a framework for looking at old things in new ways. A painter paints a still life that re-discovers beauty in a bowl of fruit or a bottle of wine.

Up to a certain age a child loves the same story to be told again and again but beyond that age he wants a new story each time. There are moods in which the familiar is comfortable and moods in which it is boring.

Many unemployed school leavers who are still living at home cannot be bothered with the hassle of claiming unemployment pay. This seems to involve going to one office for forms which have to be taken to a second office, where more forms have to be taken to a third office. Almost all government offices are organised for the benefit of the people working in them rather than those who have to use them. The result is a certain amount of hassle when anything needs to be done. There is some logic in this. If people cannot be bothered to put up with the hassle then perhaps they do not really need the benefits. On the other hand it can be said that too much hassle may simply be an intelligence filter which filters out the less intelligent who may need help most.

As society becomes more complicated every area of life becomes more involved. There are more and more forms to fill in and every form becomes part of the general hassle of being alive and of surviving from day to day. In Russian stores it is necessary to join one queue to examine the goods and make a decision. Then there is a queue for the cashier. Finally there is a third queue at the end of which the cashier's receipt is exchanged for the goods. The ultimate effect is a form of rationing by time and hassle which goes to hide the shortage of consumer goods.

It is the hassle of using public transport that encourages drivers to use their cars in cities. City authorities try to increase the hassle of finding a parking place so that one hassle is balanced out by another. This sort of policy results in a perpetual hassle whatever a person does or wherever he goes. There is a suspicion that if things are made easier then everyone will want to do them and the system will be overwhelmed.

Almost all existing tendencies tend to complicate life and to increase the hassle. There are few tendencies working in the opposite direction. Attempts to cut costs usually end up not by simplifying a procedure but by shifting more of it on to the consumer. The legal profession is an example where hassle has always been a way of life: the more hassle there is the more livings can be provided.

Outside the purity of an academic, theological or ideological world a great deal of practical action has to be based on incomplete information. So there is risk. Some people take risks because they have to; others take risks because they enjoy taking them and hope to gain substantially if they win their bet. Faced with an election a businessman may fear that if a Socialist government is elected conditions for business will be worse and taxes will be higher. So he makes a bet that a Socialist government will indeed be elected. If the Socialist party is elected he collects his winnings on the bet. If the Socialist party is not elected then his business prospers anyway. The man has seen the risk and limited it by setting up a hedge. An investor handling a pension fund fears that if interest rates rise the value of the stocks and shares in the portfolio will fall. So he hedges his risk by placing some of his investment in

interest-yielding bonds and the rest in stocks. Whatever happens he will not lose too much.

A man might place a lot of money on a certain horse to win a race. Then he has second thoughts and so places some money on the next favourite. He has hedged his bet. But this is not a true hedge because unless the book-makers are crazy he would have done as well by placing less money on the first horse.

The diagram shows a decision point. If both of the units move down one decision path all is gained or all is lost. So the major unit moves down one path and the smaller unit moves down the other as a hedge. Just as a hedge serves to limit a garden so a hedge serves to limit a risk.

Setting up an effective hedge is not the same as doing nothing, which it might appear to be if one were simply betting against oneself. The head of a business corporation might make speeches in favour of one Presidential candidate and secretly give campaign contributions to the other. This is hardly the same as doing nothing.

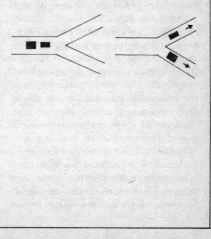

There exist hierarchies of angels (with the archangels at the top), of priests and of organisation people. A hierarchy is a sort of organised pecking order in which, except at either extreme, you are more important than someone and in turn someone else is more important than you. The basis of this 'importance' may vary. In the case of a priesthood the basis may be special knowledge or sanctity but it is just as likely to be organisational: a bishop is superior to an ordinary priest because the hierarchy above has so decided. In an organisation a hierarchy is a way of handing down decisions and control so that a few people at the top can keep a close watch on those below. Most organisations have a pyramid-type hierarchy with fewer and fewer people at each level until at the summit there is one man who is boss.

In education a curriculum is said to be hierarchical if there is a basic core from which subordinate material develops. Also if each section depends on the previous section then the material is said to be hierarchical and the correct sequence must be followed. In the world of living creatures there is a hierarchy of forms ranging from the most primitive to the most developed (man).

A hierarchy implies superiority and domination. A chain of communication, in which one person passes a message to the next person who in turn passes it on, is not hierarchical unless the person who passes on the message has more right to pass a message down than to receive one back. It is just possible to imagine a circular hierarchy in which each person is superior to the person on one side but not superior to anyone else. Messages would pass round and round the circle always going the same way. There would be no extremes because the ends would be joined: the lowliest being superior to the most senior. This is similar to the type of organisation that occurs when cells develop to form an organism. Once the organism is formed, however, a new hierarchy develops: controlled by the nervous system and by the hormones secreted by the glands.

What tends to happen in hierarchies is that the organisational position becomes indistinguishable from the person filling it, whether that person is competent or not. A position does not by itself confer competence, merely a position from which incompetence can be exercised.

Homeostasis means keeping things exactly as they are. Life is only possible because the human body uses the principle of homeostasis. The acidity of the blood, its salinity, and the concentration of different elements like calcium must all be kept within very narrow limits otherwise the body stops functioning. A relatively small increase in potassium in the blood will stop the heart. Through the intestines, the kidneys and the lungs the body adjusts its intake and its excretion in order to maintain things at exactly the right level: in order to maintain homeostasis. The thermostat in a house operates in a simpler way as a homeostat since its purpose is to maintain the homeostasis of the atmosphere in the house, at least as regards temperature. If it were operating fully as a homeostat it would control the humidity of the air and possibly also the ionisation as well.

If you were growing plants using hydroponics you would have to take care to add to the water all the nutrients and trace elements that the plant required. By your efforts you would have to try to maintain the homeostasis of the plant-growing environment. When a person is unable to produce enough insulin to maintain the homeostasis of his nutrition system we have to add insulin by injections and the condition is known as diabetes.

Keeping things in a state of homeostasis can be done from outside as in the case of hydroponics and diabetes but it is usually done by inbuilt self-adjusting mechanisms that make use of feedback principles. For example passenger liners have stabilisers. If the liner begins to roll this is detected and a signal is sent to operate the stabiliser which acts to tilt the liner in the opposite direction so neutralising the roll. The Wright brothers were the first to fly because they designed wing-tilting mechanisms which the pilot could use to maintain the 'homeostasis' of his aeroplane.

Society has all sorts of inbuilt mechanisms to maintain homeostasis. But homeostasis means keeping things as they are when they are at the optimum level. We have no way of knowing that everything in society is already at the optimal level.

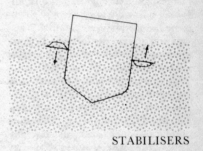

STABILISERS

The body has a variety of communicating systems. The most obvious is the nervous system. Nerves carry to the brain the signals coming from the eyes, ears, tongue and skin. Nerves carry from the brain the signals that activate the muscles. In addition there are nerves which act on the blood vessels, stomach, bladder and the heart itself. But nerves go to specific places and carry specific messages. For more general effects there is a system of chemical communicators that are put into the blood stream from the glands. These communicators, messengers or hormones act on individual cells and alter their development and metabolism.

Women develop breasts because the female hormone oestrogen acts on the potential breast tissue. If men are given this hormone, as they sometimes are in the treatment of prostate disease, they also tend to grow breasts. The best known hormones are the sex hormones which cause the development of the sexual features at puberty and also regulate the reproductive functions of the body. There is a growth hormone which causes growth itself. Too much of it causes gigantism and too little leads to dwarfism.

Each gland has its own pattern of hormone secretion but the activities of each gland are controlled by the central pituitary gland which decides how much of each hormone is required. In turn the pituitary gland is controlled by nerve impulses from parts of the brain which indicate to it the state of the body and the state of the world around. The stress syndrome is caused by overstimulation of the glands in an attempt to cope with external stress. We now know that external stress, such as overcrowding, can cause marked changes in gland secretion with effects on fertility and behaviour.

Hormones are a subtle form of communication. They are almost like a smell in the sense that they travel in all directions. Focused communication is achieved not by the focused message (as would be the case with a telephone line or a nerve) but by the special ability of some cells to respond to the hormone. It is almost as if a code message were to be broadcast on the radio for everyone to hear while only those who knew the code were able to respond.

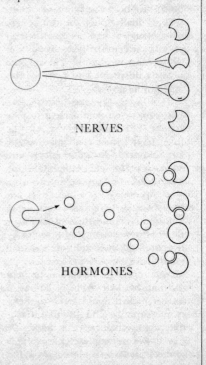

NERVES

HORMONES

You are steering a motorboat going down a river. For some reason there is a considerable delay between your movement of the steering wheel and the turning response of the boat. To avoid a floating log you turn the wheel to the left. Nothing happens so you turn it more to the left. Still nothing happens so you turn it fully to the left as far as it will go. By now the boat is beginning to respond to your wheel turning. So gradually it turns more and more sharply to the left. When you see this you correct matters by turning the wheel back. Nothing happens so you turn it further back. Still nothing happens so now you turn it fully to the right. The boat now starts to respond and gradually turns fully to the right even though you now have the wheel back in the centre. So you compensate by turning to the left. So the boat swings wildly from side to side. This is the hunting process.

The hunting process occurs in a control system when there is a delay between the output and the response. In a true hunting process the oscillations become larger and larger until eventually the system breaks down. The process tends to occur in government attempts to control the economy. In times of inflation there is a restriction of the money supply. This leads to a fall in investment and eventually a recession. At this point the government is tempted to increase the money supply in order to check the unemployment which is politically unacceptable. Such an increase in money supply would tend to lead to an inflation even worse than before. Today governments are rather more sophisticated and understand that the lag-time in the system is such that attempts to correct matters immediately can lead to a dangerous hunting type of oscillation.

To avoid hunting one needs to speed up the feedback. Unfortunately in many systems the lag-time is unavoidable (you cannot sell a car before you have produced it). The alternative is to take only small steps at a time and wait until the effect of each has become obvious. But to do this you have to know the system and like the driver of the motorboat have faith that a small turn on the wheel will eventually carry the boat clear of the floating log.

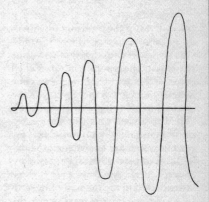

Idiosyncrasy is the term for individuality in those situations where the individual view is considered of less value than that of the group or the established doctrine. An idiosyncratic view is one which is not part of the trend or of the establishment. It is not strictly predictable. It is a view which stands out because it is made by an individual for reasons which are known only to himself. It is suspected that the reasons are entirely personal. Wherever people are expected to toe the party line or to subscribe to the general view the idiosyncratic view is regarded as an unfortunate aberration. There is a touch of eccentricity about it.

A committee has been set up to inquire into the financing of public transport. The two main lines of thought are that the money should be found from the local taxes and that fares should be raised to an economic level. The idiosyncratic view of one of the committee members is that motorists should be paid to leave their cars at home: they should be paid for preferring to use public transport when they could be using their cars. His argument is that with fewer cars on the roads public transport would be quicker and more cost-effective.

Idiosyncrasy is not a matter of numbers. At a committee meeting such as the one suggested above, one member may have put forward a view that represented an established line of thinking. The fact that only one member put forward this view would not have made it idiosyncratic. What did make it idiosyncratic was the fact that the view was peculiar to that individual; there were no followers or proponents outside the committee putting forward that particular point of view. A person who can be relied upon to act as an individual rather than a mouthpiece runs the risk of being idiosyncratic.

Idiosyncrasy has many uses chief of which is to give a token appearance of democracy. Occasionally idiosyncrasy can serve as the random mutation element so necessary for evolution. Most often it is dismissed as mere eccentricity with the suspicion that an individual's motives are rarely pure in matters where group pressures count.

A man stands in front of the mirror shaving with his right hand. The image in the mirror seems to be shaving with the left hand. It is sometimes asked why, if things are reversed from left to right, they are not reversed from top to bottom. The answer is that they are. If man was uniformly circular we could say that the mirror man was actually standing on his head and still shaving with his right hand. The real explanation is that the image in the mirror is not looking back at the shaving man but away from him. But since the image is only two-dimensional it appears to be looking back at the shaver. Draw a face on a piece of tissue paper and hold it up so that the face is looking in the same direction as your face (that is away from you). If you now look through the back of the sheet the two-dimensional face is looking towards you as well, face to face.

An image is a reflection but a reflection altered by the characteristics of the reflecting surface. Distorting mirrors in fun fairs make people look fat or thin, tall or short, long bodied or long legged.

The image that concerns most people is the reflection that they see in other people's minds. A politician is very sensitive about his image. A corporation is also sensitive about the face that it shows to the public. There is a profession of image-builders whose task it is to create images for politicians and corporations and to project these images. On the whole it seems to be a successful and able profession.

Some people's public images seem very sensitive whereas others' may be very stable. One politician may seem able to survive any manner of disaster in both his political and private life. Another politician only has to make one mistake, like calling a Pole a Polack, for his career to be damaged. For any public person there seems to be a limited range of possible images which the public is prepared to accept. They will not accept an image that is created outside this range; instead they will fit the image into the nearest stereotype. To avoid this the image-makers have to step in first and provide the most acceptable positive stereotype.

The French scientist Pasteur discovered the principle of immunisation by accident. He was investigating the effect of cholera in hens. One of his assistants had been careless about preparing the material that was to be used to infect the hens. As a result only a weak infection was transmitted to the hens. The hens survived instead of dying. But what was remarkable was that they showed a complete resistance to any attempt to infect them with a full dose of the germ. So the practice of immunisation by giving a weakened form of the antigen (the infecting material) was established. The principle is now widely used for polio, typhoid, rabies, measles, whooping cough and many other diseases.

The principle is that an exposure to a weak dose of the infecting agent allows the body to learn how to make antibodies to this agent. With future infections the antibody system goes into operation at once and overcomes the infection. Diseases like chicken-pox establish their own immunity insofar as one episode of the disease confers immunity against further infection.

In situations outside medicine prior exposure in a small dose can immunise a person against a severe reaction when the full dose of something harmful is presented. Whole populations can be immunised against strong reactions by repeated small doses. For example a certain callousness may follow repeated reports of violence. Similarly strong reactions to a famine in a distant land are prevented by frequent exposure to smaller incidents. In areas such as these habituation, de-sensitisation and immunisation tend to overlap.

The carefully controlled political leak is a standard immunisation procedure. It is leaked that there is to be an increase in taxation. There is a certain amount of opposition but it cannot be very strong because you cannot seriously oppose a rumour. Finally when the opposition has died down the measure is really introduced. It is difficult to revive with full fervour the original opposition and in any case there has been time to prepare counter-arguments or adjustments. Again this is as much a process of de-sensitisation as of immunisation. The difference between the two is that in immunisation the defence system is prepared and in de-sensitisation it is exhausted.

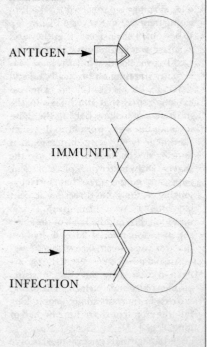

ANTIGEN →

IMMUNITY

INFECTION

It is assumed that man responds to the stick and the carrot. The carrot is the incentive. A man can be forced to go in a certain direction by threatening him if he does not or rewarding him if he does. Animal trainers tend to use reward more than punishment. Punishment might be suitable for building up a general fear or respect but is not effective for training specific activities. You cannot get someone to do what is right by punishing what is wrong. In training a rat to run a maze the administration of an electric shock every time the rat takes the wrong turn will not be as effective as rewarding the creature when it takes the right turn.

Professor Skinner of Harvard University claimed that any behaviour could be 'shaped' if it were broken down into small enough steps and if each right step was rewarded as it was performed. This extreme form of behaviourism is supported by animal training experiments. There is, however, a difference between rewards used as reinforcement for conditioning behaviour and rewards used as incentives. With the conditioning reward the person or animal does not actually anticipate the reward: he simply feels that the intended reaction is the right one. With incentives a person anticipates the reward which is clearly in mind as he works towards it. A boy who is promised a new bicycle if he scores highly in an examination knows what he is working towards. The girl who is promised a large sum of money if she does not smoke until she is eighteen years old also knows the incentive.

Money is reckoned to be the most easily handled incentive since it represents all sorts of agreeable things that can be obtained in exchange for money. Money is also tangible and an increase in wages is more easily measured than an improvement in working conditions. And yet there are increasing doubts as to whether money is really so effective an incentive. In some countries the tax structure is such that an increase in wages is immediately eaten up by tax. It is also felt that unless a person is poor the extra amount of money means little since expectations rise to meet the available amount and there is not much that can be done with money as such. Status, leisure time, work flexibility and job interest may prove better incentives although less easily handled.

The Pharaohs are said to have married their sisters in order to preserve the dynasty and to prevent the emergence of rival claimants. In modern cattle breeding the same bull fathers cows that will later be inseminated with his semen. Most cultures have a taboo on breeding between members of the same family. The Greeks and later Freud made great play of it in the Oedipus situation concerning a man who, in ignorance, married his mother.

The basic objection is that if there is no input of genes from outside the family circle then the stock will deteriorate. This does not seem to be the case with cattle but it is with ideas. In-breeding organisations that rely only on their own advice (like the public service or civil service) suffer the gene deterioration that one might expect. The incestuously bred cattle develop a purity of strain which makes them suitable only for particular demands. Similarly in government service those people are promoted whose ideas best fit the current trends of the service. This produces a pure breed that may be unresponsive to the changing needs of society. The effect is to be seen in the academic world and in the general world of education. Those pupils who best play the existing game are eventually selected to run the game and in turn choose those who are best at playing the game. The game (for game read education) becomes an end in itself. There is nothing wrong with this provided the relevance of the game to the needs of society remains high and provided that useful innovations are not automatically excluded by the incestuous breeding of ideas.

Any closed system that propagates by incest or internal fertilisation has the advantage of purity but the disadvantage of lack of adaptability. If the army is run only by generals, medicine only by doctors, universities only by academics, law only by lawyers, politics only by politicians, then such systems end up by being run for the sake of those running them rather than of those they are presumed to serve.

In general we seem to pay too little attention to the genetics and breeding of ideas and attitudes. If we did we should try to lessen the incestuous habits of so many organisations.

In times of inflation prices rise. Indeed, the degree of inflation is usually shown by the percentage rise in an assortment of retail prices sometimes called the Retail Price Index. In a rough way this indicates the rise in the cost of living. Wage demands and negotiations are related to this rise in prices shown by the rise in the index. In order for living standards to be maintained the rise in wages should equal the rise in the price index. If wages were automatically increased by this amount then wage demands would no longer be necessary in order to keep up with inflation. Some countries like Switzerland do in fact run such a scheme. The wages are said to be indexed because they rise in line with the rise in the retail price index.

Indexation can be extended to cover other matters. For instance someone who invests his savings might find that when he comes to draw them out again their purchasing power has fallen dramatically as a result of inflation. Indexation of investments protects against this by increasing the value of the investment in keeping with the percentage rise in inflation. Such indexation of investments is used in Israel and also in the United Kingdom, where a special class of indexed bonds is available to older people. In Brazil practically everything is indexed.

Indexation removes the fear and panic from inflation because money is guaranteed its storage value and wages are guaranteed their purchasing power. All the inflation mechanisms that are fuelled by fear are controlled by indexation. On the other hand indexation can itself perpetuate a moderate degree of inflation because it prevents the fall in the standard of living that might be required to end inflation. In Brazil the indexation approach was successful in reducing an inflation rate of about one hundred and sixty per cent per annum to sixteen per cent.

Wherever there is change an index of that change can be obtained by averaging out the change. For instance there may be an index of industrial growth obtained by averaging out growth across different sectors of industry. There may be an index of drug usage obtained by taking into account the number of prescriptions and the quantities of each drug prescribed.

Indexation is the process of keeping level with the index by making equivalent changes.

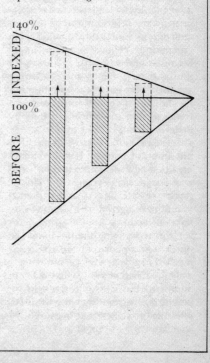

The inertia of a mass is its reluctance to move. In Newton's terms inertia can also refer to the tendency of a body to continue in a state of uniform motion in a straight line unless acted upon by some outside force.

Inertia is the willingness of things to stay exactly as they are unless moved by sufficient force. We know that this is so in physics and yet we are surprised when it turns out to be the case with organisations. Why should a large organisation change direction simply because someone with a new idea thinks that it ought to? Measured against the mass of the organisation the individual's efforts must seem like trying to alter the course of a tank by throwing a ball-bearing at it.

Inertia is not a matter of opposition but simply of inaction. It is often imagined that new ideas are vigorously opposed and hence defeated. This is rarely the case. The ideas are listened to and even agreed with, but nothing happens because there is no mechanism for overcoming the inertia of the system. An opportunity to change is rarely the same as a reason to change.

The education system has a lot of inbuilt inertia. The subjects taught are taught not because they are of direct relevance to society but because they have always been taught and there are teachers trained to teach them. In many countries the school-leaving exams are geared to university entrance requirements. Like a rocket plunging through space because it has developed movement in a certain direction, the system continues in a straight line along its original course. And it is no one's fault.

The problem with inertia is that it seems to make change by gradual evolutionary progress impossible. It seems to force change into the cataclysmic clash mode. To overcome inertia force must be exerted by a body of significant force and mass. This type of change is wasteful and destructive. Perhaps the answer is to find the sensitive nodes in the system and to exert pressure for change at these points.

Periodically the West German government finds that its administration is infiltrated by spies from East Germany. There is a flushing out and then the process starts all over again.

Perhaps the most powerful weapon the police have against narcotics gangs is to infiltrate them with their own agents.

The famous Centre Point office block in London had been empty for so long that outraged citizens were determined to occupy it as a gesture. But the building was guarded by security guards. One of them, however, opened a window and let the demonstrators in. It seemed that the demonstrators had infiltrated the security service.

Infiltration implies the filtering in, amongst the genuine members of a group, of outsiders who to all appearances are members of the group but whose allegiance lies elsewhere. It is extremely difficult to guard against since there is no way of knowing what is going on in the mind of an applicant. Paradoxically the more suspicious a group is of a new member the more surely will they accept him once the suspicions have passed.

It is often claimed that the power structure of one or other union has been infiltrated by Marxists or Fascists. This is of course infiltration but perfectly legitimate political infiltration. If their supporters are the only ones who can be bothered to turn up or vote at meetings they have a right to be elected. (This is quite apart from the political dilemma as to whether a group that does not believe in the democratic system has a right to use that system for its destruction.)

The purpose of infiltration could be

that of information feedback to an outside body as in the case of spies. The purpose could also be that of hidden influence on decisions. Sabotage is another function. Legitimate political takeover is a further possibility. Finally the infiltrators may be 'sleepers' who once infiltrated do nothing for several years until a situation arises in which they are 'activated' to perform their role.

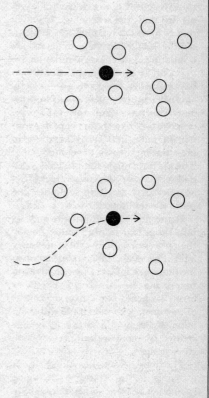

Inflation seems to suggest that something is getting larger. In fact inflation means that the exchange value of money for goods is falling. To compensate for this the face value of the money is inflating. The causes of inflation are many and various. Imported inflation happens when the goods produced by another country, such as oil, become more expensive. This raises the price of goods derived from or depending on these imports. Wages rise to meet this increase in the cost of living. This in turn raises the price of goods and services. So the cost of living rises again. Wages catch up again and the spiral is established.

If the government tries to pay its bills simply by printing more money then prices rise and the value of money falls. The same thing happens when the money supply is increased by a rapid increase in credit. Credit is created when a bank gives overdrafts to customers who then trade with each other by using the artificial money created by the overdraft credit: book entry money.

The most damaging thing about inflation is the positive feedback element. The wage–price spiral is only one of these elements. The other is the rush to invest in houses and gold and other goods which are supposed to be inflation-proof. This sends up the price of these items so fuelling inflation. Interest rates, unless controlled, also rise in order to compensate for the fall in money values and this raises the cost of borrowing so putting up prices yet again. Almost all the reactive interactions in inflation tend to make it worse.

Attempts are made to control inflation by controlling the money supply (credit), by controlling prices (with food subsidies) and by controlling wages. Successful control of inflation tends to lead to a recession and a rise in unemployment, so governments are perpetually having to balance one against the other.

A modest rate of inflation tends to benefit the government since more tax is collected as incomes rise into higher tax brackets. Furthermore taxes take a slice of inflated capital values.

Inflation destroys the storage value of money and also the contract value. Both can be protected by indexation which removes the fear element of inflation but fuels the process.

Most of the systems we know depend on communication. One thing affects another because they are in communication. The complex interactive systems that make up society arise from the complex lines of communication. The self-organising and self-stabilising properties of biological systems arise from the communication between the different parts, whether by nerve or by chemical. The diagram shows that the easiest form of communication is to bring two things into contact one with the other. If this is not possible then we try to establish a channel of communication between the two things.

We always tend to suppose that troubles arise because there is too little communication. Yet sometimes the opposite may be the case. A person who touches a live electric wire risks his life because communication is too good. A house which loses a lot of expensive heat through the walls and roof does so because the communication between the air outside and the air inside is too good. To overcome this excessive communication we introduce the concept of 'insulation'. The diagram shows how we could interrupt communication simply by pushing two things out of contact with each other. The other approach is to introduce some insulation between them in order to stop or diminish the communication.

Insulation is not the same as isolation. Isolation suggests removing all communication between something and its surroundings. Insulation implies slowing down the communication with regard only to one type of communication. We may wish to insulate the income of pensioners against the effect of inflation. We may wish to insulate the foreign exchange rate of currency from the greed of speculators. Some people are hypersensitive and go through life in a sort of raw-skinned agony. We might want to insulate them from this over-communication but would risk insulating them as well from the benefits of this sensitivity.

When we talk so much about the advantages of communication we sometimes forget to think about the advantages of insulation.

In the thinking of the Greek philosophers cause and effect were quite distinct. It would have been unthinkable for the effect to turn round and act upon the cause. The simple relationship between cause and effect is shown in the diagram. One thing acts upon another: the footballer kicks the ball; the boiling water boils the egg; the scissors cut the paper; the bomb destroys the building.

As soon as we leave the world of physical action and consider people the idea of simple cause and effect is not enough. A mother smacks a child but the child's behaviour has an effect on the mother. Two people are arguing: they each have an effect on the other. A boy gives his girl-friend a present. She is affected by his kindness and he by her delight and appreciation. In the biological world interaction is much more common than one-way action. Sometimes the interaction is a mutual exchange of action and effect. At other times action goes one way but is returned through a loop that involves another party. Both these possibilities are shown in the diagram. All feedback situations involve interaction.

Interaction suggests communication. Communication channels are rarely one-way. If the channel exists it can usually be used from either end. Communication is a form of action so wherever there is communication there is likely to be interaction.

Sometimes it is important to know the extent of the interaction. For example when two drugs are given to a patient it is important to know whether they are going to interact. They could interact in three ways: the second drug could neutralise or reduce the effectiveness of the first; the second drug could exaggerate the effect of the first; the two drugs might together produce a totally new effect. Each of these processes can happen the other way round with the first drug affecting the second. Even outside medicine any two actions which might separately have a pure effect, when acting together might produce unsuspected consequences.

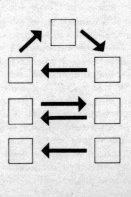

The concept of an interest rate forms the basis of capitalism. Someone borrows a sum of money and pays the lender an interest rate of five, seven, ten or more per cent per year for the use of the money. Why is he paying this interest rate? We can find a variety of reasons. If the borrower was not paying any interest rate the lender could just as well keep the money under his bed or in the bank; there would be no point at all in lending the money. The fact that the borrower is paying an attractive interest rate makes it attractive for the lender to lend the money instead of trying to use it himself to generate more money: the interest rate competes with other uses of the money. There is a risk that the borrower may not be able to repay this money and so the lender might lose it all. In practice the loan would be secured against something owned by the borrower but some risk is usually present. In the end the simple rationale is that if there were no interest rates then no one would be encouraged to lend money.

It is not, however, beyond the bounds of human ingenuity to devise alternative incentives for lending money. For example it might be possible to guarantee that money which was lent out would not lose its value. Thus money stored under a bed or in a bank might lose money with inflation and the only inflation-proof storage system would be to lend it out (at no interest rate). In practice money would be lent to a central government bank which would guarantee to protect it against inflation. This bank would then lend it out without interest to different commercial enterprises. In times of severe inflation this is what does actually tend to happen insofar as interest rates (especially after tax) do not even preserve the value of the money.

In a totally free market interest rates would fluctuate with the supply and demand of money, being high when there was much competition for limited funds and low when funds were plentiful. In practice central banks fix the interest rate to give the official cost of money. Adjustments in this interest rate are one of the very few instruments available to government for controlling the economy from moment to moment. Such adjustments control the flow of money from country to country and also within the country. But in turn expectations about changes in interest rates cause trouble in the system.

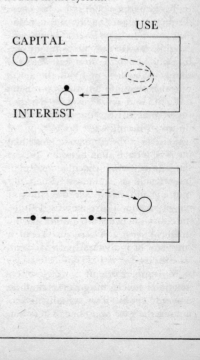

USE

CAPITAL

INTEREST

In a tiny island like Malta quite different dialects can be found in villages that are less than half a mile apart. This seems very strange for half a mile is well within walking distance and there are no natural boundaries to keep people apart. The diagram shows how there can be two centres of influence, perhaps market towns, drawing people towards them. People in the countryside go to one or other. There must come a point where the circles of influence are actually touching. At this point a person in one circle of influence will be very close physically to a person in another but far apart in terms of how he is influenced. Although the two people are functionally standing 'back to back' we can regard this point as an interface between the two spheres of influence.

An interface occurs where one system comes directly into contact with another. The interface between a mighty multi-national company and the public may be in a series of small shops in which individuals decide whether or not to buy the goods being offered. In a more specialised way it may come in the stockmarket where investors decide what price to put on the shares of the company. There may be no interface at all between students and university authorities, except in the teaching situation which has nothing to do with the way the university is run. There may be no interface at all between the public and the medical service it receives except in the case of individual patients being treated by doctors.

We suppose that there is a close connection between the governed and the government but if we actually look for an interface we find none. There may be an occasional letter to a newspaper, a Congressman or a member of Parliament. A few people may even know such a person. Editors and journalists may write 'on behalf' of the public. But the actual interface is limited to the infrequent voting booth which provides only a blanket either/or choice.

The interface between two systems is usually at the edge rather than the centre. It is surprising how little attention, care or design thought is given to interfaces.

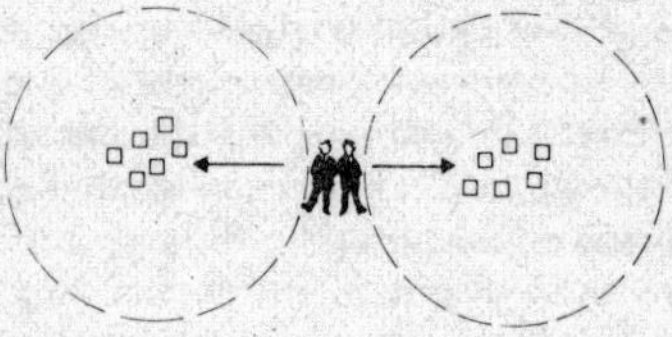

In times of boom retailers stock up with the goods that are selling fast because they do not want to run out of the items in demand and so have to turn customers away. Since everyone else is also selling fast there is a reason for holding even more goods in stock than usual to serve as a sort of cushion in case delivery is slow. For the same reason manufacturers build up supplies of raw materials in case these become difficult to obtain because of competition. The competition will also tend to drive prices up so this is another reason for buying larger quantities than usual.

When the boom starts to turn into a recession the process goes into reverse. Everyone stops buying and starts to run down their accumulations or inventories of goods. The retailer finds his sales are falling off so he does not order fresh stocks but runs down the large inventory he has, being worried that he will not be able to sell all he has accumulated. Because the retailers are not buying the manufacturer has to cut back on his manufacturing. He therefore orders no more raw materials but uses up the inventory of materials he bought during the boom. In short everyone is running down their inventories so actual sales figures look far worse than they really are. For example the retailer may be selling ten per cent less than usual but his ordering from the manufacturer may have gone down by fifty per cent. Similarly the manufacturer may be using twenty per cent less material than before but his ordering of raw material may be down by sixty per cent. Everyone reacts to these poor figures and the recession is intensified because investment plans are stopped and workers

are laid off. Finally the inventories are run down and everyone starts buying again. And the whole cycle restarts.

In any system with an uneven flow there have to be reservoirs or inventories to even things out. The manufacturer has to produce at a steady pace in order to get the most out of his machines and workers. But sales may be very uneven: for example three quarters of all toy sales occur in the three months over Christmas. So the goods are stocked in a warehouse to await customers orders. Everyone tries to cut down inventories as much as possible because idle goods represent idle capital.

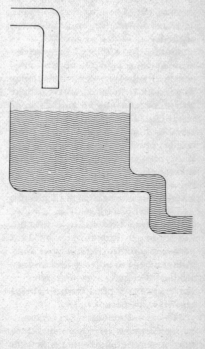

Perhaps the concept of investment is the most difficult to understand and yet the most important. An organism naturally moves towards what is attractive, towards what is needed for the moment. The idea that you may have to move away from what is attractive in order to profit later is unnatural. Most religions are investment devices. They set up structures which help people to perform things which appear to be contrary to their own immediate interests for the sake of reward in a next life. A martyr is asked to do nothing less than give up his life in order to gain salvation. This is quite an investment. Some people suffer fasting and discomfort to the point of self-mortification in order to invest in the purification of their souls.

A chicken faced with a bowl of grain separated from it by a wire net will try to get through the wire. In a parallel situation a dog will move away from the bone in order to find his way around the net. A young man at university may spend his time studying while his friends outside the university are out on the town every night. Supposedly he is investing in his future since a good qualification might get him a better job (no longer as true as

it used to be).

A farmer may forgo the immediate use of some money in order to pay interest on money that has been borrowed to invest in a tractor. If the investment is sound the pay-off will be more effective farming. Children can be seen as parents' investment for old age. The children are expensive to bring up and require a lot of care and attention but then they are supposed to support their parents when they are too old to support themselves. Life insurance is an investment in which a small sum is put by each year with the promise that on death (or at a certain age) a lump sum will become payable.

Investment is the basis of capitalism. The stockmarket and other capital markets are merely devices for selling shares in an investment or inviting new investments.

Any situation in which reward is delayed and does not immediately follow the effort is an investment situation. A man who plants trees which he himself will never see is investing in his children's happiness. Gamblers are compulsive investors.

JARGON

Huntsmen wear red coats which are always called 'pink'. White horses are never called white horses but always 'greys'. Polo is played on horses which are always called 'ponies'. There are any number of language clubs whose members automatically recognise each other and non-members by the private language that has grown up around some sport or activity. An extensive private language has grown up around the use of citizens' band radio by drivers on the freeways in the United States: 'smokey bear' or simply 'smokey' refers to a police patrol car. The army has its own private language in which 2 i/c means second in command. Medicine has another private language which can vary from hospital to hospital: TCI written on an outpatient's notes may mean To Come In while MI may mean myocardial infarction.

One might expect to find a difference between the jargon of 'language clubs' where the strange words are cherished as being the basis of the club and the jargon of a profession which is supposed to be only a convenient communicating device. In practice there may be no such difference. A scientist will use as much jargon as he can in his field to show that he fully belongs to his pro-fessional club. A teacher will use expressions like 'learning environment', 'reinforcement', 'Piagetian model' to show that she too is up to date.

Those who object to jargon should realise that there are times when a new word is required in order to describe in a simple and direct way something that is important. An engineer who is denied the use of the expression 'aerofoil section' would have a hard time explaining the concept on each occasion. A doctor who was denied the use of the term 'immune reaction' would have an equally hard time. A motor mechanic may have to talk about carburettor jets even if the listener knows nothing about carburettors.

The important point for the user of jargon to remember is that it is his business to communicate and not only to describe. He is showing, not showing off. Any communicator must be conscious of the listening powers of his listener and the use of jargon should be kept to a minimum, and explained when used. Conversely the listener may have to make some effort to grasp essential jargon in a field.

IN

A metal key is carefully shaped so that it fits the lock and opens the door. Instead of the metal key we can turn our thumbs into keys by having a metal plate on to which we press our thumb. The plate records the fingerprint and is pre-programmed to open the door only if the correct thumb is used. A much simpler, but less foolproof method, is to have a set of numbers which are used in sequence in order to open a combination lock. Finally we can have a 'time' lock. With a time lock there is no key but the knowledge that the door will open exactly at thirteen minutes and twenty seconds past three o'clock if a finger is placed on a button precisely at that time (if the finger is placed there before the lock will remain closed). In this case knowledge is the only key.

Once you have opened the door of the house you can enter and enjoy the amenities of the house. Once you have opened the door of the bank vault you can remove the money (honestly or otherwise). There is no limit to what is made possible even by a fairly simple key. There is a similarity between a key and a trigger: in both cases what follows has been set up beforehand and is only released. The key or trigger permit access but play no part in causing what follows.

Ancient languages have remained a puzzle for centuries until the chance finding of an inscription which relates the unknown language to a known one has unlocked the code. Once the key has been found to a code all else follows. The key-stone of an archway is the stone that locks a pile of other stones into an arch.

If everyone were to have a key to a door there would not be much point in locking the door; a latch could be used to stop it blowing open. A key suggests a privileged access. It suggests that the communication channel is restricted to those who have the key. In fact the functional purpose of a key is not so much to open things up for some people as to keep them closed to everyone else. A key is a form of organisation whereby access control is put on an information channel.

Since only hens lay eggs, chicken sexing is a very important profession. It is not easy to tell the sex of a chicken that is only a few days old. In England bands of highly skilled Japanese chicken sexers go from farm to farm identifying the sex of young chickens. Any mistakes which they make are replaced by the person who has sold the chickens as all hens. Chicken-sexing does not appear to be something that you could learn out of a book. Knowing how to do it is what matters. This know-how comes from experience and possibly from working with other experienced people.

Huge industries like paper making and steel making are not as scientific as might be imagined. In some respects they are more like crafts, depending on the know-how of certain skilled workers. Whisky blending, tea blending and tobacco blending are much more obvious examples of the importance of know-how.

Know-how is a mixture of information, experience, trial and error, imitation and learning. A Japanese company setting out to make dyestuffs will buy the know-how from a Swiss firm under a licensing agreement. A businessman who has worked for years in the Middle East will be eagerly sought out for his know-how regarding business in that area.

In certain technical subjects such as chemicals or electronics the know-how may consist entirely of technical information but in most other cases it is actual experience that matters most. The apprenticeship of a student to a master was a useful method of passing on know-how. Famous painters like Rubens had studios full of pupils who learned directly from the master, and painted many of his pictures for him. At one time plumbers, doctors and lawyers all learned their professional know-how through apprenticeship.

The simplest way to acquire know-how is to buy it by hiring someone who has it. A person with know-how in a certain field has a sort of intellectual capital which has gradually accumulated over the years and has acquired a cashing-in value. It also happens that a great mystery is made of know-how in certain fields where anyone may be able to acquire the know-how in a few weeks.

You turn the steering wheel of a car and the car moves to the right or to the left at once. It would be very difficult to drive if there was a lag of five seconds between the movement of the steering wheel and the response of the car. In many situations, however, there is a noticeable lag-time between an action and its effect. The government may take action to encourage industrial investment, for instance by lowering interest rates, but there is a lag-time of months or years before this gives rise to an increase in jobs. A corporation may invest money in research but it may be several years before this investment gives any tangible result and several more years before anything comes on the market. The lag-time is very long. On the other hand the savings that are made by firing members of the staff are quickly reflected in the expenditure accounts: the lag-time is short.

Control of complex systems would be relatively easy if there was no such thing as lag-time. A government could wait until it was clear what needed to be done and then do it with immediate effect. Because lag-times can be very long (perhaps ten to twenty years for energy decisions) there has to be a lot of guessing and speculation and extrapolation of trends. Thus occurs the extraordinary paradox that the biggest and most important decisions have to be made on the flimsiest of evidence, because they have to be made so far in advance.

One year there is a shortage of beef so farmers are encouraged to go in for beef. There is a lag-time of three to four years before the effect of this decision comes to market. By then there is no longer a shortage of beef (because the poor weather has passed, consumption has fallen and too many people made the same decision) and there is a glut. Prices fall and cattle are shot instead of being marketed. Trade cycles, business cycles, economic cycles all arise from lag-time. Because there is a lag-time it is difficult to see what decisions other people are making until the effects emerge. So everyone makes parallel decisions (to grow beef, to build, etc) and when this is at last noticed it is too late to change.

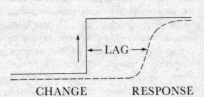

CHANGE · ← LAG → · RESPONSE

Laissez-faire is the opposite of control, intervention, over-reaction and direction. In a laissez-faire economy it is government policy to allow free play to the working of the market forces. Instead of price and wage control there is a free-for-all on the basis that after an initial period of turbulence the situation will sort itself out.

The arguments in favour of laissez-faire are numerous. Control does not allow the system to stabilise in the optimal state. Control of only one aspect distorts the system so that eventually control has to spread to all aspects. Control is bound to be unfair. Control only stores up tensions and distortions that are then released all at once when the controls break down. Controls only reflect artificial pressures and favour special interests.

The arguments against laissez-faire are equally numerous. In a free-for-all society the powerful are going to become more powerful and the weak are going to become weaker. The optimal state achieved in a free organisation may be optimal only for a small section of society. A free market tends to be short-sighted with a rush for immediate gain and little interest in long-term investment. The emphasis is not on stabilising the market but on out-witting competition in a fluctuating market. The main argument against laissez-faire, however, is that society has become too complex. For example the stockmarket crash of 1929 was entirely due to a laissez-faire attitude in an area (a secondary market) where this might have seemed reasonable before. Since then the tight regulations of the Securities Exchange Commission in the USA have made unlikely a repetition of this crash.

Laissez-faire extends outside the purely economic field. It extends into the fields of literary censorship and non-criminal morals. Homosexuality between consenting adults used to be a crime in many countries.

Laissez-faire is a misnomer because there is always some structure within which the action is to be free. The argument is really about how much should be done to tighten up that system. At one extreme is a tight system within which everything is controlled and at the other is a free-for-all. In between there are envelopes of structure within which there is freedom to choose.

A father is busy putting decorations on to the Christmas tree but as quickly as he puts them on his two-year-old son pulls them off. He is about to put the child in a play-pen when his wife suggests that it might make more sense to put the tree in the play-pen and leave the child outside. Instead of keeping the child away from the tree one can keep the tree away from the child. Lateral thinking involves moving sideways to look at things in a different way. Instead of fixing on one particular approach and then working forward from that the lateral thinker tries to find other approaches.

You cannot dig a hole in a different place by digging the same hole deeper. A committee that is convinced that parking meters are the only way to control city parking will spend its time deciding what meters to use, where to put them and how to patrol them. A lateral thinker would look at other approaches: letting people park anywhere they liked so long as they left their headlights on; giving people licences which would allow them to park free in town on only one day a week and so encouraging car sharing; visible licences that the motorist would pay for if he wanted to park anywhere in town.

Our thinking traditions are very firmly based on logical thinking in which we start off with a certain way of looking at things and then see what we can deduce from that. This can be called vertical thinking since it involves building on what is accepted as traditional. Vertical thinking is for using ideas and lateral thinking is for changing them.

Most of our thinking does not take place at the logical stage but at the perceptual stage which precedes this. Lateral thinking is to do with changing perceptions and finding new ways of looking at things. Lateral thinking is the practical process of creativity. There are various deliberate techniques such as the use of stepping stones (produced, for instance, by reversing the usual situation) and random word provocations. Lateral thinking turns creativity into a tool. In a patterning system such as the mind provocation is as important as analysis – and more important for changing ideas. The concept of lateral thinking was originated by the author in 1966.

Lag-time refers to the delay that follows after an action has been taken and before the full effect takes place. You move the steering wheel of a ship but there is a lag before the whole ship responds. Lead-time refers to the time that has to elapse before the action can take place. You start to think about turning to the port side, you consider it, you give a command to the helmsman and eventually he turns the steering wheel.

The lead-time for a decision to build a new airport may take many years. There have to be analyses and assessments, political decisions, environmental considerations, a search for sites, public inquiries and so on before the actual decision is taken. The problem of lead-time can more than double the difficulties created by lag-time. At least with lag-time the decision or action has been taken. With a long lead-time there may be delay before the action can be taken and then a lag-time before it has any effect. A decision has to be made about the building of a new hospital. The lead-time is three years. In that time the cost of building the hospital has doubled.

It can happen that a decision that is worth making cannot be made because the lead-time is too long. If the lead-time on closing the stable door is too long the horse will have escaped by the time the door is closed. Nothing much can be done about lag-times because the nature of a system and the delays at each stage inevitably result in delay. For example a cut in interest rate could not result in more jobs until money has been borrowed and new tools bought and installed. But lead-times can be speeded up considerably.

It is often a criticism of the democratic system that lead-times on decisions are far too long. The dilemma is that a short lead-time may be unfair to some people, and we tend to feel that the nature of a decision is what matters, not the speed with which it is made. This may not always be the case, however: if a slow decision costs twice as much as a fast one the speed does matter.

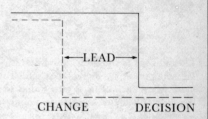

LEAD

CHANGE   DECISION

Liquid is ready to flow at any instant. When a person has money that can be used at any instant he is said to have liquidity. The money may be in an old sock under the floorboards or deposited in a bank under conditions of immediate withdrawal. The opposite to being liquid is to be illiquid. A person may invest all his savings in a house. Should a sudden need for money arise (to set up a business, to pay medical or legal bills, to invest in something more attractive) he would have to sell his house. If the market is slow it might take him a long time to do this. It might also be that the house market is in a slump and he would lose a lot of money if he had to sell quickly. In practice he would probably borrow money against the value of the house by taking out a mortgage. An investment company that had invested in two-year bonds would not be able to take its money out again to invest in something more favourable and the cost of borrowing money to do so would make it pointless. Money invested in stocks and shares is liquid in the sense that these can be sold at any

time but the market for those shares may be in decline and instant sale would involve loss of money. A truly liquid position involves money that can be used instantly without any loss of value.

Liquidity applies equally to assets other than money. A film actor under an exclusive long-term contract to a studio has illiquid assets. A pop star with a long-term recording contract may be in a similar position. Liquidity is a matter of keeping options open. Ideally it might seem sensible always to be liquid but money kept under the bed earns no interest. If when interest rates are high a person can invest on a long-term basis at the high interest rate then he will be better off than if he had followed the week to week fluctuations in interest rate. Similarly an artiste with a long-term contract may be better off than if he had relied on freelance employment. A man who never marries keeps his marriage options open but may never enjoy such benefits of marriage as children.

If the sole purpose of staying liquid is to choose the right investment then the liquidity is, by definition, temporary. One can of course try to maintain some liquidity by arranging that longer term investments are staggered so that some funds become liquid in rotation. As might be expected everyone prefers to keep options open and yet enjoy the benefits of security.

A small donkey is standing in a field with two panniers across its back. More and more hay is loaded into the panniers and across them until it reaches up in a mountain above the tiny donkey. Eventually the owner drives the donkey from the field and along the lane. The donkey does not appear to have much choice. A load is something that is to be carried.

The Great Blackout occurred in the United States when one evening in the mid-1960s almost the whole of the North-eastern corner lost all its electricity. Lights went out. Elevators stopped. Electric ovens grew cold. And it is claimed the birth rate rose. What had happened was that by a freak coincidence an excess load had caused some power stations to drop out of the supply system. This shedding of the load put a higher load on others which in turn shed the load by dropping out. So the chain reaction continued with the load growing progressively larger until it was shed entirely.

A load is usually imposed from out-side. A work load is the amount of work required to be done. The size of the work load can sometimes be physically measured: for instance the number of insurance forms that have to be checked. But there is also a subjective element. The same physical work load may be considered excessive by one person and moderate by another depending on expectation, previous experience and personality. Asked to carry a heavy box of parts up some stairs one person might struggle to carry up the whole box and complain of the load. Another person might empty some parts out, carry up the half-filled box and then make a second trip to carry up the remainder. Expertise, efficiency or work style will affect the way the work load is perceived. The load itself remains the same: the amount that has to be done.

Any organisation has certain fixed overheads (rent, telephone, heating, administration costs). It may choose to divide these costs and to 'load' them on to different activities that are earning money. In general a load or loading is anything which has to be carried.

A searchlight fastens on to a bomber. The bomber dives and weaves about in an attempt to evade the searchlight. But the searchlight is 'locked on' to the bomber and stays with it. Computers were first developed in the Second World War as a means of allowing anti-aircraft gunners to lock on to aircraft and to shoot them down.

A coastguard radar scans the seas until it detects a vessel. The radar is then locked on to the vessel while the coastguard cutter approaches it to determine its business. Any search procedure is likely to end in a 'lock-on'. The searcher and the searched-for are locked together. The search is over; the effort is now directed towards preventing the discovered object from escaping.

Rumours spread because the people listening to the rumour become locked on to it. The rumour is so interesting, whether it happens to be true or not, that it is worth repeating. The original version is more interesting than any modification so the listener, and repeater, remain locked on to the rumour.

A lock-on is a type of positive feedback effect: because something hap-pens the likelihood of it continuing to happen is increased. The wandering attentions of a young man in springtime become fixed on a lady and lock on to her charms. The more attention they get the more desirable they seem, even to the point of obsession.

Psychological studies tend to show that once a person has made a choice he is likely to perceive that choice as even more attractive than before it was made. This is known as cognitive dissonance. A woman chooses purple as the colour of decoration for her dining room. Instead of having doubts and second thoughts she comes to like purple even more and to defend her choice. Once a choice is made the emotions of the chooser tend to lock on to the object of the choice.

It is the basis of self-organisation that some connection may be made casually or by chance but once it has occurred it becomes more difficult to undo it than it was to bring it about.

A puppet-master manipulates his puppets. His puppets are mere tools in his hands. A skilled manipulator operates in much the same way but uses people instead of puppets. A manipulator succeeds in getting his way in the end, but never by forcing it on people. Instead he plays on their ambitions, fears, loves and hatreds until they find themselves doing exactly what he wants them to do.

The secret in judo is not to oppose the enemy's attacking force but to work with it and turn it to your own advantage. Similarly the manipulator turns the wishes of those he manipulates to his own advantage. A skilled manipulator will also re-set his goals to equal what people are capable of achieving and then gain credit for the result.

Manipulation is a sort of control but it is hidden and takes advantage of the system rather than imposing solutions on it. A skilled politician can manipulate events to suit himself. If an unpopular issue is about to arise he can divert attention to a more immediate crisis and then slip the contentious measures through with a great show of reluctance. A skilled lawyer can manipulate the feelings of the jury in such a way as to generate enough reasonable doubt to free his client.

When the volume of trade in a particular stock is very small it is possible to manipulate the stockmarket price by buying up the stock through a third party. It is claimed that the price of works of art can be manipulated in this way through a collector paying unnecessarily high prices for the works of an artist he has patronised.

The highest skills of manipulation are undoubtedly to be found in politics, not so much in the front line as in the behind the scenes wheeling and dealing, where bargains and promises and votes and people are juggled with skill and purpose. Juggling is a skill and so is manipulation. It is a skill we regard with suspicion because we cannot see it in operation but are only aware of its results.

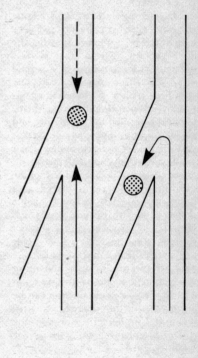

We are inclined to think of things as averages or as uniform chunks. But quite often things are not uniform at all. A man might be paying a marginal tax rate of ninety per cent. He may act as if he were paying that amount of tax on all his income but in fact it is only on the last slice or margin. Margin is easiest to understand in terms of 'what happens next'.

The diagram shows a graph relating cost and effect. In the first part we look at a slice or margin showing the area where a huge increase in costs will only produce a small or marginal increase in effect. Imagine a company spending money on advertising its products. When almost everyone knew about the product the company could go on spending more money on advertising but the extra money spent would only produce a small increase in effectiveness. In the second part of the diagram the margin is placed at a different point. Here we could imagine a steel mill with certain fixed costs: keeping the furnaces going, keeping the men on the payroll, paying rent for the factory site. All the costs have to be paid irrespective of the amount of production going on. In this situation a great increase in production can be achieved with little increase in costs. Or, to put it another way round, the cost of producing extra steel is very small.

Instead of thinking in terms of averages or wholes, we can think in terms of 'margins'. This means considering the results from the next small increase in effort or spending.

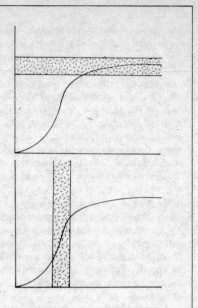

It is remarkable that whilst commercial organisations spend a great deal of time on marketing, governments spend very little. Politicians are acutely conscious of the importance of projecting a suitable image but their efforts are as crude as those of early advertising and a far cry from sophisticated marketing strategy.

A stall in a street market is an interface between buyer and seller. The buyer has genuine wants. At which stall is he going to satisfy them? The stall-holder can rely on position, display, price, type of foods, and personal charm. All these go into the marketing mix. On a more sophisticated level marketing covers very much more than advertising. The choice of goods, the target market, the pricing structure, the choice of retail outlets and the packaging are all part of marketing. The marketing specialist is acutely conscious of buying habits and buying needs. For example most children's toys are not bought by children at all but by adults for children. A child may like a toy after he knows what it is but at the point of sale the toy must be able to demonstrate (in model form or on the box) what it is about. Much of men's clothing is bought by wives for their husbands and this goes for other things like soap and shaving cream.

The marketing specialist has to decide what end of the market to aim for: low cost and high volume at the lower end or high cost and small volume at the upper end of the market. It is the aim of every marketing man to avoid falling between the two stools, where the item is too expensive for the lower end of the market and not of good enough quality for the upper end.

Once a certain proportion of the seats on an airliner have been filled the rest of the seats could be sold at a low cost and still be profitable. The same applies to hotels and cinemas and any situation where fixed costs have to be covered and any excess constitutes profit. But how does one market these extra seats without destroying the market for the full fare seats?

How much attention does a government pay to marketing its services or policies as distinct from advertising them?

INDIFFERENCE

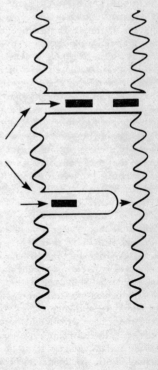

In terms of communication the media are the means by which the communication is carried out. The media should carry the message in a neutral or passive manner. In practice this means that the public is asked to accept that the media have no wish or intention to alter the content of the message. Nevertheless the structure of the media can cause considerable changes without anyone ever having tried to change anything. If you stand in front of a moving steamroller and it rolls you out into a ribbon it is no use claiming that the steamroller was only acting according to its nature and had no evil intentions.

People never listen to what a person is saying on television because they are looking at his face, assessing his charm, disagreeing with his manner. This is no fault of television or the interviewer. Newspapers can carry speeches and articles that would have been ludicrous if they had been read out by the writer to an assembled audience.

In America a schoolchild might spend twenty thousand hours watching television and only ten thousand hours in school. Both are media for communication. Television may be able to afford to select the best communicators but only a schoolteacher can notice whether or not a child is listening. If you watch something passively then that something has to contain the action: and violence is the most reliable form of action.

A medium can never be neutral because like any other structure it affects what it contains. But a medium can be neutralised because it cannot escape from its own structure.

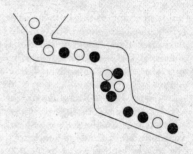

A system acts according to its own nature and for the purpose defined by that nature. A child is playing: he attempts to poke scissors into the electric power points; he makes interesting ink-patterns on the carpet; he attempts to drink from the liquid detergent container. All these activities arise directly from the nature of the system: child–exploration–environment. Fortunately there is another system which lies outside the child system: this is the mother or nanny system. This outside or meta-system operates according to its own nature which is child care.

Primitive tribes quickly establish a system of beliefs, taboos and laws. Without this meta-system everyone would act according to their own individual systems which might be based on immediate gratification, self-indulgence and impulse. The meta-system lies outside these individual systems and overrides them in favour of society and a longer time base. For example an individual may only collect enough food for his immediate needs but the meta-system may require him to collect enough to store for the winter as well. To some extent the success of societies has depended on the strength, and the nature, of the meta-

systems they have set up.

An individual goes to see a psycho-analyst and is told that his troubles arise from the way his mother treated him when he was young. This explanation or 'story' becomes a meta-system for the individual and can explain or guide his actions independently of his mood of the moment.

Religion is the prime example of a meta-system that has served to override man's small view of himself and given him aims and values he might not otherwise have developed. The internal logic of the religious meta-system is based on its own nature, and not on the needs of man. Outside religions strictly so called, ideologies, philosophies and moral concepts have also served as meta-systems.

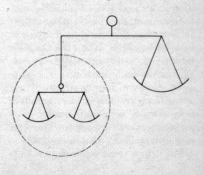

Missionaries have a sense of mission (or else one must suppose that they enjoy the way of life). Astronauts are sent on a mission to land on the moon. A sales mission is sent to Iran to try to sell frozen chickens.

Extremists and terrorists seem to be people who need a sense of mission. There has to be something to be achieved, a goal towards which efforts are directed. It is the mission that gives sense, direction, excitement and urgency to life. A mission is the best treatment for boredom, indecision or fuzzy values.

There are people who have missions connected with establishing something new like an exotic variant of an Eastern religion or a new alphabet that makes learning to read easier. These positive missionaries have a hard time because few people will listen to them. Unless they achieve something there is no satisfaction from the mission. Negative missionaries have a much easier time. To hate the establishment and to be hated in turn is already an achievement. To be treated with as much importance as one treats oneself is a confirmation of the mission. To be pursued and to avoid pursuit is again an achievement. To throw bombs, hijack or even be destructive in lesser ways is also achievement. Because the potential for achievement is so considerable, negative missions tend to thrive if they are conducted with any skill. To be against the building of a new airport or by-pass gives a much stronger sense of mission than to be for it, especially if it involves being against the government or a mindless establishment that seems invulnerable in other respects.

Boy scouts used to have missions.

Street gangs create their missions as they go along. The pursuit of a mission is much more durable than the pursuit of pleasure. The problem is that society is no longer so good at providing missions. Almost everything is either done or so impossible to do that positive missions never get going. That leaves only negative missions to absorb the missionaries.

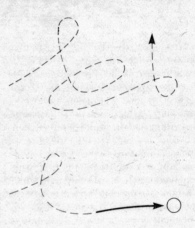

Imagine a television set which at the back has a series of small drawers rather like the drawers in antique writing desks. Each little drawer has a red indicator bulb on it. One day the television set breaks down. Instead of phoning for the TV repair man you look at the back of the set. You notice that the red light is shining on one of the drawers. You pull out this drawer and take it along to the TV shop where you are given a replacement drawer. You take this back and plug it into your set which now works again. In effect each drawer contains one working module. The TV set has been built out of such modules and whenever one module fails it can be replaced without any need to examine the whole set and all its intricacies.

Modular furniture consists of units that can be put together to form sofas or armchairs or casual chairs. Modular kitchen units can be put together to form cupboards, work surfaces or wall units. In a modular system the modules do not have to be interchangeable. The essential point is that the modules are separate but can be assembled to give the required effect. Modular housing might consist of basic modules (bathroom, kitchen, bedroom, living room) which could be put together in different ways to give houses with as many bedrooms as required.

The difference between a modular system and an ordinary system is that the modular system consists of separate units whereas an ordinary system consists only of ingredients which have no existence of their own until they are put together to give the final system. Modular units have the advantage of ease of design, manufacture and assembly. With modular systems the units may be the same although the final product may be very different. It can be a way of combining mass production with variety.

In many education courses it is fashionable to have modules which the pupil can choose and assemble in any way he wishes. This gives the element of flexibility without involving the teaching staff in the work of designing individual courses for each student.

The terms amplitude modulation (AM) and frequency modulation (FM) are familiar in the radio world. The diagram shows that there is a basic carrier wave which is transmitted. This basic carrier wave is then altered or modulated by the waves caused by the electrical translation of speech or music. This second wave is superimposed on to the basic carrier wave. The sound wave can alter the amplitude of the carrier wave as shown in the diagram. This is amplitude modulation. Alternatively the sound wave can alter the frequency of the basic carrier wave and this is frequency modulation. At the receiving end the sound wave is disentangled from the carrier wave and the speech or music is heard through the loudspeaker.

In its general sense modulation implies that one ongoing process is being altered by the superimposition of another ongoing process. We would not call it modulation if the second process simply served to increase or decrease the first process. The suggestion is that the pattern of the second process is added to the pattern of the first process instead of affecting the first process directly; for example the effectiveness of a salesman may be modulated by the pattern of his domestic life. At any one moment the effectiveness may be increased or decreased but the overall effect is that of adding one pattern to the other. The pattern of teacher employment may depend on the general economic climate and availability of government money for education. But this pattern may be modulated by the fluctuations in the birth rate which result in baby-bulges.

With modulation it is always im-plied that there is a basic ongoing process which is modulated by a second process. It may, however, be difficult to decide which process is modulating which. It is easy to decide that the basic trend towards ever increasing house prices may be modulated by interest rates and employment fluctuations. But it is less easy to decide whether economic circumstances are modulating political beliefs or the other way round. In a true modulating situation the two patterns are simply added but do not interact.

A ball rolling down a slope gathers momentum. A car rolling down a hill out of control gathers momentum. The momentum is indicated by the efforts that would have to be made to bring the ball or the car to a halt. In an exact sense momentum refers to the product of mass × velocity. In a more general sense momentum means the continuing energy of anything that has been set in motion.

A rumour may gather momentum because the more people who know it the more people there are to pass it on. The same applies to an epidemic. Support for a piece of legislation, for instance on abortion, may gather momentum as more people come to know about it and more politicians find it convenient to get on the bandwagon.

A ball rolling down a slope will have enough momentum to carry it over bumps and along a horizontal or even uphill stretch until the slope is re-established. The main usefulness of momentum is to carry a movement through a period in which energy is being given out rather than taken in. An ideology may derive its energy from opposition. If there is no opposition there may be a 'flat' patch and only the momentum built up before can keep it going.

When we talk about the momentum of a ball on a slope we acknowledge that at any moment the momentum is derived from the velocity and the mass. It does not matter whether that velocity was achieved rapidly or slowly. When momentum is used in a more general sense there is a feeling that the momentum acquired over a short time has a greater force than that acquired over a long time. For example a new left-wing group that took several years to reach a membership of five thousand has less momentum than a group which achieved that membership in only six months. The suggestion is that the 'speed of spread' is the relevant velocity rather than the actual size of membership.

Anything that is happening has the energy of that happening. That energy can be met by opposing energy and cause a clash or it can gradually leak away through lack of any further intake of energy. It can happen that a movement set in motion for a particular purpose acquires so much momentum that it keeps going by itself.

It sometimes happens that when a powerful argument is followed through it is found in the end to rest on some-one having a 'moral obligation' to do something. The convenience of the 'moral obligation' label is that it can be applied to anything which one person considers another ought to do.

A legal obligation is defined by law. Other obligations such as technical or business obligations are defined by the circumstances. For example in build-ing a suspension bridge there is an obligation to be sure that the wire ropes are strong enough to support the weight of the roadway and also to take precautions against resonance oscilla-tions caused by the wind. In business there may be an obligation to take note of the buying brackets of the public in terms of lower end of the market, middle market and upmarket. A product which was sloppily posi-tioned would do badly.

With a moral obligation it is a matter of a person saying: 'I, on behalf of the rest of society, feel that our usual way of doing things makes it necessary for you to act in a certain way.' An indi-vidual sells a painting to a gallery for a small price. The gallery discovers that the painting is by a famous painter. Does the gallery have an obligation to go back and pay the seller an in-creased price? The probable answer is that the gallery does not have this moral obligation since it is the gallery's own expertise that has added the value to the painting. So the gallery sells the painting to a collector for a large sum. Later it is found that the painting is actually a forgery. Does the gallery now have a moral obligation to reimburse the collector and take the forgery back? This would seem to be the case since the gallery is using its 'expertise' in offering the painting as an original. The gallery could argue that it acted honestly and that in law the buyer should have had the painting checked. If the gallery now suspects that the original seller knew it to be a forgery, does the original seller have a moral obligation to reimburse the gallery? Probably not, because the original seller made no claims for the painting but simply took advantage of the gullibility of the gallery.

Moral obligations express notions of natural justice and fairness even when these are not given an exact legal form. For example if a person falls ill a year before he qualifies for his pension there may be a moral obligation for the pension to be granted.

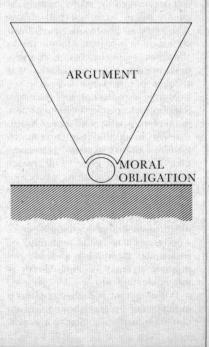

Frederick the Great of Prussia was a general who used to win battles which had in fact been lost. Quite often his loss of men and equipment was greater than that of his opponents. He may even have been forced to yield ground. Yet he emerged the victor because the enemy troops were demoralised and fled whereas his troops maintained their morale and treated themselves as the victors, with the result that everyone else was also prepared to treat them in the same way.

Morale is spirit, confidence and ego. The opposite of morale is dejection, depression, apathy and loss of confidence. It is said that in a tennis match a sudden change in morale can completely reverse a game. One player might have been winning easily and then suddenly the opponent regains his morale and goes on to win. If morale is bad in a factory then there is absenteeism and a high turnover of workers. There will probably be strikes and the quality of work and productivity may be low. Morale is intangible but real.

When morale is high discipline is unimportant because the momentum of morale carries a soldier or a worker to do what needs doing. But when morale is low there has to be something else which gets things done. The most effective thing is habit and the most practical habit is that of discipline: something is done because it has to be done.

During the Second World War it was said that both in Britain and in Germany morale was actually raised by the air raids. This paradoxical result was the opposite to what had been expected. It was thought that the raids which rendered ordinary citizens helpless would sap their morale. Instead the common and now visible enemy seemed to give them something to fight against, and coping with the situation increased their morale.

Morale in peacetime seems to depend a great deal on leadership. But it seems difficult for leadership to emerge except during a crisis. This is why politicians tend to treasure the crises that arise. Uncertainty and a slow erosion of confidence seem the most common factors in the loss of morale.

A games company is deciding whether to manufacture a new game. The game is complicated and has a large number of plastic pieces. The cost of production is calculated and this figure is multiplied by a multiplier of five to give the approximate selling price in a shop. It is decided that this is much too high, so the game is rejected. The multiplier of five covers such things as distribution costs, retailer's mark-up, promotion costs and profit. Instead of calculating each of these every time, a standard multiplier is used.

Economists use a multiplier to calculate the effect of an increase in wages (or a cut in taxes) on consumer spending. Office managers use a multiplier to calculate the true cost of adding another member of staff: it may be two or three times the actual wage that is to be paid.

Whenever we want to express a relationship between two things we can do it in different ways: we can say that A tends to increase or decrease B; we can say that there is a one to one relationship and that a ten per cent increase in A will result in a ten per cent increase in B; or we can say that the relationship is governed by a multiplier so that the value of A must be multiplied by X to give B.

A multiplier need not mean an increase. It is possible to multiply something by 0·75 and so obtain a decrease. For example the relationship between industrial investment and employment may have this sort of multiplier. A great deal of invested money may result in relatively few jobs (because much of the investment is in machines that will actually take over jobs). Such a multiplier may vary from industry to industry and may affect government investment policy.

Few corporations know the multiplier relationship between advertising expenditure and sales. This is hardly surprising because the relationship is not straightforward and may vary from time to time. But in deciding whether to spend money on advertising, salesmen or price-cutting some sort of multiplier decision may have to be made. In such cases a multiplier is a measure of the effectiveness of certain courses of action.

Muscle is power. Our will to do something is signalled by complex nerve impulses to our muscles. The muscles convert the signals into real action. If the muscles are weak the action is weak. If the muscles are paralysed, for instance with curare, then no effort of will can get anything done. Traditionally the underworld gang has had muscle-men whose business it is to carry out the heavy work. Such men have been characterised as coarse and stupid, perhaps only because they have been used more for their brawn than their brain.

A lot of people have ideas but very few have the muscle to put them into effect. A large food company has the marketing muscle to launch any new product. If the product is of any value at all it will probably succeed. If the same product were to be launched by a smaller organisation it would almost certainly be a failure through lack of marketing muscle. A large group of chain stores have buying muscle. The group buyer can insist on a low buying price because the selling potential of his stores is so important to the manufacturer. A major advertiser in a newspaper can often flex his advertising muscles in order to influence editorial decisions.

There are many different sorts of muscle. There is decision muscle, for example where planning permission for a new development is granted by a decision of the planning officer. There is communication muscle where some body controls either the media communication or distribution communication as in the example of the chain stores. Then there is financial muscle, political muscle and establishment muscle. Establishment muscle is the silent power of acceptance or rejection exercised by any club-like group.

The importance of muscle in society is usually underestimated. For example the critical muscle of a single theatre critic in New York can decide the fate of a play that has cost thousands of dollars to put on and involves the reputations of many people.

Muscle is not quite the same as power. Muscle is an established part of a structure. Power is dominance. Muscle may be used to achieve power but power by itself cannot develop muscle except by borrowing it.

The negative feedback is concerned with stability. Most biological systems only exist because they have set up negative feedback loops which preserve their stability. If your blood pressure rises special receptors in some of the arteries are stretched by the rise in pressure. Nerve impulses then go from the receptors to the brain centre that controls the diameter of the peripheral blood vessels and the vessels are relaxed. The pressure is reduced. On the other hand if the blood pressure falls then the negative feedback system sends messages that tighten up the blood vessels and speed up the heart and so the pressure tends to rise again to the normal level.

In a negative feedback loop what is fed back opposes or subtracts from the original action, and so protects the stability or status quo of the system. With a steam engine if the pressure rises in the boiler we could put in a simple escape valve to let off the excess pressure, or we could put in a pressure detector which would sense the rise in pressure and send a signal that would turn down the fire; if the pressure fell the signal would turn up the fire. In this way the pressure in the boiler could be kept steady. In the early days of steam engines there were times when the engine went faster and faster until it wrecked itself. So a governor was invented. This consisted of some heavy balls attached to a rotating shaft. As the shaft rotated faster and faster the balls were flung outwards by centrifugal force. As they moved outwards they shut down the flow of steam to the piston and so the engine slowed down.

A thermostat offers a simple example of a negative feedback system.

If the temperature in a room rises this is detected by the thermostat which sends a signal to turn down the central heating. This is much more effective than opening a window and leaving the heating unaltered. If the temperature falls the thermostat sends a signal to oppose this fall in temperature and so turns up the central heating.

Society, civilisation and culture tend to preserve their stability by a negative feedback system that tends to attack new ideas.

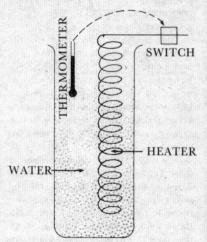

If you draw on paper a diagram of a communication system you will find that there are points which seem to collect more lines of communication than other points (as shown in the diagram). Like the knots in a net these points can be called nodes. A node is a point where things gather together.

In any communication system or organisation the nodes have special importance. The nodes are control points. If the node exerts any influence on the communication that is passing through the node then the node has control over much of the communication. Even if the node passively passes on the messages that flood in, the speed of processing can matter. The nodes can become bottlenecks for information or for decisions. A node is somewhat like a traffic junction in a busy town. Since so many roads converge at this point there is a much greater chance of a traffic jam than elsewhere.

A node is also a weak point or a sensitive point. Anyone who wishes to damage a system will seek out the nodes and attack them. Anyone who wants to take control of a system will try to gain control, by infiltration, of the nodes. In most revolutions an effort is first made to take over the local radio station. This is an obvious communication node. Control of the radio station means that government messages can be blocked and that revolutionary exhortations can be transmitted to the populace.

In an organisation the node is not necessarily the most senior position nor the most publicly visible. Quite often a relatively humble position is more important as a communication node than a senior one. In a local

authority strike in London a handful of computer operators were able to throw the whole system out of gear. They refused to prepare the demands for local authority rates and so virtually stopped the finances of the authorities.

The only way to reduce the importance of a node is to by-pass it. Where a market town because of its historic position draws in to itself all the roads of the neighbourhood the congestion can only be relieved by a deliberate by-pass. The creation of the by-pass immediately reduces the congestion and the importance of the town which may now become a backwater. A by-passed node suddenly loses influence.

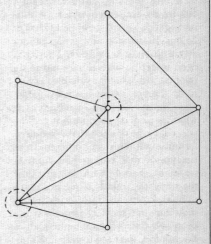

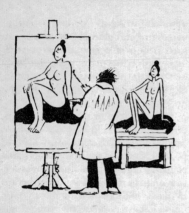

Scientists are searching for the ultimate laws of nature. Philosophers are searching for the ultimate truth. Artists are searching for the ultimate beauty. Improvers are searching for the ultimate good. Yet all the time life has to go on. All decision and action cannot await ultimate knowledge. There is a need to get on with things and to do the best with what is available. Trying to do the best with what is available, and under existing conditions, is what is known as optimising. The practical type of mind that is required for optimisation is very different from the type of mind required for ultimate searches. Faced with a practical situation the mind concerned with ultimates retreats into criticism to show how far short of perfection the proposals fall. The optimiser realises this but feels the need to get something done.

An agency that is advertising instant coffee has its budget cut. One response would simply be to cut the equivalent amount off its planned advertising. Another response would be to see where the cuts would matter least, thus protecting the strong points. A third response would be to reconsider the whole campaign and to try to optimise the advertising under the given conditions: would it be better to reduce the number of insertions and still keep large displays or to keep up the number of insertions but reduce them in size? Perhaps there could be a totally different approach using radio instead of press.

A developing country has few doctors: what is the best way to optimise their use? One alternative would be to establish a few highly equipped centres of excellence to which gravely ill patients would be referred. Another alternative would be to abandon highly specialised medicine (such as open heart surgery) and to concentrate on village medicine where the same amount of money could make a huge difference. This was the choice made in Tanzania. Of course it would be nice to be able to afford both approaches but in actual circumstances a deliberate optimisation is preferable to a half-hearted approach to both.

Optimisation is too often viewed as a compromise which interferes with the pursuit of perfection. This is a dangerous attitude which in practice amounts to dogmatic imperfection all round.

If a microscope enlarges an object ten times then there will be an order of magnitude increase in the visual size of the object. If the enlargement is one hundred times then the increase will be two orders of magnitude. If the enlargement is one thousand times then it will be three orders of magnitude $(10 \times 10 \times 10)$.

Dealing with magnitude and size is difficult. That is why we have created a whole system of mathematics and measurement. It is not enough to say, 'People are hungry, give them some food.' It may be necessary to calculate how best the available food can be spread amongst the hungry people and the amount of transport required to deliver the food to where it is needed.

We might assume that since it is possible to land men on the moon it should not be difficult to fly them to planets in different star systems. Yet the distances and problems may be several orders of magnitude greater. For health we need sugar in the blood and we also need vitamins but the amount of sugar that is required is several orders of magnitude greater than the amount of vitamins. An order of magnitude difference usually means that two things are not comparable on the same scale: the temperatures found in a furnace are one or two orders of magnitude greater than those found in the human body and the temperatures found in the sun are several orders of magnitude greater still.

Most people realise that a nuclear war would be far more destructive than previous wars but few people realise that the destructive power of hydrogen bombs is many orders of magnitude greater than that of con-

ventional weapons. Merely to say that something is greater or very much greater does not give the same sense of reality as saying an order of magnitude difference (provided you know that an order of magnitude is a '× 10' difference). The difference in energy required to carry a load by road as compared to rail is roughly an order of magnitude difference.

'An order of magnitude' is a way of bringing a sense of mathematical proportion into ordinary language.

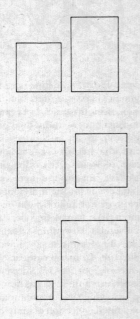

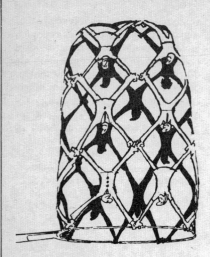

a mixture of both characteristics. The essence of organisation is predictability. Predictability is obtained by establishing rules, roles and relationships. The space between individuals is more clearly defined than the individual himself. In a fishing net the functional part is the actual hole which allows the water to pass through but not the fish. Yet the existence of the net depends on the strands and knots. So in an organisation the emphasis is on the strands and knots that connect the individuals. Western religions and ethical systems have depended heavily on the idea of creating the virtuous man who would do everything properly and according to the rules. In the East, Confucius insisted that the correct role-playing of relationships (between father and son, between ruled and ruler) was much more important. If everyone played their role properly then society would function, whether or not the individual souls were virtuous.

The organisation man in a large corporation knows how to play the organisation game because his soul is no longer in his individual body but part of the corporate soul that floats everywhere between the individuals working in that corporation. When individual cells come together to form the organisation known as a sponge they lose their individuality because they no longer need it.

However one tries to define organisation one is likely to find that the definition is inadequate. Is organisation a collection of individual units that are able to act as a single unit? One can imagine an organisation of ants each of which is carrying out a specific task but where there is no overall tendency for the individuals to act together in attack or flight or just movement. We can define organisation as a set of relationships which enable individual units to act together for a purpose. In many cases, such as clubs, the sole purpose would seem to be the survival of the organisation. We end up by saying that an organisation is an organised collection of individual units: in other words a large unit is created by the organisation of the individual units.

The human body, a motor car, society are all examples of organisation. The first of them is self-constructing and self-organising, the second is externally constructed and the third is

The parameters in a situation are the dimensions that are being measured, noticed or taken into account. For example if a study of depression is being undertaken the parameters may include an estimate of stress, family background, IQ, climate, inflation rate, etc. In some way or other all these would be measured in order to give an internal structure to the situation. The parameters involved in designing a table are the measurements, the strength of the material, the physical appearance of the material and the expected selling price.

A situation is defined by its parameters. Parameter is different from perimeter. A perimeter simply sets the external boundary but tells nothing about what happens within the boundary. Parameters set internal boundaries rather as the bones in a skeleton determine the final shape. Someone may be instructed to keep within set parameters. This means to keep within set measurements or guidelines. For example the parameters defining a new type of medical service may include an overall cost figure, a figure for capacity and an estimate of competence (cost, number of patients to be treated, standard of treatment).

A negotiator is told by his supporting committee that the negotiations must be carried out within certain parameters: cost of living, preservation of differentials in wages, redundancy agreements, revision clauses. The government may lay down certain parameters for permitted wage increases, for example six per cent in one year.

What parameters are to be used for selecting a new headmaster? These might include age, years of experience, qualifications, size of previous school, expected salary, etc. There is an overlap between boundaries, requirements, measurements, constraints and parameters. We think of a boundary and a perimeter as running round something. When the measurement occurs within the object, it can be just as crucial to its definition. For example one of the parameters in sorting eggs into sizes might be the length from top to bottom, another might be the weight.

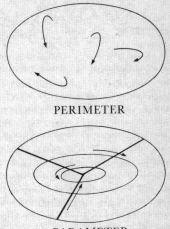

PERIMETER

PARAMETER

This is a most important word, but one that is very difficult to define. Most people think of a pattern as a design on a dress or wallpaper. Any design might now be called a pattern but originally the word meant a re-peating design. The paper patterns that are used in dressmaking allow the dressmaker to repeat the shapes that are necessary for making up that particular dress.

A psychologist might be able to identify a particular pattern of be-haviour in a juvenile delinquent. A wife may learn the pattern of be-haviour of her husband when he comes home from work. A bird-watcher may be able to describe the courtship pat-tern of an osprey. Wage negotiations between a union and a major cor-poration might always follow the same pattern of threat and counter-threat.

Both recognisability and repeat-ability suggest prediction. On a piece of wallpaper if one of the shapes was covered up you would be able to pre-dict from the pattern what the shape must be. If you know the pattern of behaviour you can predict what the

bird, the husband or the negotiator is likely to do next.

A pattern means that things hang together, are linked up, occur to-gether in a recognisable, predictable sequence. In contrast to a 'group' there may be no logical reason why things happen in that way but if they do a pattern is formed. Language is based on patterns. There is a pattern of sound which we recognise as the word 'girl'. There is a pattern on paper which does not look at all like a girl but which we recognise as being the spelling of 'girl'. As soon as we see the word or hear the sound a whole pattern of experiences and images may be unlocked in our minds. There may in fact be several different patterns depending on the circumstances. It is the natural behaviour of the brain to form patterns. That is the mechanism of mind (as I describe in my book *The Mechanism of Mind*).

A pattern has something in common with a group, a cluster, a constellation, a syndrome, an organisation, a struc-ture: in all of them there is a coming, and a staying, together.

What is the pay-off? When is the pay-off?

A corporation is persuaded to spend a lot of advertising money in sponsoring golf tournaments. The money is spent but not much seems to be happening to sales. The marketing director wants to know from the advertising manager when the pay-off can be expected. The investment has been made: the result of that investment is awaited.

An electronics company spends a lot of money on basic research into the conducting properties of glass. More and more money is spent but as yet there is no pay-off in sight. In a field like electronics, however, the pay-off could be so large that the investment is worthwhile.

A suggestion is made that the top tax rate in a country should be reduced from eighty-three per cent to fifty per cent. Obviously there would be a small fall in revenue. What would the pay-off be? There would be more incentive and people might work harder. There would be less need to work out tax avoidance schemes and the actual tax yield might even rise. Less time, effort and brains would be occupied in trying to minimise the tax bill. There could be a reduction in the staff required for dealing with the higher rates of tax. Together, all these advantages would constitute the pay-off.

A senior government official in a developing country accepts a bribe from a maker of agricultural machinery. In return he persuades his government to buy tractors from a particular source. The pay-off is made into a numbered bank account in Switzerland.

The reward, benefit, advantage, profit, return on investment and gold at the end of the rainbow are all pay-offs of different sorts. A person puts coin after coin into a poker machine in New South Wales. Each time he pulls the handle in anticipation. He is waiting for the big pay-off.

In some form or another the pay-off is the reason for all action. Even the most apparently selfless actions can sometimes be found to be based on a pay-off in the next world.

Athletes train hard for the Olympic Games. Their aim is to reach peak mental and physical condition during the Games. It is sometimes said of tennis players that they have peaked too early in the season and that their play has become tired and stale by the time they reach Wimbledon. With politicians in an election campaign the great fear is that they will peak too soon. If a politician peaks even a matter of days before polling day this can lose him votes. A person who appears a winner too soon loses the enthusiasm of his workers and the votes of those who are simply voting against the opposition.

American businessmen are very conscious of actresses, writers, football players and pop artists who are deemed to have peaked. An investment is worthwhile if someone is seen to be moving towards the peak because the potential is limitless. But if someone has already peaked then the investment is likely to be wasted because a second peak is unlikely; the trend can only be downwards.

This attitude towards peaking comes directly from the stockmarket. If a particular stock has been rising it is a good investment. Then the peak is reached and at once people start selling in order to cash in their profits. The stock slides down the other side of the peak. The value of the stock itself has not changed at all. What has changed is the whole composite attitude of people towards the stock. Similarly with a performer the talent may not have changed at all but if the attitude of everyone else involved has changed then a peaking effect can be seen. A performer may be full of promise for a long time but as soon as a flash of fulfilment is exhibited then promise no longer has any value. But what about the talented performer who gets better and better? It all depends on what happens after the first success. If another success does not follow fairly soon then people talk of 'peaking'.

Any accelerating process is bound to peak sooner or later because a fall-off in acceleration immediately sets in motion the process of deceleration and then downward acceleration.

Hens on a perch have a definite pecking order. One hen can peck another without being pecked back. The second hen then pecks the one below her and so on down the line. An order of importance has been established and the token peck is only a way of reminding others to stick to the established order of things. The same thing happens in the animal world when animals live together in packs, herds or family units. There are aggressive signals, like a dog baring its teeth and snapping, and there are submission signals, like a dog turning its head to expose its jugular vein. Like the pecking of the hens these signals are used to make obvious the pecking order. If two animals attack the same piece of food then the animal senior in the pecking order displays his seniority and the other one stands back.

The pecking order is established by actual combat and by the display of will. In a combat or a threatened combat one animal or the other stands down and this establishes the pecking order between these two. When this has been done across the whole group a single line of relative importance has been established. From a social point of view the system is useful because squabbles are automatically solved by reference to the pecking order instead of by ad hoc fights. It also seems a fair system except at either extreme. In between an animal gets kicked by the animal above but has a chance to kick the one below. At the extremes the top animal gets kicked by no one else and the bottom animal has no chance to kick anyone. From an evolutionary point of view it is supposed that the method ensures that the toughest and most strong-willed animal has the pick of the mates and so establishes the best breeding strain.

In the human world pecking orders are established by subtleties of rank and importance rather than by actual combat. An employee may be quite happy if his official pecking position is above that of a fellow although his actual working position is below. The establishment of an honours system, as in the United Kingdom, is a clever device to separate official pecking orders from actual pecking orders based on competence or personality.

Trial by jury is supposed to be trial by one's peers. In psychological terms one's peers are one's fellows. What a teacher thinks of a child may be different from what his peers think of him. The teacher may think of him as bright because he answers all the questions in the expected way. His fellows or peers may consider him dull because outside the set lessons he does not seem very bright. Assessment by a peer group sounds more formal and more serious than assessment by one's fellows or contemporaries.

A businessman may seem to the public to be particularly able but inquiries amongst his peers may suggest that he is more of a public relations expert than an able businessman. There are, of course, problems with peer group assessment of this kind because jealousy is liable to creep in. Peers are quite likely to disparage anyone who seems to claim to be better than they are.

The General Electric Company of America studied its own laboratories to see how information and ideas were handled. They found that the best way to detect the 'ideas man' was to ask everyone to suggest a person who seemed to be a source of ideas. This peer group assessment quickly identified the 'ideas men' who tended to be easily recognisable by others.

With the exception of trial by jury most assessments in life are not carried out by peer groups. School examinations, job interviews and promotion assessments are all carried out by someone in authority who has an idea of the qualities required and then looks to see who possesses those qualities. If we were to use peer group assessment it could work the other way round. The peer group would separately assess the qualities that were required for a particular job (after all they were doing the job themselves) and the qualities shown by their peers. Later a selection match would be made. When attempts are made to let pupils assess themselves and each other they tend to be more severe than the teacher would have been. This is probably because they do not have enough experience to set realistic standards or expectations.

Perception refers to the way we see the world. It is supposed that out there is a real world and of this we can see glimpses according to the acuity of vision with which we are equipped. It is supposed that some of us are looking at the world through cracked, distorting or clouded glass, or that we happen to be short-sighted. The perceptive person is supposed to have very good vision.

Throughout history philosophers have argued about perception: is there a real world out there or is the world we presume to see an illusion created in the mind? Is a tree there when no one is looking at it? Is the colour of a tree there when no one is looking at it? This philosophical puzzlement is of little practical value. It is known that we can see things clearly when they are not there at all: under hypnosis and when suffering from hallucinations. It is equally clear that we may fail to see things which are there even when our sight is not impaired: by failing to notice them. The world is a mass of potential patterns and things to notice. How many people notice the characteristic separation of the second and third finger in most El Greco paintings? It is difficult to notice at first but very obvious once it has been pointed out. Many people appreciate the proportions and symmetry in a Georgian building but if asked to draw such a building will usually place the windows in the wrong position. To see is not to notice. We can only notice something if we pay specific attention to it. And we can only pay attention to something if we have some preconceived idea of where to look.

In the process of perception patterns gradually build up in our experience. These patterns allow us to see the world in a particular way, and in doing so we reinforce the patterns. We see mainly what we are prepared by experience to see. In a way we are trapped by these established patterns of perception. That is why we sometimes need to use 'lateral thinking' to help us escape from the obvious way of looking at things.

The philosopher Kant believed that there were built into the mind certain fixed ways of looking at the world. For example the notion of 'cause and effect' was one of the these fixed ways and we imposed it on the world.

The important point to note about perception is that most of our thinking takes place in the perception stage.

Some countries like France have a centrally planned economy. Others, like the United Kingdom, believe in guided drift with adjustment as required. If you believe you are sailing a boat on a lake then you have to decide exactly where you are going and how you are going to get there. If you believe you are sailing a boat down a river then you might prefer to take full advantage of the current and its vagaries and do just enough steering to keep off the rocks and clear of the river bank.

The problem with plans is that they always have to assume that surrounding circumstances will remain much the same. An agricultural planner deciding how much encouragement to give the beef industry must assume that people's preference for beef will continue. It is possible to make contingency plans and to believe that if beef prices rise then less people will eat beef but such contingency plans become very complicated because they have to take into account inflation, wage rises, price rises of competitive protein sources and virtually every other condition of the economy.

Another problem with plans is that they cannot take account of unforeseen events such as the sharp rise in oil prices that occurred at the beginning of the 1970s. A plan only deals with extrapolations of known trends. Sometimes the unforeseen event wrecks the plan. At other times the unforeseen event offers a great opportunity which the rigidity of the plan cannot use to advantage. If there were to be a sudden breakthrough in solar energy technology would it be possible to transfer the resources that had been allocated to long-term investment in coal and nuclear technology?

There are those who claim that it is better to set up sensitive systems of anticipation, adjustment and self-regulation rather than to have long-term plans; this is the way the human body works. The only problem is that the lag-time from sensing a problem to putting it right may be five, ten or twenty years (for instance in energy) and during that time the people will have to suffer a worsening crisis. Investment in steel production, hospitals or roads has to be made ahead of acute need.

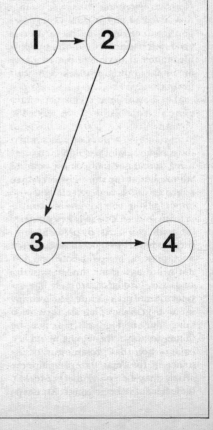

A new brand of cigarette is introduced with much image advertising. Sales rise and continue to rise. Then the curve starts flattening off. Finally it levels out. Eventually it starts to decline. But the flat part of the curve may be steady for quite a long time. This is a plateau.

A new novelist writes a book which gets a lot of attention and even some sales. The book is generally agreed to be of a high literary standard. Each year the writer produces another book of about the same standard. The writer has quickly reached a plateau of achievement and is able to sustain this. There are no peaks. In contrast a pop group might produce a mixture of good and bad records so that the profile of their achievement is more like a mountain range with valleys and peaks.

When something seems to sustain itself at a steady level we talk of a plateau effect. Very often, in business, people talk of a plateau effect when they mean that sales have stopped rising and are actually on the point of falling. But at the time when they are not increasing and not falling the owners of the company talk about a plateau and seek to sell the company before the fall starts. By definition any rise that has ceased goes through a very brief plateau period before the fall starts, just as a stone thrown into the air passes through an instant of zero velocity until it accelerates downwards.

In a genuine plateau state two things may be happening. It may be that new factors are coming in but are balanced by those going out. For instance in the cigarette example, new people may be trying the brand but those who have been using it are dropping out at the same rate. The overall effect is a plateau. On the other hand the novelty and initial advertising campaign may have caused some people to switch brands who have then remained loyal, but they have been followed by no new recruits.

A plateau may also mean that within defined limits there may be fluctuations but these do not move outside the limits.

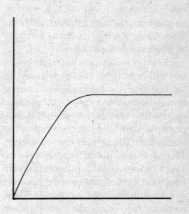

A toaster, a television set, a hi-fi player or a washing machine exist in their own right but can be plugged into the electricity supply. A switchboard operator can plug into a conversation that is being routed through the board. In a modular-designed computer if one module fails the engineer simply plugs in another module.

Plug-in means connecting up but it also implies that the unit is complete and exists on its own before it is plugged in. It also implies that the connection is not permanent but may be unplugged at any time.

There is a sharp contrast between two different types of organisation. In the first type the system is constructed as a whole: the various connections are made and the system gradually emerges. Until the last connection has been made the system does not exist. This is a centralised type of system. The alternative type of system is one in which each unit is organised separately as a functioning module. These modules can be plugged in or taken out at will. The connection between the modules is one of communication rather than organisation. The system is a decentralised one.

A complicated machine can be built up out of different plug-in modules. If something goes wrong a diagnostic procedure identifies the faulty module and this is replaced. The procedure is much simpler than having to analyse the whole system and put the fault right. It is also possible to have back-up modules so that if one module is not working it can be by-passed by another which takes over the function.

In its technology society is moving towards the plug-in principle because it is easier to operate. In human terms, however, it is more difficult to apply. A person who has to move house in order to find a new job cannot easily plug into a new set of friends. This is becoming much easier with the increasing uniformity of culture especially amongst young people, and with special interest groups or clubs which can provide plug-in points. Taken too far, however, total plug-inability can mean a loss of individuality and identity. There is also the problem of plug compatibility.

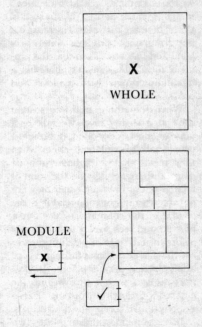

WHOLE

MODULE

The word 'lateral thinking' which I coined in 1967 to describe the type of thinking that was used to change concepts and perceptions is now in the *Oxford English Dictionary*. Just as 'no' is the operative word of logical thinking so the invented word 'po' is the operative tool of lateral thinking. Po is derived from such words as hy*po*thesis, *po*ssible, sup*po*se and *po*etry. With an 'hypothesis' we put forward an unproven idea in order to give us a working basis for devising experiments. With 'possible' we suggest that something which is not yet may come about in the future. With 'suppose' we set up an imaginary situation in order to see what effect it will have. With poetry we put together words and images in order to produce an effect that may only be apparent after we have assembled the images. In all cases there is a provocative use of ideas. To indicate this provocative use we can bring in the word 'po'.

In lateral thinking there may not be a reason for saying something until after it has been said. In a logical world that is not permitted: the reason for saying something should precede the statement. But in the patterning world of perception we may have to use a provocation in order to bring about a change in patterns. When we have used the provocation the new way of looking at things may suddenly become clear. The word 'po' serves as an indicator to show that the idea is being used as a provocation not as a logical description based on experience. For example in solving a river pollution problem we might say: 'Po the factory should be downstream of itself.' That is not a logical statement but it is a provocative one. From the provocation comes the idea that factories should be required by law to have their intake from the river downstream of their outflow, so that they would at least get a sample of what they were discharging.

Essentially 'po' is used as a de-patterning device. This may mean putting together provocative ideas to see what happens. It may also mean breaking the pattern between a statement and the usual judgement response. For example in an argument 'po' means that one side is prepared to accept the point of view of the other side as a 'point of view'. Po may mean that we allow ideas into our heads to interact with other ideas already there, rather than turn them away with a 'reject' judgement at the gate of consciousness.

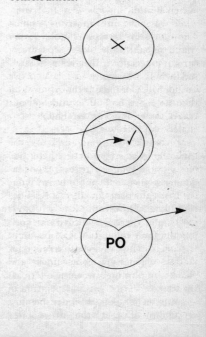

There are two poles to a magnet: north and south. The description comes from the idea of regarding the earth itself as a huge magnet with a North Pole and a South Pole. The only definition of the North Pole is that it is at the opposite end to the South Pole, and vice versa. To polarise an issue is to create two opposite poles and to push everything towards one pole or the other.

Jesus Christ polarised the situation when he told his followers that whoever was not 'with him' was 'against him'. A similar type of polarisation happens naturally with any strong group especially if the group is based on beliefs which are novel. You are either inside or outside the group. You can no more be half in and half out than something can be half in and half out of a drawer.

In some situations, such as the attitude to free enterprise, there may be a whole range of attitudes. For instance some people might be in favour of free enterprise for all but essential industries. Others might be in favour so long as there was a curb on excess profits and exploitation. Others might be against free enterprise except for small village-type operations and backyard farming. In political terms it is difficult to deal with a spectrum of opinions. If you thunder against capitalism or preach the virtues of free enterprise you have to be definite in what you say. You cannot keep saying 'within limits' or 'with safeguards' or 'under certain conditions'. So the situation is polarised into 'for free enterprise' and 'against free enterprise'. Everything is pushed to one extreme or the other and in the end there are only the two sharply polarised positions slanging each other. Once the positions have formed then any fluidity is lost because someone leaving the free-enterprise camp must, necessarily, be going to join the other camp. There are no longer any official intermediate positions.

Yet most often it is in these intermediate positions that there is to be found most effectiveness, most happiness or whatever other benefit is valued. Polarisation is a most efficient device for excluding solutions while offering the maximum opportunity for emotional display and ideological fireworks.

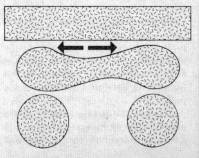

to obtain the views of a small sample of people (from 1,000 to 10,000) and to take these as representative of the views of the whole population. The fact that public opinion polls have proved wrong in their predictions on several occasions does not mean that they are inaccurate measurements but that they cannot be entirely reliable predictors. If someone declares on Monday that he is going to vote Republican and then sees the result of a poll which shows that most people are going to vote Democrat he may well decide to join the majority. In any case an accurate recording of his view on Monday does not prevent him changing those views by Friday. If, however, public opinion polls were used to indicate agreement or dissent about some proposed legislation then they would be accurate *at that moment*.

Democracy is supposedly based on the will of the people who periodically vote to elect their government. No one seems sufficiently enthusiastic about democracy to take the process one stage further. The main reason for electing a politician is that it would be physically impossible, outside a village community, for everyone to vote on every issue. So the elected politician is a sort of package of votes that can be applied to an issue. But if, with modern telecommunications technology, it suddenly became possible for everyone to vote once or twice a week on matters of importance would this be welcomed by governments? The answer must be that it would not for we already have such a device in the poll.

Modern statistical sampling techniques are so sophisticated that within a narrow margin of error it is possible

There are several objections to such an extended government system. The phrasing of the question could make a huge difference. For example in Italy a poll asking whether people wanted to change the law which allowed divorce had people voting 'no' and believing they were voting against divorce whereas they were voting for it. The media presentation of the issue would strongly affect voting and the media is by no means impartial. People might have little information or experience on which to base a vote (supposing politicians to have more). If government was just an administration of multiple polls where would any initiative or leadership come from? Even so the sheer efficiency of polls suggests they should have a larger place in decision making.

In a negative feedback the effect of an action is fed back to oppose that action. In a positive feedback the effect of an action is fed back to increase that action. A child eats some chocolate. The effect of this action, the taste, results in an increase in the action and the child eats more and more, until he feels sick when the negative feedback takes over. A cat purrs when it is stroked and the purr encourages the stroker to go on stroking. Love and sex depend very much on positive feedback responses from the people involved.

Leaves are being blown along a street. A few of them pile up behind a small stone. This creates a bigger obstacle and more leaves pile up. The increase in size of the obstacle allows it to catch even more leaves and so the effect continues in a positive feedback manner. The same thing happens with drifting snow. The snowball effect is similar. A small snowball collects more snow and becomes bigger. As it becomes bigger it collects even more snow and becomes bigger still and so on.

A few people catch a disease. The disease spreads to their friends and neighbours. There are now more people with the disease so it spreads even more. A positive feedback loop or a vicious circle is set up. The effect increases the likelihood of the effect. So the spread of the disease makes it even easier for it to spread and an epidemic is set up.

In times of inflation prices rise. In order to preserve their standard of living people demand higher pay. This higher pay puts up prices even further. So more pay is demanded and the inflationary spiral or positive feedback effect continues. In times of inflation interest rates tend to rise to preserve the value of money. This makes it more costly for industry to borrow money so prices go up and inflation increases. The exchange rate for the currency of a country with high inflation falls. So imported goods become more expensive. The cost of living therefore rises. This is followed by pay rises which push up prices, resulting in more inflation which in turn leads to a further fall in the exchange rate. Industry finds it harder to make a profit so fewer people are employed. This means that fewer people have money to buy goods and the recession gets worse, so perpetuating the cycle.

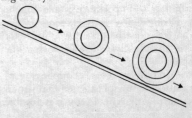

The American philosopher William James was the first to treat 'pragmatism' as a way of behaving. In fact he had derived the basis of the idea from another American, Charles Peirce, and had somewhat distorted the original meaning. Philosophers had been primarily concerned with the nature of truth. Was truth something which had to come from divine revelation? Was it implicit in certain axioms? Was it something that could only be found in such areas as mathematics? William James maintained that the truth of a statement depended on the 'cash value' of that statement. In other words if holding a statement to be true made a practical difference to life then that statement could be regarded as being a true statement. This approach cut right through the metaphysical speculations and endless word-games in which philosophers had entangled themselves. It could be argued that James was not referring to 'truth' but to 'meaning'. An untrue statement, in the sense of a lie, can have meaning and can affect life considerably but nevertheless remains untrue.

In a more general sense pragmatic behaviour is the sort advocated by the first political realist Machiavelli who wrote a book advising the princely rulers of Renaissance Italy on how to behave in order to increase their power and maintain their thrones. The book is full of pragmatic and realistic advice. For example Machiavelli did not have strong religious beliefs but, as a pragmatist, he was in favour of his rulers encouraging religion as a means of keeping the people occupied and setting their minds on the next world rather than this.

The opposite of pragmatism is idealism. An idealist is someone who works towards a fixed ideal or idea of how things ought to be. An idealist is often a statesman. In contrast a pragmatist reacts to the situation of the moment. What he does is not governed by some general plan or ideal but by the need to solve the problem under his nose. Indeed, in order to solve this problem he may undertake actions which go against what had appeared to be his general policies. Harold Wilson is often accused of having been the most pragmatic of English prime ministers.

Life would be impossible unless we assumed that most things were predictable. At a crossing we have to predict that other cars will stop when the red light is against them, otherwise we should never be able to drive. We predict that people's behaviour will fall within our expectations which are based on their usual behaviour. A manufacturer has to predict the cost of producing an item in order to arrive at a selling price. This prediction is quite easy if everything is stable and only machines are involved, but is made more difficult if he has to predict the price of raw materials and labour as well as the productivity of the labour. Even if he only uses machines he predicts that they will go on working.

There is the normal prediction when we assume that things will continue to happen just as they have happened in the past. This sort of prediction is really an assumption. We expect that in the absence of any unusual or untoward event things will continue in the same way. A man does not expect to get fired when he walks into his office in the morning. A wife does expect her husband to come home in the evening. The difficulty is that if there is a small but steady drift in a new direction it is not easily noticed. Each day is predictable because it is going to be similar to the previous day. But if a person were to go to sleep for three years and then wake up he would be unable to predict what the next day might bring. That is why people who move into government or positions of authority can be so bad at predicting the mood of the people or the effects of their actions.

The other kind of prediction is actually a guess. We have no reason to expect something to happen in a certain way but we want to guess. A person betting on a horse race tries to predict the winner. A political journalist tries to predict the outcome of an election. In both cases there may be evidence or indications (such as polls) which can affect the prediction. In ancient cultures the high priests acquired great authority by being able to predict eclipses and thereby seeming to control the heavens.

The whole of science is aimed at understanding nature so that we can control and predict it.

A filibuster is when a politician talks and talks until he has talked away all the time available to discuss an issue so his opponents never get a chance to make their views heard. In effect the politician has taken over the communication channel: he has pre-empted it.

The diagram shows three different ways in which one party can oppose another. The first is by a head-on clash. The second is by trying to restrain, cage or imprison the opposition. The third is by seeing which way the opposition is about to move and by getting there first and so pre-empting its activity. Nowadays political parties are becoming a little more sophisticated and are starting to move towards pre-emptive tactics rather than opposing ones.

Politicians are also managing television interviews better. The interviewer sets out to give the politician a hard time and asks a question which is designed to run contrary to the politician's own thinking: 'Don't you think it is quite wrong that we should spend so much on foreign aid when there are very poor people in our own country?' Instead of defending the foreign aid spending the politician says: 'Yes, I completely agree with you.' This pre-empts the interviewer who cannot very well say: 'But you are not supposed to agree with me!'

At an auction sale one bidder may put in a high bid in order to shut out all other bidders who are not immediately prepared to pay that price. Had the bidding risen in gradual stages such bidders might well have reached the same price but the sudden jump is off-putting.

Pre-empting means to get there first: to do what someone else is going to do before they do it. It implies taking over a channel of communication or activity and so denying its use to others. A man who knows he is going to be sacked gets in first by resigning. A man who is going to be accused of a serious crime gets in first by pleading guilty to a lesser charge. A politician who knows that his opponent is going to make a major speech gets in first by saying the same thing in a minor speech.

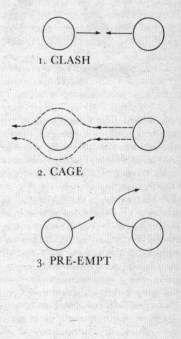

1. CLASH

2. CAGE

3. PRE-EMPT

There is much concern that the ancient and beautiful city of Venice is sinking into the lagoon on which it is built. There are many prescriptions offered for saving the city: permanent dams to keep out the Adriatic sea; temporary dams for peak conditions; reduction in the industrial development in the surrounding area; reduction in the extraction of water from the ground in the surrounding area, and so on.

A patient goes to a doctor with some symptoms and is happiest if she can come away with a prescription for some pills. She feels, at least at first, that the doctor has diagnosed the condition and prescribed the correct treatment.

Economists are always prescribing remedies for the current economic crisis. It puzzles some people that for each economist there is a different prescription. Such people think that the disease should be recognisable and the treatment accepted by all. After all economics is a matter of fact not of opinion. The different prescriptions arise from different understandings of the basic process involved in the economy. Unlike science the background conditions of the economy are continually changing so that a prescription that was right for Keynes in the 1930s may be disastrous now. It is almost as if the human body were changing rapidly from year to year and doctors were being asked to keep on treating patients for the same illness.

A prescription is a specific cure offered for a specific problem. The more detailed and specific the cure the more credible it seems to the patient. Witch doctors' remedies which require the patient to go through elaborate active rituals are more likely to be successful than general advice because the patient is more involved in his own cure. At first sight a psychoanalyst does not appear to be involved in prescribing. It seems that he is just diagnosing the background to the situation. But in fact he is prescribing an 'explanation' or organising story which is just as much a form of treatment as a bottle of pills.

In most situations, however, people are more ready to offer explanations and analyses than actual prescriptions. No one can be proved wrong on an explanation but a prescription may not work.

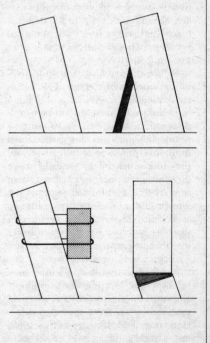

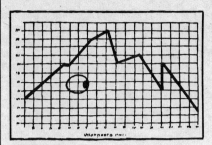

The difference between a frontal view and a profile view of a human face is that the profile view is two-dimensional. At one time it was fashionable to draw silhouettes. They were almost always profiles. A frontal silhouette would not have shown much that was individual: being just a broad outline with two ears and a pile of hair. But the profile with its individual shape of nose, slope of forehead and chin could be personal even though it was two-dimensional.

When we display data on a piece of paper it has to be done in two dimensions. A graph is a two-dimensional relationship. In another form of display quantities are shown in bar form as a histogram which may be upright or on its side as shown in the diagram. The profile of this data display may be sufficient to characterise a person or a situation, according to the various distribution of quantities.

Airline booking clerks were at one time told to watch out for the typical hijacker: they were given a profile of characteristics. Customs officials build up a profile of what potential smugglers may look like. Scientists could put together the profile of the man most likely to suffer a heart attack: over forty years old; takes little exercise; smokes; family history of heart

attacks; raised cholesterol levels in the blood; aggressive in nature, etc. This profile would be constructed by looking at a large number of cases of heart attack and seeing how often certain features occurred amongst them. The features that occurred very often would be put together to give the 'profile'. The same could probably be done for men who beat their wives. Just as a set of features in an individual profile is said to be indicative of the person, so a set of features in a statistical profile is said to be indicative of a situation.

Profile can also be used to indicate the shape of an outline curve relating something to time (or to another thing). For example the sales of a book could have a sharp profile, a steadily rising profile or a step profile, as the diagrams show.

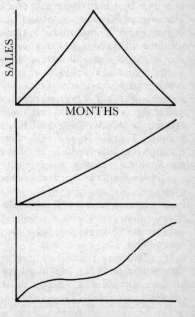

Karl Marx believed that with the coming of the industrial age the worker became able to create a surplus value far beyond his subsistence needs. This surplus value was not reflected in the worker's wages but went to increase the capital of the capitalist. From this it would follow that all profit is the result of stealing or at least exploitation. The industrialist would argue that profit is not really profit at all but funds which have to be used for specific purposes. He would argue that profit is as essential to industry as is fuel to an engine. From the profit have to come the funds for reinvestment and buying the new tools that will increase productivity and keep the industry competitive with its rivals. From the profit also have to come certain reserves which act as a cushion in bad times keeping the industry going until things improve. Finally the profit is an inducement to other people to invest money in the industry and so create jobs for workers. This last argument is somewhat circular for in a non-capitalist economy the state would provide the capital without such inducements and on grounds other than profitability.

It can be argued that irrespective of the moral position of profits they have an immense value as indicators of efficiency. A company is doing poorly and a new dynamic management team takes over. The profits soar. It is obvious that the management is much more efficient. As soon as one admits that there is a scale of efficiency in management then profits acquire a value as an indicator of efficiency. Efficiency in management must surely be of use to society. If ten people sit around idle because poor management has not ensured an adequate supply of materials that cannot be good for them or for society. Poor management may increase employment in the short run but reduce it in the long run if an industry cannot survive competitively. But if profits are the managerial gods then surely the supreme act of worship must be the 'rip-off' situation where management sets out to make as much profit as possible without any special scruples. Clearly this is what the early capitalists did with so much gusto.

There are profits to be made from producing goods and services in an efficient manner. There are less justifiable profits to be made from buying and selling pieces of land where temporary ownership is the only contribution made by the profiteer.

Technically the proletariat covers those people who have no possessions other than their children. Marx and Lenin and early Communists advocated the 'dictatorship of the proletariat' on the basis that this class of people would seem to have been most exploited by capitalist society and also most capable of the revolutionary protest that was to overthrow capitalism. Both Marx and Lenin and most subsequent revolutionaries have, however, been staunchly middle-class. During his most creative period Marx lived in London very much as a middle-class Victorian, though rather poorer than most, and is supposed to have indulged in such middle-class habits as fathering a child by his maid. It was always understood that the dictatorship of the proletariat was to come about under the guidance of an avant-garde élite who would do the necessary thinking – a thinking based on political subtlety as much as on class outrage.

There can be little doubt that the success of capitalism was due to the vigour of its ability to exploit everything in sight, especially workers. Taxation, regulations, welfare services and government controls of various sorts have put a ceiling on exploitation and raised living standards all round. Nevertheless a protest against the system has to be framed as a challenge on behalf of the oppressed, and the proletariat will always continue to fill this role no matter what proportion of the population they form. In most industrialised countries the middle class is by far the largest section of the community and yet the appearance is always given that it is but a thin strand squeezed between the upper class and the mass of the proletariat.

By definition the proletariat are supposed to represent the mass of the people since the capitalists can only be a small fraction. But in fact the vast improvement in living standards over the last half century has meant that there is an infinity of gradations, so that people at each level are conscious that their standard of living is slightly better than that of someone at a lower level; in other words, that they have something to lose. Almost by definition anyone with something to lose is middle-class.

In the United Kingdom in 1976 public expenditure accounted for over sixty per cent of the gross domestic product (GDP is the sum of all goods and services produced). Public expenditure is the spending of the government on such matters as education, defence, health care, legal services and the like In the United States government expenditure has increased seven times as fast as the growth in population. In most countries government expenditure already takes between a third and a half of the gross domestic product. All the estimates indicate that this is bound to increase. In fact it is estimated that in Sweden by the year 2000 government expenditure will equal one hundred per cent of gross domestic product; in other words all the money produced through goods or services would be completely taxed to support government spending.

The growth in public expenditure arises from several causes. People expect the government to do for them what they might otherwise have done for themselves; the government takeover of education and health services is an obvious example. What is more, when the government takes over, the average quality (if not the peaks) increases since people who could not hitherto afford a good education or advanced medical care now become entitled to it. In certain fields such as medicine the advances in technology make things more expensive. If a difficult operation is possible it still has to be paid for. If expensive drugs can cure an illness then they must be used. The cost of technical advances is also obvious in defence where a single fighter plane may now cost millions (or up to a thousand times what it cost

forty years ago). The regulations and controls set up by government require people to handle them. For example there are some 86,000 people employed in the United Kingdom to collect tax. Finally it is claimed that there is no way of measuring efficiency in a public organisation. A commercial firm has to show profits in order to survive. In order to create this profit the firm has to compete in an open market against other firms which can lower their prices if they are more efficient. Inefficient people get sacked. None of this applies in the public service where a need for more money is met by raising taxes or borrowing.

Just as the resources of the world are now regarded as limited so too are the taxable resources of a country.

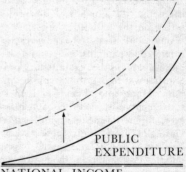

Electrons are presumed to be spinning in fixed orbits around the nucleus of the atom. There are only a certain number of these orbits and if an electron jumps from one orbit to another then a quantum (or several) are released or absorbed. In this case it is energy which is released in definite packs or quanta. In more general terms a quantum jump means that something happens by steps. For example, to be effective rises in salary have to take place in quantum jumps. A gradual rise would not be effective in conferring new status. If a person is to be promoted then the new salary must be at least a quantum jump above the old one. The same thing happens with pricing. A publisher or a manufacturer of games thinks in terms of quantum jumps for the selling price, dividing his market into the lower, middle and upper ranges and finally the luxury bracket. Through all these stages there is not a smooth increase in price but a series of jumps.

Escalation can involve quantum jumps. For example in a domestic dispute if one party hurries off to see a solicitor that is a quantum jump of 'dispute seriousness'. In a conflict, if shots are fired then that is a quantum jump of involvement.

In setting the advertising rates for publications there is a series of quantum jumps depending on the circulation; for example there might be one rate below 10,000, another rate at 50,000, yet another rate at 100,000 and so on. In between the quantum steps there is no rate increase. In building a hospital or a school the process may involve quite large quantum jumps of cost. It may not be economical to build a school only a little bigger than the present one. If the building reaches a certain size then it needs equipment, such as heating, which would equally serve a much larger building. Similarly the equipment needed for a hospital, such as X-ray facilities and operating theatres, imposes a quantum effect.

Pregnancy is a classic example of quantum jumps. No one can be a little bit pregnant. Each foetus is a quantum jump. Animals can have one, two, three, four or more offspring in a litter but they cannot have one and a half or two and a quarter.

The importance of recognising situations in which change occurs by quantum jumps is well understood by anyone who has to deal with expenditure and planning.

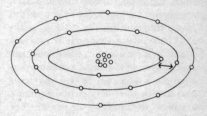

There seem to be noticeable differences in the queueing habits of different people. It is said that in Britain if three people happen to be standing outside a store a queue will form behind them. In Italy or France if there is a queue at a bus stop it represents no more than the starting line in a race in which everyone tries to get on the bus at the same time.

When you go to a shop in Russia you queue to have a look at what you want and to choose the size or colour. You then get a ticket which you take with you to join the queue at the cashier's counter. Eventually you pay the required price and are given a receipt. You take this receipt and join a third queue at the end of which the receipt is actually exchanged for the goods you have bought. In a supermarket in the United States you choose what you want off the shelves, pile it into a basket and wheel the basket to the check-out point. If there are a lot of check-out points or the store is not very busy you may not have to queue at all. In a few supermarkets in Japan you insert a magnetised card to release the goods you want from a compartment. A computer system adds up the prices and sends you a monthly bill (or

you pay the total as you walk out). The amount of queueing required is determined by the organisation of the system.

It would be possible to eliminate queueing if everyone could have what they wanted exactly when they wanted it. If there were enough supermarket check-out points to cope with the busiest shopping peak there might be no queueing, but at off-peak times these check-out points would be unused and the cost of setting them up and staffing them would be uneconomic. Queues can indicate a bottleneck that needs to be removed or may be a way of evening out peak and off-peak demand. Bus queues are supposed to be a way of sharing out limited seating according to length of waiting.

In a fluid system the build-up of pressure speeds up the flow. Unfortunately this does not happen in a queueing system.

When you throw a pair of dice the numbers come up in a random fashion. The numbers on a roulette wheel come up in a random fashion. This means that there is no discernible order, sequence, pattern or way of predicting which number will come up next. If twenty red numbers occur in a row at roulette the next number is just as likely to be red as black.

A random event is one which is not related to or caused by surrounding circumstances. A random check on income tax returns means that there is no set pattern for working through all the returns but an unpredictable system of picking out a few returns and checking on these.

You may watch a child walking down the street and now and again hopping in an apparently random manner. You might consider the manner random because you cannot see the pattern (within the sequence of hops themselves) or because you cannot relate the pattern to anything in the street itself. Yet the pattern of hops may not be random at all: the child may be humming to herself a hopping song which you cannot hear. Events may appear to be random yet may have a pattern we have not yet detected. Conversely events which really are random may seem to be full of order and significance. Since the mind is able to ignore or create meaning of its own accord, independently of the events, perceived meaning is not the same as actual meaning.

Random access to stored data means that any part of the data may be wanted at any time. This is in contrast to a sequence of data in which the tenth item in the sequence would only be required if the first nine items were required first.

The use of a random word is one of the techniques of lateral thinking for generating new ideas. The problem in question is held in juxtaposition with a totally unconnected word which serves to trigger off new lines of thought. The word is introduced at random but once there sets off ideas which now create links.

In a world where everything seems to be changing we sometimes need to know just how fast things are changing. 'Rate of rise' refers to an imaginary graph in which the increase in something is related to time. The time base may be in minutes, days, months or years. The diagram shows a rate of rise in house prices of twelve per cent over a year. This means that at the end of the year a house will cost twelve per cent of the starting price above the starting price. We can talk about a steep rate of rise or a shallow rate of rise. Another diagram shows a steep rate of rise with regard to the price of sugar but a shallow rate of rise with regard to the price of milk. It must be remembered that an actual rate of rise may only last for a week or a month. When a rate of rise is given over a full year it is either the average rate of rise over the year (smoothing out the humps and dips) or the increase at the end of the year related to the value at the beginning.

You are driving a car at a steady speed. If we relate your speed to time we find that it has no rate of rise so we draw a flat curve. But to reach that steady speed you had to start moving at some time in the past. So the other line in the graph shows how there was a steady rate of rise in your speed from zero speed when you were stationary to the steady speed you have now achieved. But if instead of looking at speed we were to look at how much ground you had covered for every second we would find that as you accelerated from rest you covered more and more ground for each second that passed (this follows naturally from the fact that your speed is increasing). So if we draw another

graph showing the increase in distance against time we find that it gets steeper and steeper. In other words there is an accelerating rate of rise. This simply means that from moment to moment the rate of rise is increasing.

Rate of rise applies in the same way to rate of fall. An inflation rate of ten per cent per annum means that the purchasing power of money has fallen by ten per cent after one year. An accelerating rate of inflation means that each month the actual rate of rise of inflation increases so that the purchasing power of money accelerates downwards as shown.

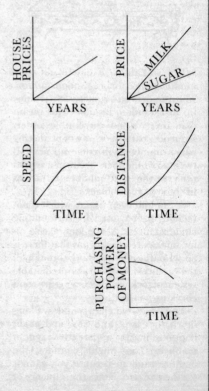

You can describe a scene from the opera or from a film. You can describe the scene of the crime. You can describe the general scene at your place of work or the political scene in your own office. A rationale is simply the description of a logical scene. All the logical reasons are laid out and they add up to a scene. Rationale is a sort of plural for 'reason', indicating not simply a collection of reasons but the way the reasons fit together into a structure.

Just before an election the state government in New South Wales reduces the price of petrol by reducing the tax element. The rationale seems fairly obvious: an election gimmick to show a willingness to reduce the cost of living. Of course, it can backfire: if it is possible to reduce the price at this point was it not possible to reduce it earlier? A library introduces a new rule which says that people always have to take out two books at a time; it is no longer permitted to borrow only one. This seems a strange rule and the borrowers cannot see the rationale behind it. In fact the rationale is that checking books in and out is expensive and time-consuming and it is hoped that if borrowers take two at a time they will halve the issuing time.

Rationale is the logical basis for some action undertaken with a specific effect in mind. It is not a summation of the reasons used in an argument; rather it is the logical explanation of something that is being done. What is the rationale of changing over to a decimal currency? It makes calculations much easier. What is the rationale for driving on the left-hand side of the road in countries like England and Japan? There is no real rationale ex-

cept that it would be expensive to change over (and what indeed is the rationale for driving on the right-hand side, except that more people do this?). Supposedly there is also the historical reason that it allowed two horsemen meeting in the road to have their sword hands free to smite each other, or else to shake hands.

Quite often a logical scene is constructed to surround and support a position that has been adopted for quite other reasons (emotional, political, etc). This creation of a rationale after its conclusion is known as rationalisation.

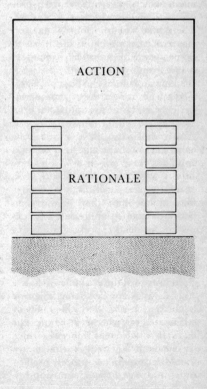

A lion does not regard as raw the meat which it is given to eat in the zoo. A lion in its natural surroundings does not regard as raw the zebra which it strikes down and eats. We only regard meat as raw because we know that we shall be cooking it in order to eat it. A raw recruit may be a perfectly capable carpenter, teacher or lawyer but in the eyes of the army he is raw because he has not yet been taught army skills. Both the raw meat and the raw recruit await a processing that is going to make them more useful to their user.

Scientists talk about raw data when they mean a mass of simple measurements which have not yet been processed to yield an idea or an answer. There might be a lot of raw data on cigarette smoking habits but it has to be processed by statistical techniques before any relationships between smoking and illness can be shown.

We tend to regard raw data or experience as of little use until it has been processed to suit the use we have for it. A man looks at a glass not as a raw experience of shape and light but as a drinking vessel which he is about to drink from or about to refill with beer. It is characteristic of Eastern religions and philosophies that they try to persuade man to appreciate raw experience instead of seeking always to process it into something of practical use. The emphasis is on the 'is-ness' of something (be it a glass or a relationship) instead of the usefulness.

The way we process something raw is always self-ish. We cook things to our own liking whether it be meat or data. It could not be otherwise since we decide the use we want. Ideally we should let experience process itself in order to give us the maximum appreci-

ation of that experience, but this is difficult to do. We tend either to hurry along with the processing or else to make an effort to appreciate the rawness itself. Somewhere in between lies the true state of perception that allows experience to organise itself to yield up its full value.

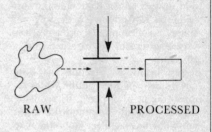

RAW   PROCESSED

Traditionally trade unions have preferred to be reactive: that is to react to whatever happens. The most natural reaction is one of opposition. The reaction may also be to proposals that are put forward but again the distinction is between putting forward a proposal and reacting to it. Being reactive tends to be a stronger position because anyone who puts forward a proposal risks its rejection.

Most educational material is reactive. Pupils are faced with material they have to absorb or react to. Most thinking is reactive rather than projective. A pupil is given a mathematical problem and told to use all the information that is given. He reacts to the material and comes up with the answer. Unfortunately this sort of reactive thinking is of limited use in life outside school. Very rarely is all the material presented. Often material may have to be collected, gaps filled in by guesswork, what is relevant sorted out. Furthermore many situations require initiative and planning. It is not enough to wait and then to react to situations as they develop.

The reactive thinker tends to be critical rather than constructive. If he were inclined to be constructive then probably he would not have had to wait for a reactive situation in order to put his ideas forward. The reactive thinker waits for a crisis whereas the constructive or projective thinker plans ahead to avoid the crisis. There is an obvious disadvantage in this. When a crisis does develop the reactive thinker makes a fuss about it and then gains an equivalent credit if he succeeds in settling the crisis. The projective thinker, unfortunately, who plans ahead so that no crisis ever develops does not get any credit for solving a crisis which no one else can see. The moral is fairly obvious: bad government tends to gain the most credit.

Many industrialists are far more reactive than they would like to admit. They react to competitive pressures but rarely to market opportunities. They are more content to let things emerge than to seek them out. They are more willing to have change thrust upon them than to initiate it.

A piece of information is said to be redundant when it adds nothing to what is already there, when it can be removed without making any difference. You are giving instructions to a motorist: 'Drive along for exactly one mile until you come to a church in the middle of the road, then you turn immediately to the right, in a northward direction, following the sign to Hopeville.' Turning to the right, turning in a northward direction, following the sign to Hopeville all say the same thing. Two of them would seem to be redundant. Similarly proceeding until the church was reached and driving for exactly one mile also say the same thing unless there was a nearer church. In practice, however, this logical redundancy can be useful in stressing a point.

The type of information handling that goes on in the brain is very different from that within a computer. In the brain system there is a great deal of redundancy whereas in the computer it is kept to a minimum. This is because in the computer the more that can be done with less the cheaper is the process. In the brain, however, the great amount of redundancy means there is a greater tolerance for mistakes. If information is handled in parallel by different systems then a mistake in one will be overruled by the others.

A man may lose his job because there has been a fall in orders and he is declared redundant. In another factory the same fall in orders has not resulted in any redundancies. The management of the second factory believes that the market will change soon and wishes to keep its men. In both cases the extra men are redundant to the immediate production needs.

But in a wider context the men in the second factory are not redundant to the longer term production needs (at least as estimated by the management).

Redundancy depends on the definition of need. Logical redundancy in information means that the message can be transmitted perfectly without the redundant information. But perceptually the repetition may be useful and even necessary.

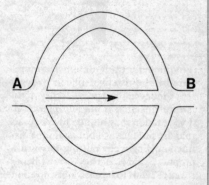

The regulator on a boiler keeps the steam pressure constant. The regulator on a watch keeps constant the marking of the passage of time. Regulators are devices that are set up to control matters. The control may be automatic by means of a negative feedback system or it may require such human intervention as the turning of a stopcock or the opening of a valve.

Economists are forever grumbling that there are very few effective mechanisms for regulating the economy. Some argue that the money supply provides the best regulator. Others prefer the rate of interest. Still others prefer taxation alterations. A few find a use for price and wage controls. The problem is not so much that the regulators do not work but that in working they use mechanisms which are politically unacceptable. For instance a regulation of the money supply to control inflation works to some extent by increasing unemployment. It is rather like a medicine with unpleasant side-effects. It would be nice if these side-effects were absent but sometimes they are inseparable from the effectiveness of the medicine. In that case care has to be taken (as it is with anti-cancer drugs) to give just the right dose that will cope with the illness but not itself kill the patient. The use of the regulator has itself to be regulated.

In ordinary affairs there are very few regulators. The inner conscience developed by centuries of Christian morality is one. The regard of our fellows is another. The fear of the law is a third. All these are more in the nature of pressures or influences than actual regulators. None of them can be turned up or down to combat rises or falls in pressure. Nor is the problem one of regulating individual conduct as much as regulating the attitude or mood of society as such. Originally, and even today in primitive cultures, art operated as the regulator of social mood but in industrialised society that function has disappeared.

We are rapidly approaching the situation when our mood will be regulated by chemical pills: 'uppers' for when we are depressed and 'downers' for when we get over-tense. It is already happening on a large scale: anti-depressants and tranquillisers head the list of prescriptions.

The behaviourists believe that behaviour can be shaped by the suitable use of reinforcement. In his famous experiments the Harvard psychologist Skinner trained pigeons to tap out a simple tune on a toy piano. He did this by breaking down the required movements into simple steps. Each time a pigeon, by accident, took the right step the behaviour was rewarded or 're-inforced' by a present of grain. In this way, step by step, the complex behaviour was built up or shaped.

Animal trainers use the same method. They reinforce the desired behaviour of animals by small rewards of food. Theoretically negative reinforcement or punishment should not be used.

Attempts have been made to condition good social behaviour of delinquents by using token money as a reinforcing reward whenever socially useful behaviour was shown.

It is pointed out that if a child is given a sweet to stop it crying this acts as a reinforcement for the crying and actually aggravates such behaviour (a sort of negative investment). If students are rewarded with publicity and importance whenever they demonstrate this again acts as a form of reinforcement.

Reinforcement is a form of conditioning. It is not suggested that the behaviour is carried out simply to obtain the reward: the chain of behaviour is set up by reinforcement at every step. Once the chain is set up, however, it seems to be the desirable way to behave. A teacher in a classroom can obtain exactly the sort of response she wants by reinforcing (with a nod of approval) the type of answer she expects and ignoring the others. After a while the children learn to play the education game.

If the claims made for reinforcement are true then it is a powerful method for shaping behaviour. It must also be observed that many of the things we do in society may actually be reinforcing and shaping behaviour which we do not require. A child who is naughty to gain attention finds that attention reinforces his misbehaviour.

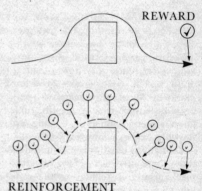

REWARD

REINFORCEMENT

A manufacturer of women's underwear does research into the change in the shape of women. It seems that since the advent of the contraceptive pill women have increased the size of their bust. The research may consist of carrying out measurements on a sample of women or of buying such measurements from an organisation like the armed services which has had to obtain the measurements in order to supply uniforms.

A pharmaceutical company sets out to do research on the control of blood pressure. It hopes to come up with a drug that will control and lower blood pressure. High blood pressure is a common and dangerous disease and there are good profits to be made in such drugs because they have to be taken every day of a patient's life. A drug seems promising but much further research has to be done to find the best dosage; to see if there are any side-effects; to investigate the effects in pregnancy; and to find if the initial beneficial effect wears off with time.

A Shakespeare scholar undertakes lengthy research to check whether a particular sonnet attributed to Shakespeare could have been written by someone else.

Research may be done in a library or in a laboratory or in any other place where effort might be rewarded with information. Sometimes the research has a specific information-accumulating function: for example someone might be asked to do research on family businesses. At other times the research is termed basic since the purpose is the further understanding of natural phenomena. Scientific research usually sets out with an hypothesis and then attempts to find out whether there is evidence to support the hypothesis.

Ideally a scientist hopes, with his research, to accumulate enough evidence to prove his hypothesis. Then he hopes to get further evidence which will disprove the first hypothesis and so drive him on to an even better hypothesis. In practice this rarely happens and scientists, being human, are more inclined to look only for the evidence that will support their own idea.

The need for research is obvious but there is too often a hope that research alone will solve all problems.

You are pushing a young child on a swing. You wait until the child is right at the end of a swing and then give a little push. If you get your timing just right you can get the child to swing higher and higher by using small pushes. If, however, you get the timing wrong and push before the end of the swing has been reached then you will slow the swinging down. Older children learn to swing themselves by moving their legs forward or backward at just the right moment.

A professor of physics demonstrates resonance by hanging a solid iron ball on a wire from the ceiling and giving a student an ordinary drinking straw. The student has to blow at the ball through the straw and get it swinging. If the student gets his timing exactly right the heavy ball can be made to swing backwards and forwards in ever increasing arcs just by the tiny pressure of his blowing through the straw. The process is shown in the diagram. In effect the swinging ball collects and adds up all the separate inputs.

A famous physicist once said that given a pea-shooter and an exquisite sense of timing he could demolish Tower Bridge in London by shooting a pea at it in time with its own swing or resonance. Soldiers are always told to march out of step when they come to a bridge because the rhythm of their left-right step could cause the bridge to collapse by setting up resonances.

Resonance depends on the natural characteristics of the system: the swing of the child; the pendulum effect of the iron ball; the vibration of the bridge. If an input is put in at just the right moment then the natural oscillation will be set off and increased. If you flick a fine wine glass it gives a note. It is said that by hitting exactly the right note an opera singer can cause such a glass to break. A radio receiver resonates in tune with the wavelength sent out by a particular station.

An artist could be said to have an emotional resonance with his public if he was so tuned to their emotions and perceptions that his work amplified these into a visible form.

Some countries like Australia are rich in natural resources: the ground is full of minerals like iron and uranium; the climate is good for agriculture in many parts and there is enough space. Other countries like Japan have few natural resources: no energy, no minerals, little land for agriculture.

It is becoming fashionable in schools to have 'resource' areas. These resource areas contain books, cassettes, records, pictures and other material which the pupil may want to consult when he is working on a project.

A resource is something which can be turned into value when required. It is something which occurs rather than something which has been deliberately stored in a place. It is something which needs processing or exploiting. Resource implies potential.

Reserve, reservoir and resource all refer to something which can be used at some time in the future. Reserve implies that the use is being deliberately held back, as reserve troops in a battle or the reserve power in an engine are held back. Reservoir implies storage just as a water reservoir is a way of storing water so that it can be used as required. In contrast a re-source means something that is there without having been put there. Before it can be turned into actual value there must be a decision to tap the resource and also the means of doing so.

Resources may not always be recognised as such. For instance Japan may be low in natural resources but may be high in labour resources insofar as the culture is said to encourage the habit of hard work and long vision. An organisation may be unaware of its own resources whether of people, property or reputation.

Some resources are self-renewing but others are finite and can be used up. The problem then is whether to keep the resources or to exploit them, and if so how fast.

A government minister resigns because there has been a scandal in his department and he accepts full responsibility for it even though he has known nothing about it. A commanding officer accepts responsibility for the men under his command. At a war crimes trial a soldier disclaims responsibility for his actions on the basis that he was merely carrying out orders. An attempt is made to make parents responsible for the vandalism carried out by their children.

Trade unions have traditionally refused to accept responsibility because they sense that they would then become vulnerable. It is safer to retain the role of protest and opposition. In some countries, however, this is changing and unions are taking on direct responsibility for work conditions and discipline and perhaps in time for investment decisions. Where this is not mere tokenism the appointment of union representatives to the boards of corporations is an attempt to involve unions in the responsibility of decision making.

Responsibility means no more than taking the blame. Political parties spend a considerable amount of time arguing about who is responsible for a recession. A doctor is responsible for the treatment of a patient. An architect is responsible for the design and safety of his buildings. An editor is responsible for the libels of his reporters.

Avoiding responsibility is a common strategy. President Truman is said to have had a sign on his desk reading: 'The buck stops here.'

The real problem with responsibility is that the focusing of blame is not equally balanced by a focusing of the means to get things done. Many people seem to be in a blame-only situation. The best they can do is to survive and not get blamed for mistakes. They have little power to do anything positive or constructive. In fact they are scapegoats that have been tethered to the system. In ancient days the woes of a tribe used to be decanted on to a goat which was then driven out into the desert. To some extent the Watergate scandal served as a ritual purgation of this sort. The original scapegoat however was never technically guilty.

Rhetoric was the art used by a Greek orator. It has come to refer to the language of a 'wind-bag' and is used whenever the style of writing or speaking takes precedence over the actual content. A rhetorician asks questions only when he knows the answer: 'Who has led us into this situation? We know who, don't we?'

The tricks and devices of oratory are valid enough but when the balance between style and substance is upset in favour of style we talk of empty rhetoric. Just as we discount advertising so we also discount rhetoric.

A politician may make a long speech and at each moment he seems to be talking sense and to have the audience with him but at the end it is clear that nothing of any substance has been said. It is not difficult to talk in generalities and good intentions: 'We shall do all we can to raise the workers' standard of living; we are firmly committed to a policy of cutting out wastage in government expenditure; we are very much concerned with the rising crime rate; we are pledged to uphold the democratic process; we are, in short, pledged to do or acknowledge or be aware of all those things which might retain the interest of our supporters and pacify our opponents.' Often rhetoric amounts to declaring at great length and in detail: 'We are determined to solve this problem by finding a solution to solve this problem.'

In Tibet classical disputations between the monks on theological matters were highly formalised. There was a specific gesture to accompany a positive point, there was a different gesture to indicate a break in the argument. Rhetoric is often ritualised in a similar way, not with gestures but with the use of questions and escalating clauses (moreover . . . moreover . . . moreover . . . but . . .).

Rhetoric is a sort of verbal massage that is pleasant and reassuring while it lasts but is not intended to leave any mark afterwards.

A great deal of rhetoric is usually to be found in law courts since the significance of a fact or two could not sustain the whole ceremony.

RIP·OFF

206

Legitimate profit is at the opposite pole from a rip-off. Nevertheless there is a point where the borderline between the two is blurred. A legitimate profit is one which allows for reinvestment and proper rewards for those who have made possible the enterprise. A rip-off is based on the sole ethic of 'what you can get away with'. Its rationale is the notion that no one is under an obligation to buy and that if they choose to do so they must have made their own assessment of value. This assessment has nothing whatever to do with the objective values involved. For example there is to be a Rolling Stones concert and the tickets are sold out within a few hours of the announcement. Some ticket touts buy up tickets and then offer them for sale just before the concert at fifty times the real price. The real price is based on the costing of the whole tour. The ticket tout's price is based on what he can get away with. No one is forced to buy the tickets. If they value them so highly then that is what the tickets are really worth to them.

The sale of paintings and other works of art depends to some extent on this approach. The value lies in the eye of the buyer. The buyer, if a museum, buys at that price because it is not possible to buy at any other price. The dealer sells at that price because he has had to buy at a high price and the bigger the difference the more profit he makes. The buyer, if a speculator, wants to keep the price high in order to protect his investment. All this is perfectly legitimate.

The problem arises when the rip-off is not based on a buyer's valuation but on a misled buyer's valuation. An agent selling plots of land on a tropical

island can paint a picture that is far from reality. Of course the buyer could have checked it out for himself. The rip-off specialist feels no responsibility towards the buyer: if the buyer is gullible that is his fault. Since the whole of society works on some sort of mutual credibility the rip-off operator cashes in on this reserve of trust.

This approach can sometimes amount to blackmail: for example where a specialist puts a 'rip-off' price on his own services compelling the patient either to accept it or go untreated.

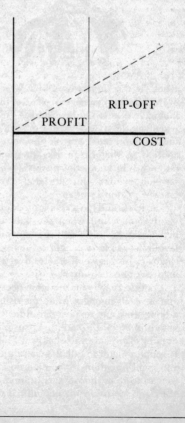

When Euclid was teaching his geometry he made it clear to a royal student who must have been rather bored that there was no 'royal road' to geometry. The royal student would have to follow the same road as the other students.

A road is a route that has been prepared and smoothed over. At one time there may have been a very good reason for putting the road in that particular place. Later the initial reason may have disappeared but the mere existence of the road is sufficient to justify its use.

There are roads in the sky and roads on the sea. The flight paths of airliners are carefully plotted so as to avoid collision, reduce distance and pay some attention to the wishes of the countries which are overflown (especially in the case of supersonic aircraft like the Concorde with its supersonic bang). Shipping routes or sea 'lanes' are also well established.

Roads are convenient. For one thing the surface is much smoother. The ultimate in smoothness is the railroad where the smoothness of the metal rails is the smoothness of the road: that is why it takes only a fraction of the energy required on a normal road to move the same load by rail. Apart from the smoothness a road implies that other problems have been overcome: bridges have been built over rivers; swamps have been filled in. There are also signposts and road maps. All in all a road is a device for solving problems in advance and for simplifying decisions.

By their very nature roads are conventional. They go by fixed ways to fixed destinations. If we proceed along the set road we will end up at the set destination. In our approach to problems if we use the set road we will end up with the established solution.

In life the difficulty has always been to decide how far to use established roads and how far to try new ones.

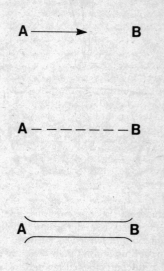

Trapeze artists in a circus use a safety net. Society is under a moral obligation to build safety nets for those who, through no fault of their own, are unable to compete well enough to keep themselves alive. It may be a matter of physical or mental handicap or a combination of circumstances which makes it impossible for a person to earn enough money to support himself and his family. There are times when the circumstances of society change so that many more people, hitherto capable, find that they are out of work and cannot earn a living.

Political doctrines diverge considerably over the question of safety nets. On one side there are the doctrines which support free enterprise and personal effort and insist that individuals should take responsibility for themselves instead of turning to the state to solve their problems. This free-market, competitive type of outlook needs to be accompanied by an efficient safety net to catch those who cannot compete and therefore cannot survive in such a society. The main criticism of such doctrines is that the safety net procedures are usually less than adequate since there is a reluctance to provide funds for such a negative purpose as help to those who cannot compete. The opposite doctrine is to make the state responsible for the welfare of all its citizens: health, education, housing, work, etc. In this case the aim is to direct more help to those in greatest need. In both cases the problem has always been to distinguish between those people who really need help and those who find it easier to accept help than try to compete. It is probably true that some people who are receiving hand-outs from the state do not deserve them but how large this proportion is remains uncertain. It is equally true that many people simply could not survive without state aid. The next problem is to decide how much help is enough. Should the help be just enough to keep the people alive or sufficient to give them a life that is comparable to that of their fellow citizens?

If the first function of any society is to survive and the second is to improve the living standards of its members then the third function must be to provide safety nets for the less able members. Much of politics is about how best this can be done.

Architects, town planners and engineers often build small-scale models of what they plan. It seems a sensible thing to do. Instead of going ahead with the expense of a full-scale operation the model can be built and then the project can be judged. The scale may be one thousandth, one hundredth, one twelfth or one quarter which means that each measurement on the model is one quarter (etc) of what it is intended to be in real life. Unfortunately it does not follow that something which works well in the scale model will also work well when the model is scaled up to full scale. For instance a building that seems very pretty when you look down on the model on a table may be boring when you look up at it from the street because you are looking from a different angle and can only see one part at a time.

A cube may be made at one-tenth scale. This means that in real life the cube will be ten feet long instead of one foot in length. But the area covered by one face of the cube will not scale up from one square foot to ten square feet but to one hundred square feet. So the amount of material required will go up one hundred times. Similarly the volume of the cube will not increase from one cubic foot to ten cubic feet but to one thousand cubic feet – a thousandfold increase even though the scale is one tenth. This is why the successful engineering principles used in the design of insects cannot be scaled up to apply to larger creatures.

An advertising campaign is planned. In a discussion between the advertising agency and the client the client asks what the time scale is: is the campaign to last for a week, a month, a year or several years? Health department officials may be having a discussion about the nature of a vaccination campaign: is it to be full-scale? Scale refers to size, whether of time or anything else. But it includes not just the size of something but the whole 'universe' of size. Within this universe everything is to scale. It is like looking down a telescope from the wrong end: the world is complete but everything looks much smaller. To ask on what scale is this being done, is to ask what is the size of this happening? The answer is usually small-scale or full-scale.

When we read our eyes scan along the lines picking up information as they go. When we reach the end of one line we go back and start at the beginning of the next. The television set works on a scanning principle. A spot of light scans very rapidly across the surface of the tube in a regular pattern covering one line after another and then flying back to the top to start all over again. As it scans across, the intensity of the spot is altered by the signal coming from the transmitting station. In this way a black and white picture would be transmitted. The basic process is similar for colour television except that each colour is treated separately.

A sailor scans the horizon for land or for another ship. A semicircular radar aerial moves round and round as it scans the sky or the sea for metal objects that will reflect back the radar waves and show up the object as a blip on the radar screen.

A scan is a fixed pattern of search or movement that covers the area in question irrespective of what it finds.

The sailor sweeps his eyes backwards and forwards over the horizon. This may be a true scan. But when the sailor finds another ship his eyes fasten on to it and follow its progress. This is no longer a scan. In contrast the radar scan continues irrespective of what has just been shown on the screen.

There is a suggestion that the brain-waves which we can pick up with an electro-encephalogram represent a scanning system in the brain. It is supposed that this scanning system takes a look at the different parts of the brain and puts together what it sees to give an overall output.

The difference between a scan and a random search is that the scan is methodical whereas the random search may go over some areas repeatedly and others not at all. Furthermore a scan is not meant to be a search for something specific but a way of seeing whatever is there. You may search the horizon for a ship or scan the horizon to see what is there.

The overture has come to an end. The audience sit expectantly in their seats. The curtain goes up to reveal a magnificent stage setting with realistic trees and houses and a fountain in the middle of the village square. The audience burst into applause. The scene is set. The opera is about to begin.

The policeman jumps out of his car and hurries across to the scene of the accident. The truck has smashed through the front of the shop. The driver is slumped forward in his cab. No one in the shop has been injured. There is glass everywhere and the sidewalk is covered with groceries.

In each of these examples there is an element of 'stop-frame' or freezing of the situation. Something has happened or is about to happen. The observer wants to take it all in at once in order to understand and react appropriately. He wants to get a clear picture of the scene, of the setting.

It is easy to see that the term 'scene' can apply to a physical setting as in the case of the opera scene and the scene of the accident, but it can apply equally well to other situations. A new executive appointed to a company may take his secretary out to lunch in order to find out from her about the 'scene'. A situation is something that

may arise from moment to moment and then change. A scene is more stable. A scene is the background picture within which and against which things happen. A description of the scene may outline the people involved, structure, trends, moods and style. A person who wants to get to know the scene wants to get to know it clearly. He does not necessarily want explanations or interpretations.

If it is not possible to take in the scene all at once the observer may have to build it up or piece it together as he goes along. The ultimate aim is a clear overall picture of the setting. Clarity and full coverage are what matter. Such coverage should always be complete as regards breadth but details and depth may depend on requirements. A person who has to take immediate action may not require as much depth as someone who has to live in the scene.

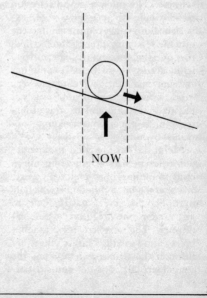

A bank is screening applicants for a job in its computer department. The job is an attractive one and there have been a large number of applicants. The first stage is to screen the applicants and to select out the ones who might be suitable. The interview and selection stage would then follow. Age, experience and salary requirements come into the screening process. So too does the question of security for anyone with access to a bank's computer system is in a position to carry out very subtle forms of fraud or theft, such as paying a tiny amount from each account into a fictitious account controlled by him.

Metal screens are used to separate out different sizes of gravel for use in road building and concrete work. Each screen has a different size of hole in it. The first screen has big holes so all except the biggest stones get through. The next screen has smaller holes and so the stones that get through the first screen but not the second are all of a determined size.

The purpose of the screens is selection. The characteristic of the screens is determined by the selection requirements. The bank's mental screens for selecting the right person for the computer job were designed to let through only those applicants with certain basic characteristics. So selection may be in terms either of what gets through a screen or of what does not.

A population may be screened for diabetes by taking a urine sample from each person and testing it for sugar content. Those people who show sugar in their urine are then tested further for diabetes. The purpose of a screening test is to narrow down the number of people who need to be tested in a thorough fashion since this costs time and money. For that reason screening tests tend to be simple to use and cheap. I once designed a whistle device for use as a screening test for one type of lung disease.

A screen is used for sorting or separating. Whether the selected group is the one that gets through the screen or the one that does not, depends on the nature of the screen. It is just as easy to have a screen that picks out the unsuitable as the suitable.

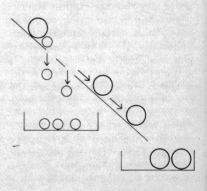

The concept of a 'seed' is the most powerful and fascinating concept there is in biology. A seed is insignificant in size. Thousands and thousands of similar seeds may be produced. A seed can lie dormant for years, even thousands of years. But from each seed can grow a huge tree capable of producing millions of further seeds each one like the original. A seed is a packet of organisation. Once germinated it organises energy into the production of substance and form, and further organising structures.

Research foundations are always interested, or at least purport to be, in 'seed projects'. These are small-scale projects which once started generate a tremendous growth and keep growing by themselves without further support.

Certain conditions are required for a seed to germinate. Unless these conditions are met the seed is wasted. That is why plants produce thousands of seeds and why there are millions of spermatozoa in sperm. One seed, however, is enough, provided it falls on fertile ground. We often talk about the seed of an idea which may be implanted in a person's mind many years before it suddenly emerges as a definite idea or action.

A seed is a starting point but one which differs from others. A journey of a thousand miles starts with one step but that step is not a seed. A seed is deemed to contain the organising potential for all else that follows. For the same reason there is a difference between a trigger and a seed. A trigger may be insignificant compared to what it releases but its force is exerted on circumstances outside itself.

A seed may appear insignificant in size but the organising potential it contains is huge.

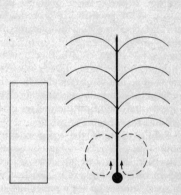

SEED

A self-fulfilling prophecy is a prophecy which itself brings about what
is prophesied. Imagine that the value
of the pound sterling is in decline. The
economic pundits prophesy that it will
fall even further. This prophecy itself
destroys confidence and the pound
does fall even further. So the prophecy
has itself brought about what was
prophesied.

Business depends to a considerable
extent on confidence. An investment
decision is partly based on facts and
partly on an emotional interpretation
of the facts. One businessman might
complain: 'Orders are only up five per
cent on last year.' Another might
enthuse: 'Orders are already up five
per cent on last year.' People who talk
in terms of depression lower their own
morale and soon find themselves in a
genuine depression.

Publicity about the steep rise in
house prices makes genuine house
buyers rush to buy at once before
prices rise any higher. It also brings
in speculators who see a possibility of
profit in the rising prices. Both events
tend to make the prices rise even
further in a self-fulfilling manner.
Exactly the same thing can happen in
reverse. Publicity about falling house
prices encourages people to hold off
buying in case prices should fall
further. So home owners have to
lower prices further in order to encourage buyers.

A financial correspondent of a weekend paper picks an industrial stock
which he feels is likely to rise. So many
people take his advice that the stock
does actually rise.

A self-fulfilling prophecy is a
special form of positive feedback or
vicious circle. A dilemma is created

because no matter how genuine and
objective a forecast may be the very
credibility of the forecast will alter the
event.

A different type of self-fulfilling
prophecy is to be found in religious
sects who forecast the end of the world
on a particular day and then climb to
the top of a mountain to await the
end. They pray to God to avert the
disaster. When the appointed day
passes they have the choice of acknow-
ledging their error or marvelling at the
effectiveness of their prayer.

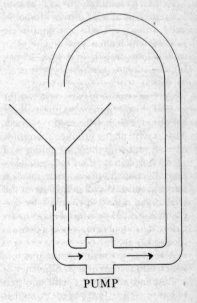

PUMP

The diagram shows four ways in which a process may be limited. In the first there is a natural boundary or container. A river may flood its banks and may spread until it reaches a low hill. A forest fire may spread until it comes to the barrier of a fire-break.

In the second illustration a process may be halted because it is opposed by counter-measures. For example the spread of crime may be countered by reinforcement of the police force. An epidemic may be countered by a massive vaccination campaign.

In the third illustration the process is self-limiting because it runs out of steam. For instance in a small community dishonesty is self-limiting because sooner or later everyone gets to know about the behaviour of a dishonest man. The growth of government expenditure is eventually self-limiting because there comes a point when no more money can be generated by increasing taxation.

But there is another form of self-limitation. This is illustrated in the fourth diagram. Here the process itself generates a force which eventually counteracts the process. For instance advertising causes a fall in credibility since people expect advertising to extol the virtues of a product. Eventually this credibility falls so low that even a true description is not believed. A boom in property prices is also self-limiting. As the price rises so speculators buy more and more but eventually there are no new speculators and the ones who bought early are anxious to sell in order to realise their profits. So the price starts to level out. This encourages more of them to sell before it falls. This causes it to fall. More people are anxious to sell in order to

realise some small measure of profit and so the fall becomes steeper. The cycle, however, is not symmetrical as many people who bought houses actually wish to live in them.

Demonstrations can be self-limiting because after a while everyone becomes bored with them. Protest can also be self-limiting as after a while it becomes in itself an establishment. The difficulty is to detect which processes need to be checked because they are self-fuelling or self-fulfilling and which can be neglected because they are self-limiting. It also matters how much damage they cause before being limited.

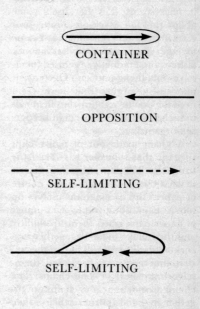

CONTAINER

OPPOSITION

SELF-LIMITING

SELF-LIMITING

St Thomas Aquinas was probably the most influential Christian thinker there has ever been. He constructed logical proofs of the existence of God. One of these proofs referred to God as the ultimate organiser or designer. The argument was that everything had to be organised and this called for an organiser. In turn the organiser had to be organised and so on back to the original organiser who had to have existed from eternity: this was God. If something is organised we tend to feel that an outside influence must have organised it at some time. But it need not be so. The concept of a self-organising system is important because it now seems that life itself came about through a self-organising process whereby different chemicals came together in a more or less chance fashion and gradually organised themselves into living patterns. Of course it may still be argued that there was a need for God to organise the chemicals in such a way that they could become self-organizing.

A chain made out of paper clips suggests that someone has taken the trouble to link paper clips together to make a chain. It is not in the nature of paper clips to make themselves up into a chain. But if you take a number of paper clips, open them up slightly and shake them all together in a cocktail shaker you will find at the end that the clips have organised themselves into short or long chains. The chains are not as neat as chains put together by hand but nevertheless they are chains. A teacher can organise her class into groups by assigning each child to a specific group and picking the group leaders. She could also tell the children to organise themselves into groups of five and then let them get on with it in a self-organising fashion. The diagram shows an object that has a magnet out on a prong and two metal plates on the bulb. If we shake up a number of these objects we find that they tend to organise themselves into the arrangement shown. Once the magnet comes into contact with the metal plate it tends to stick there. In other words once something has happened it does not un-happen as easily. It is this asymmetry that is the basis of self-organisation.

In the way our mind deals with the outside world in terms of perception we can find a self-organising system.

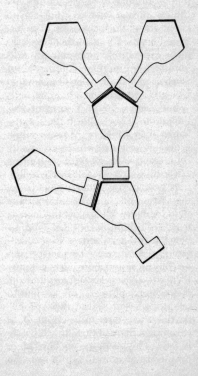

'All profit is justifiable because if something is worth doing then the worth must be somewhere discoverable in the result. This added worth we can call profit.' This is a typical example of word-play in which 'profit' and 'worth' are too easily ,equated. Most arguments and disputes are fundamentally about the meaning of words or semantics. For example someone else might argue about profit: 'All profit is theft because the surplus that is produced at the end of an operation must have been stolen from those whose efforts have contributed to its success.' Here 'profit' is equated with 'surplus'.

St Anselm's famous proof of the existence of God went as follows: 'God is perfect. Perfection must include existence otherwise it is lacking something and cannot be perfect. Therefore God must exist.' The argument is a circular semantic argument because it rests on the meaning already given to the words 'God' and 'perfection'.

Words are convenient packages of experience or ideas. When we play with words in an argument we tend to detach the word from its full meaning and to rely on a partial meaning. Obviously this partial meaning is not incorrect but it may convey less than the full meaning. A common semantic trick is to show a similarity in one area between two words and then to bring in the second word and employ all the other dissimilar meanings attached to it. For example: 'Men and women are equal human beings and therefore any difference or discrimination between them is to be condemned.' Here 'difference' and 'discrimination' are lumped together. Similarly men and women may be equal in their 'humanity' but not necessarily in their physical 'being'. Clearly men and women are physically different. Whether any discrimination should be based on this (given their equality as humans) is another matter. The argument is by no means wrong but it derives its force from semantic manipulation.

Another aspect of semantic play is concerned with vague but valued words such as 'rights', 'moral', 'unfair' and 'dishonest' which give a spurious concreteness to subjective feeling.

A person who is allergic to shellfish develops a rash or becomes violently ill every time he eats shellfish. It is easy enough to avoid eating shellfish directly but when they are an ingredient in a pilaff, stew or sauce they are often eaten unwittingly. Sensitivity to shellfish may be inborn but in many cases the person seems to become sensitised to them after eating some that have gone bad.

The Watergate scandal in the United States sensitised many people to corruption in government. Whereas a minor peccadillo would have been shrugged off as part of the game before Watergate, afterwards it would become front page news. When the reaction to something increases very sharply a process of sensitisation has probably taken place. After a political speech on race problems everyone becomes sensitised to the race issue: people start noticing the number of black or coloured faces on a bus or in a queue.

The diagram shows the relationship between money spent on recruiting advertising and the actual number of recruits for the armed services. A general fall in employment in the country sensitises the response so that the same amount of effort now results in a much bigger response. A substantial rise in pay may have the same effect.

Since most stable systems depend on communication and the effect of communication, especially in a feedback situation, the process of sensitisation can upset a relationship and unbalance the whole system. For example the delicate balance between saving and spending can be upset by the fear of unemployment. In order to provide a safety cushion in the event of becoming unemployed people tend to save more. This means less spending which in turn pushes the economy further into a recession so increasing the risk of unemployment.

A wife's jealousy may be sensitised by her finding a letter in a suit she is about to send to the cleaners. The sensitisation may be so acute that any behaviour on her husband's part becomes a cause for suspicion. If he is late home, if he has to spend a weekend travelling, if he has lunch with a woman client, these all have to be explained away in detail. Sensitisation can lead to over-reaction. The opposite of sensitisation is anaesthetisation.

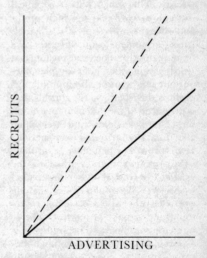

Everyone who works is on a workshop floor of one sort or another. A manager's office is a workshop for the particular sort of work that he does. By tradition, however, the term shop-floor seems to apply to the traditional work force which is thought to have no interest beyond a weekly wage in the production process. The concept is rather old-fashioned and tends to be used to suggest the voice of the unions or the unionised workers. In fact the voice of the shop-floor is more that of the shop stewards or local convenors who may or may not agree with centralised union policy.

If the management wants to install new machines it needs to discuss the matter with the men on the shop-floor who are going to be using the machines. Traditionally, however, the role of the shop-floor has been seen as one of objecting to change or being obstructive. Its role has been one of insisting on the rights of the workers and restraining the greed and exploitation of management. The time may have come, however, when the role of the shop-floor may have to be as constructive and as full of initiative as that of management. In Japan it is claimed that many decisions arise through direct shop-floor consultations amongst the workers. The decisions are then fed upwards to management and finally find their way down again as management decisions and policy. Other countries have different forms of consultation, some of them involving genuine consultation and others a mere tokenism.

Attitudes to industry have changed to the extent that industry is now seen as having two roles. The first is to supply the goods that will raise the standard of living of the general population at economic prices and with full efficiency. The second, but equal, role is to provide a livelihood for its work force. The point of clash occurs in the definition of the work force. Is it the present number of workers or the number that is needed for efficiency? Is automation acceptable if it decreases the number of workers but increases the job satisfaction of those who remain? If it is decided, as is usual, to allow the work force to decrease by not replacing those who leave, then how are youngsters to get jobs?

The concept of the shop-floor is now probably more of an obstruction than a help to industrial development.

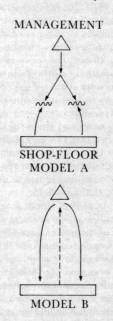

MANAGEMENT

SHOP-FLOOR
MODEL A

MODEL B

When the telegraph was first invented the British Admiralty rejected its use on the grounds that they were satisfied with the semaphore system of signalling from one hilltop to the next – using a version of the same code of arm movements kept up by Boy Scouts today. It seems likely that the railway signal is itself derived from the arm movements of the semaphore code. The Admiralty signals passed on signs which meant something to the person receiving them. The railway signal means something to the train driver. In both cases a standardised code has been set up so that a signal unlocks a packet of meaning.

Every now and then at bridge tournaments there are complaints that one or other team is cheating. It is claimed that the team has set up an elaborate signalling system to indicate the cards that are held: the way a cigarette is puffed; scratching one's nose or pulling at one's ears; shifting in the seat; moving one's gaze about the room. All sorts of natural activities can become signals once a code of meaning has been set up. A music hall mind-reader's assistant would take an object from a member of the audience and ask the mind-reader what it was. The blindfolded mind-reader on stage would identify the object. It all seemed uncanny but there was an elaborate code in the way the assistant framed his remarks: 'I am now holding up the object'; 'The object is now in my hand'; 'I have in my left hand this object'; 'Here is something which I have taken from a lady.'

Prearranged signs and signals can carry the most elaborate meanings. The sender knows what he intends to send and the receiver is on the lookout for the signal. It is a different matter when a husband and wife are out at a dinner party and the wife thinks it is time they went home. She tries signalling to her husband in various ways but he is enjoying himself and does not notice the signals because he is not looking out for them. A flirtatious woman learns the sort of signals that encourage a man's attentions. A perceptive man learns the signals of interest that are given unconsciously by a woman who is responding to his attentions. An economist is supposed to detect at an earlier stage than anyone else the signals that indicate a boom or a recession.

The sophists were paid philosophers in ancient Greece. They were paid to give lessons in logic and argument. It is very likely that the people who paid them simply wanted an audience to listen to their own ideas – since their friends probably refused to do so any longer. In this respect the sophists would be not unlike the modern psychoanalyst.

The sophists excelled in the skill of argument rather than the profundity of their thought. Most of the argument seems to have been in the nature of word-games: playing around with the nuances of meaning already implicit in a word and pretending to rediscover them through logical analysis. The sophists acquired a bad reputation for using fallacious arguments, although probably doing this no more than anyone else. Since sophists had no way of advertising their skills they must have relied a lot on professional denigration of their competitors. If you could claim that the other man's arguments were fallacious then that made you the better sophist. If everyone was doing this at the same time it is hardly surprising that the profession acquired a bad name.

Today a sophist is someone who uses intricate arguments to prove that black is white. A sophist is someone who places a greater emphasis on the form of the argument than on the content. A sophist is someone who will win an argument by forcing his opponent to defend it on the sophist's own grounds. This is usually done by insisting, at the outset, on a definition of terms: 'What do you mean exactly by justice?'; 'Define what you mean by equality.' The sophist persuades the unsuspecting opponent to adopt the definition which the sophist can then exploit. Very often there is no logical flaw at any point in the sophist's argument. But there may be many unwarranted assumptions that are taken as fact. There may also be a tendency to deal with only that small part of the total situation that can be seen to support the argument: 'Refugees are proud, they do not want help – it's an insult to help them.' The failure is not one of logic but of overall perception.

The reaction against logic which seems able to support any side of an argument by choosing the appropriate premises, is a reaction against sophistry.

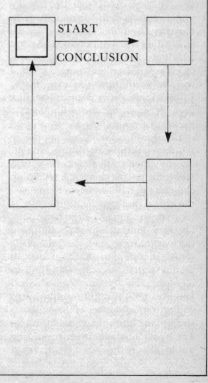

The difference between an expert and a specialist is that a specialist is looking forward in a certain well-defined direction and an expert is looking backwards in the same direction. A specialist goes on narrowing his field in order to increase his concentration of knowledge in an area. An expert is satisfied that he knows all there is to know and is trying to widen his field on the assumption that his expertise will widen with it.

It is often said that over ninety per cent of all scientists who ever lived are alive today. This indicates that the explosion of knowledge has been so colossal that there is room for all these thousands of scientists each of whom specialises in some area. The trend towards specialisation is inevitable. If you happen to be a semi-expert in three areas and someone else is an expert in only one area then he will get the job. After all if you have a brain tumour you want the expert brain surgeon not someone who is a semi-expert in brain surgery, heart surgery and breast surgery. In any field we go for the best because we see no reason why we should be satisfied with the second best. This is obvious. The problem arises in our definition of the fields of specialisation.

If you had a control problem which you felt needed electronic devices you would have gone to the electronics specialist who would have provided you with a suitable electronic control system to regulate the thickness of paper in your paper mill. But had you gone to a pneumatics specialist he would have provided you with a pneumatic control device that might have been more suitable in many ways. Each specialist functions perfectly in

his field – assuming you have made the right choice of field. But how is that choice made? If you have a pain in the eye you would go to an eye specialist but the pain may be due to some general illness. So perhaps you ought to have gone to the general doctor first. Similarly the man with the control problem ought to have gone to the 'control specialist' first.

So the way to overcome the problem created by our hunger for specialisation is to create a lot of new specialities which will be the generalist specialities. They will be specialities which cover other specialities and can make the right choice between these. But they will be specialities, not an absence of speciality.

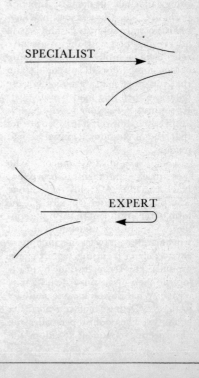

SPECIALIST

EXPERT

When white light is passed through a prism it separates out into the rainbow spectrum of colours: red, orange, yellow, green, blue, indigo, violet. Each colour represents a difference in the wavelength of the light.

There are people who seem to have definite opinions on everything. They either like things or they loathe them. They seem to see everything in black and white: they may be completely against socialism and completely for environmental protection. On any issue there are those who hold the black and white extreme views. But in between there may be a whole range of shades of grey. There may be a whole spectrum of grey responses ranging from a grey that is only just greyer than white to a grey that is almost black. There are people who are fervent churchgoers and who go regularly on every occasion. At the other extreme there are people who never voluntarily go to church even though they may be taken there when they are babies or are dead. In between the two extremes there lies a whole spectrum of churchgoing ranging from people who go quite often but not regularly to people who go only on very special occasions.

The human mind and the language it uses finds a spectrum of responses very difficult to deal with. If you are ordering a meal you cannot half order a steak because you half like steaks. A young man cannot half marry a girl because his love is somewhere along the spectrum from hate to ecstasy. People who occupy positions along the spectrum are said to be weak, dithering or undecided. Perhaps it is best to think as though there were a spectrum and act as though there were not.

It can be argued that a spectrum of responses really covers different situations and circumstances. Someone says he is not completely against pornography because he feels that it could be useful for some people. Someone else has an in-between response to military music because he likes the music but does not like the associations.

A spectrum covers a range of responses which shade one into the other without a definite boundary between them.

It used to be claimed that there had been considerable spin-off from such expensive programmes as the Apollo space missions and the Concorde supersonic airliner. It was pointed out that new ceramics had been developed and that these would be useful for cooking utensils. Another spin-off was a special material that was useful for making artificial heart valves.

It is thought that the planets originated by being spun off from the main body of the sun, to become entities on their own. The spin-off concept applies to things that happen in the course of development of something else but become useful in their own right.

There was a time when Route 128 near Boston was full of small, highly specialised, electronics companies which had been started by individuals who had been doing research at the Massachusetts Institute of Technology or Harvard University. These small enterprises were spin-offs from the laboratory work going on at these centres. The huge General Electric Company had a policy that any laboratory discovery which did not fit in with the main thrust of the research could be spun off into a separate company set up to develop and exploit the discovery.

A salesman goes to Japan to sell some machine tools. He is unsuccessful in his mission but in the aeroplane he makes friends with someone who tells him about a new textile technology. He follows this up and obtains the licence to use the technology in France. The spin-off from the trip has been useful even if the main purpose of the trip was not achieved.

In education we teach a range of traditional subjects not because we believe them to be useful but because as a spin-off we hope that we are training the pupils to think things out for themselves. Corporations tend to employ graduates not because they feel that university improves the person's mind but because the selection system that allowed them to get there in the first place must have picked out the brighter pupils. Which then is the spin-off: the selection or the university training?

Any change in circumstance or technology tends to give rise to spin-offs that can be utilised by those who are alert enough to notice them.

Hitherto the trend has been for industrial countries to go all out for expansion and growth. The increase in productivity has meant an increase in the material standard of living of the people in those countries. For example today one man can produce the food that required the agricultural effort of a thousand men two hundred years ago. Increasing worries about pollution, exhaustion of resources and the deteriorating quality of life have led many people to challenge the concept of growth and to replace it by the concept of stability. It is often not clear whether this means that all nations should stand still or whether the already-grown nations should stand still and allow the others to catch them up. If the latter is meant it is not certain that it is possible once the industrial nations stop growing.

The mechanisms of stability are varied. There can be stability through inertia when a system has so much inertia that nothing is likely to change it. The legal and educational systems in most countries have stability of this sort. There can be a stability which depends on a multiplicity of parallel structures. For instance it would be very difficult to upset a table if it were to have twenty separate legs. Such systems lack a sensitive point of change. Finally there is the stability which is brought about by negative feedback, such as the stability of biological systems. The system is a dynamic one with strong energy flow through a complex of interacting parts. Stability is maintained by a feedback system which operates to oppose any destabilising influences. In this manner through a huge number of feedback systems the human body achieves the stability necessary for survival (note for example the very small fluctuations permitted in body temperature).

As shown in the diagram the natural process of evolution passes through three stages. In the first stage there is randomness and the hexagon plates float about. By chance two of them adhere. This now makes it easier for other plates to adhere because they can fit into the 'corners'. This is the positive feedback stage. So the hexagon plate grows. But each plate releases a chemical which inhibits the stickiness of the plates. Eventually a stable size is reached and growth stops. This is the negative feedback or stable state.

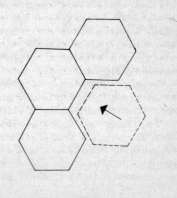

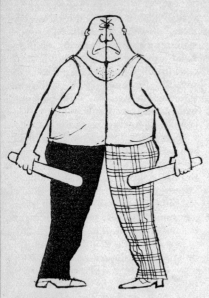

There is a hope that a future world war will be averted through the use of a nuclear stand-off. If both sides are well enough equipped to obliterate each other then it is clearly in the interest of neither side to start a war. As soon as one side appears to gain an advantage either in the power to deliver nuclear missiles or to resist them, the stand-off position can only be regained if the other side draws level again. This automatic escalation is never seen in absolute terms, simply in terms of the difference.

A stand-off occurs when two opposing sides both know that neither can win. There are many games in which the first player loses no matter what moves he makes. Each player is therefore reluctant to make the first move and there is a stand-off. Two giant corporations know that they could temporarily increase sales by cutting prices but each knows that a price-cut on one side will be matched by a price-cut on the other, so that no one gains in the end (except the consumer). A stand-off exists.

In any situation where offensive strength outstrips defensive strength a stand-off is likely to arise. If either side can use effective offensive weapons then there is no point in any side using them.

In the First World War the casualties were very much higher than in the Second World War. On one day alone on the Somme 60,000 Allied troops lost their lives. Trench warfare had reached a stand-off. Both sides were secure in their trenches but as soon as one side tried to advance it was decimated by enemy fire. It was precisely to avoid this situation that the German High Command developed the blitzkrieg tactics used in the Second World War, with Panzer-led spearheads penetrating deep into enemy territory.

In terms of import restrictions there is usually an economic stand-off between countries. If one of them imposes import controls the others retaliate and neither side gains an advantage.

There is a certain security in a stand-off situation but it is wasteful and little constructive is achieved.

Much of our thinking and most of our science is based on steady-state assumptions. We assume that things are neither increasing nor diminishing but will continue as they are. A man in good health is in a steady state (actually he is growing older every minute). A steady state implies that things will continue as they are unless there is some disturbance.

An empty space-rocket will continue to circle the earth in a steady state. There is no friction in space and nothing to alter its speed. The gravitational forces acting on it are likely to remain constant. In space because the distances are so vast and the forces so constant we can assume that things are in a steady state provided we operate over a relatively short time-period and distance. The calculations that landed men on the moon depended on predictable estimations of gravity and motion.

If you leave the plug out of a basin and turn on both taps a point will be reached when the water leaving the basin through the plug hole will equal the water coming through the taps. The level of water in the basin will appear to remain quite steady. This is another sort of steady state and bears a resemblance to the steady state that economists would like to see operating in the economy. The steadiness of the state is not invulnerable, however, for a slight occlusion of the drain may cause flooding.

A much more stable steady state is found in systems stabilised by means of negative feedbacks. Such systems are designed to preserve a more or less steady state in the face of events which would otherwise upset them. For example the temperature of the human body stays within narrow limits be-cause it is so stabilised. So does the blood pressure. If the blood pressure tends to rise it increases the discharge from a pressure-sensing mechanism in the major arteries. This inhibits the tone of the blood vessels so allowing them to dilate and lower the pressure.

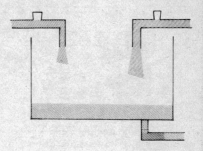

There is a fundamental difference between the English term for 'driving' a car and the Italian term *guidare*. To 'drive' something implies that the driver is providing a great deal of effort to make a reluctant creature move in a certain direction. It seems to need both hands tightly on the steering wheel and a grim expression of determination. In contrast the term *guidare* suggests that the creature has power and sensitivity and that it is willing to go the way you want it to go provided you treat it with sensitivity and understanding and lightly indicate the direction. The image is that of a driver weaving in and out of the traffic with one hand, or even one finger, nonchalantly on the steering wheel.

Steering implies a control of direction but no element of motive power. It is assumed that whatever is being steered is sufficiently equipped with its own driving force. A steering committee is not supposed to involve itself with details of day to day survival but with changes in direction and policy.

Steering is part of control but does not imply total control. Decisions as to starting, stopping and accelerating are made elsewhere.

The ingredients required for successful steering include an agreed general direction: in which direction is the river being navigated – indeed which river is being navigated? There should be some ability to see the river bank or if this is shrouded in fog to consult a chart. It is possible to steer by proceeding until the ship gently bumps a bank or scrapes the bottom and then taking correcting action, but it is dangerous and inefficient (although many organisations operate this way). Finally there ought to be some response from the steering mechanism. The effect of a delayed response with all its dangers has been described elsewhere (see 'Hunting', 'Lag-time'). There is, however, the additional possibility of a dummy steering wheel like those toy ones provided for children to use in cars so that they can enjoy the illusion of steering something that is being otherwise directed.

No one can be slightly pregnant. A woman is either pregnant or she is not.

The diagram shows a graph relating two things. We usually expect the relationship to be such that if 'a' increases 'b' will also increase. For example if we give people more food then their weight will increase. Sometimes the relationship takes the form of a step or jump. At first nothing happens, then it all happens in a rush, then nothing happens until the next step. Imagine you are dropping a bottle of water from a height and measuring the dampness of the ground. At first you drop the bottle and nothing happens. The ground remains dry. You increase the height and still nothing happens. But eventually a point is reached when the bottle breaks. The water escapes and the ground is saturated.

A child is rocking backwards and forwards on his chair at the breakfast table. Suddenly he passes the point of no return and falls over backwards.

Marketing people believe that the relationship between prices and sales are a type of step-function. You reduce the price and nothing much happens. You reduce it further and suddenly sales increase considerably. You reduce it further and nothing much happens and then you reduce it further and again there is an increase in sales. It is supposed that there are different price brackets that the buyer has in mind. When the price moves from one bracket to another sales increase but movement within the same price bracket has much less effect.

In many countries social class is a step-function. You may earn more and more money and stay within the same class. Suddenly you earn a little more

(or make a slightly different use of it) and you find yourself apparently in a different class.

The advertising revenue of magazines usually works in a step-function manner. Advertisers think in terms of number brackets (10,000; 100,000; 500,000; 1,000,000, etc) and pay accordingly. It is more natural for the human mind to think in step-function terms.

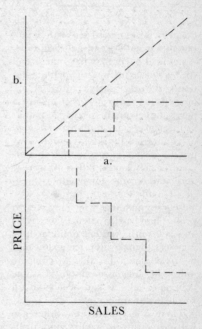

Strategy is not concerned with detail, but rather with broad policy outline. A political party may have the broad strategy of saying nothing definite but letting the other party create enemies, in the belief that voters vote against a party rather than for it. A manufacturer may have the broad strategy of aiming for the high-volume, low-profit type of sales. Another manufacturer may have a different strategy and aim for the low-volume, high-profit luxury market.

One toy manufacturer may seek to protect his ideas by patents, copyrights and law suits. Another manufacturer may seek to make his prices so low that no rival would be able to compete unless he was assured of the same volume of sales as had been built up by the first manufacturer.

There is a considerable difference between strategy, tactics and drift. Drift means floating on the tide of circumstance, making efforts only to stay afloat and to cope with immediate problems. Many successful organisations operate a drift approach even though they do not admit it. The approach is successful when the current is flowing in the right direction. Tactics are concerned with short-term problem solving and short-term objectives. If drift is concerned with survival, tactics are concerned with opportunism. Long-term policy and direction are the province of strategy. Strategy sketches the outlines of the plan which is then implemented by tactics which are themselves influenced by day to day conditions. Having an overall strategy is not without danger. The stronger the strategy the less likely is it to be changed when circumstances suggest that a new strategy is necessary. There is something of a dilemma here for if a strategy is sufficiently flexible it may be no more than tactics and yet if it is not flexible it may be a cage (especially since strategies have to be planned ahead with many assumptions and extrapolations). Nevertheless we use knives even though we know that the misuse of them can be dangerous, even lethal.

Nero and Diocletian were both Roman emperors but the way each ruled Rome was very different. Rome had a system of government with a place for an emperor. Such was its structure. What actually happened depended on what sort of person occupied this place. The diagram shows a simple structure in which one superior position controls other lesser positions. This structure is independent of the people or things that might occupy the places.

A motor car is a mechanical structure made of specially shaped pieces of metal put together in a special way. What happens to this structure depends on what fuel is put into the tank and what sort of driver takes the wheel. A trained driver will drive carefully but a person who cannot drive might crash into the first lamp-post. It is true that the structure of the car, in terms of horse-power, brakes and steering sensitivity, will also affect the way it is driven but the influence of the driver is still strong. Together the driver and the car form a system. A structure is the background to a system.

A ladder is a structure and so is a teacup. Both are 'opportunity' structures because they make something easier. Other structures are 'restrict-ing' and insist that something be done in only one way. All government forms provide this sort of structure.

A structure is made up of places, positions, points, channels of communication, hierarchies and procedures. These conditions are neutral but some structures permit only certain types of behaviour within themselves. For instance the voting system in the United Kingdom tends to preserve the two-party system. A change in structure would be required before a third party could emerge.

In summary a structure is like an egg-cup into which a variety of eggs can be inserted but all of which end up in the same condition.

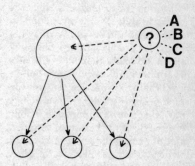

Style is important but intangible. We can recognise it and say a lot about it, except what it really is. Some painters have a style that is easily recognisable: the elongated figures of El Greco, the oval faces of Modigliani, the dream-like quality of Chagall are very easy to identify. We expect a style to be recognisable and that is why we tend to look on style as something that stands out or is different or flamboyant. Each person is his own style of being but because it is difficult to distinguish the behaviour of one ordinary person from another ordinary person we reserve the term style for the extra-ordinary. Yet when we get to know a person well enough we may detect his own individual style.

Consistency is probably the key element in style. Whatever is done fits into the established style. We may not be able to predict exactly what will happen any more than we could predict what a painter will paint, but we may be able to predict the style in which it will be done. Consistency means that the way something is done fits the style of the person or situation but it also means that each part of what is done fits in exactly with all the other parts. It is this fitting together that establishes the style. An interior decorator will have her own style: browns and whites; folk-art; or dramatic purples. There is consistency both in the way the style is used on every occasion and also in the way the different elements fit together to make up the style.

We sometimes talk of style in terms of a type. We may talk of the Western style of dress or the democratic style of government. But style is different from type. A lion is a type of animal and so is an elephant. Style means the putting together of elements in one particular way when there are very many other ways available. The difference lies not in the elements but in their use. This is where style starts to approach the basic pattern of organisation that underlies both biological and physical systems, and indeed the whole structure of the universe. That is why style is so important a word.

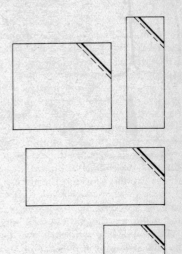

Philosophers had always been proud of the conscious mind because man's mind was really man. Descartes went so far as to say: 'I think, therefore I exist.' Freud complicated the matter by introducing a fashion for the subconscious which has become more and more entrenched. Nowadays the conscious mind is regarded as something of a window dressing for the true nature of the psyche which lurks threateningly in the subconscious.

The beauty of Freud's approach was that it denied to any person the possibility of knowing what really went on in his mind. What the person considered to be his conscious thoughts were only a disguise for the true subconscious feelings. If a person loved his father this could be a cover up for the guilt feelings that arose from his subconscious hatred of his father. If a person appeared to hate his father this could be a reaction to a subconscious love that had been frustrated. Only the psychoanalyst could sort it out for you.

Surprisingly many people rather liked this shift of responsibility to the subconscious mind. It meant that there was a possibility of uncovering a more interesting person than the one who appeared on the surface. It meant too that there was a chance of overcoming problems and weakness by revealing their subconscious basis. It meant that a person could become properly self-indulgent by making a study of his subconscious without appearing to be narcissistic. All over the United States different schools of dredgers promise to reveal the true self by breaking through the superficial persona that has been built around a sensitive ego to protect it from society.

At its most extreme the cult of the subconscious approaches the ridiculous but the basic notion that the subconscious mind contains unformulated emotions and experiences that influence our behaviour seems reasonable enough. Whether the supposed revelation of these influences actually removes them is another matter. Perhaps the creation of a subconscious scenario, whether it is true or false, provides a belief structure to support behaviour. Such a structure can be reacted against, followed, blamed or simply enjoyed.

As part of a famous experiment a series of rapid flashes advertising an ice cream were inserted in the middle of a film. The flashes were so quick that no one noticed them consciously. Yet at the interval there was an appreciable rise in ice cream sales. The potential of such a phenomenon for advertising and political indoctrination is so huge that in most countries there are rules and safeguards that prevent its use.

It is thought that when we can see a political message or an advertising slogan we can react against it and discount it, but if we do not even see it then we are supposed to have no defences. Clearly if we do not see it there could be no reaction or defence to multiple use of the message.

Subliminal communication operates like conditioning to by-pass our conscious minds. The cinema flashes were too quick for the conscious mind to grasp so the by-pass was achieved by speed. In other circumstances the conscious mind might be so distracted by something else that the subliminal message can slip through without being consciously noted. It is doubtful if subliminal communication could ever give complete messages but it could be used to build up associations. For instance a repeated subliminal communication that associated a brand of cigarette with a beautiful girl might build up an undefined attractiveness for that brand.

A husband has been slimming but his wife notices no obvious change in weight. They then visit his mother whom they have not seen for six months. At once the mother notices the loss in weight and blames her daughter-in-law for not feeding her son properly. Close contact with a situation prevents a person from noticing something that is happening very gradually. It is only if there is a gap in time that the change becomes big enough to be noticed. This sort of gradual change is also subliminal in that at each moment the change is too small to become conscious.

As with conditioning the fear is that development and use of these techniques can make people into robots who obey central commands without any consciousness of their subservience. They seem to be doing what they want to do but their actions have been conditioned or subliminally determined.

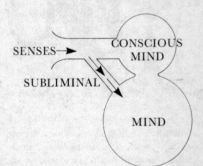

For two thousand years the syllogism was the only respectable form of logical reasoning, ever since Aristotle gave it currency in about 350 BC. The syllogism was polished, re-packaged and re-marketed by St Thomas Aquinas, the great thirteenth-century thinker who set down the logical lines of reasoning to be followed by the Church. Since in those days the Church controlled most of education and culture, syllogistic reasoning also dominated thinking throughout the Western world.

Man is mortal
John is a man
Therefore John is mortal.

Wages are an important ingredient in the cost of manufacture
Selling price is related to cost of manufacture
So if wages rise prices are likely to rise as well.

If two statements are both true then a third statement can often be made with a conclusion that is based on the other two statements. If A is related to B and B is related to C, then A is related to C.

A syllogism never gets beyond what is already implicit in the statements and what has been taken for granted in the words that are used. For instance in the example given above, to say that man is mortal is not very important since 'mortality' is an essential part of our concept of man. It is rather like saying: 'That which we know to be mortal is mortal.' Nevertheless as a device for making explicit a third truth which can be deduced (or is implicit) in two other truths the syllogism is useful.

Because the syllogism is so simple and powerful a logical device it can give the appearance of proof to what in fact are fallacies.

Men are physically stronger than women
John is a man and Anne is a woman
Therefore John is stronger than Anne.

The various possible types of fallacy have been carefully described by philosophers. The syllogism becomes less serviceable when it is a matter of dealing with probability and likelihood rather than definite statements of fact.

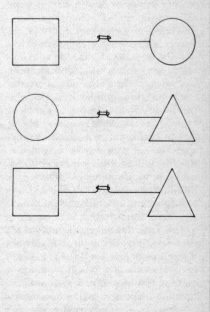

A person loses weight and finds that he is passing a lot of urine. The doctor recognises the symptoms of diabetes. Another person finds she is getting very irritable, is losing weight, has a huge appetite and cannot stand warm weather. The doctor recognises the symptoms of an overactive thyroid gland. In medicine it is often possible to work out the mechanism that accounts for the symptoms but such understanding and explanation is quite recent. Before that a doctor would recognise that a certain cluster of symptoms meant a certain disease without ever knowing the cause of the symptoms. It was a matter of habit and pattern recognition based on personal experience or the experience of one's teacher or the experience recorded in textbooks.

Whenever we suspect a disease – that is whenever something is not to our liking – we begin to look for symptoms that will confirm our suspicions. Is the rise in interest rates a symptom of worsening inflation? Is the fall in the bullion price of gold a symptom of economic recovery? Is the lack of applicants for a senior government job a symptom of a general distaste for politics? Is the rise of spending on gambling a symptom of social irresponsibility? Is the rise in teenage crime a symptom of impending urban disintegration?

The importance of a symptom is nothing to do with the actual nature of the symptom but with the meaning that our minds give to it. If we assume that the first insignificant swallow is a symptom of spring then the importance of spring is quite different from the importance of the swallow as a swallow. Since most of the time we are trying to deal with the future before it deals with us there is a hunger for symptoms that will allow us better to understand what is going to happen. Unfortunately in most cases there is no way of distinguishing a genuine symptom from a spurious one created only by a person's readiness to treat it as a symptom. Perhaps there should be an official clearing house for symptoms so that only 'recognised' symptoms could be claimed as such. But this would not work because, everyone having been made equal, the smarter operators would now start talking of pre-symptoms which presage the symptoms that are about to appear.

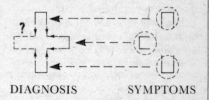

DIAGNOSIS   SYMPTOMS

In medicine there are certain well-recognised conditions we call diseases: measles, rheumatoid arthritis, gout, duodenal ulcer, diabetes. In addition there are certain rarer combinations of features which are given the name syndromes. For example in the Zollinger-Ellison syndrome excess secretion from the pancreas causes diarrhoea and multiple peptic ulcers in the stomach.

In a diabetic coma the blood sugar level is usually high since it is the failure of the insulin mechanism that has led to the coma in the first place. But there is a syndrome in which the coma is accompanied by a level of blood sugar that is not especially elevated. The distinction between a disease and a syndrome is a narrow one. If the special features occur together as a constellation within a disease group then we call it a syndrome. If the features occur together and appear to combine elements from different diseases we also call it a syndrome. If the features occur together and we are not sure how definite the relationship is we call it a syndrome at first and then when the relationship is clear we may call it a disease.

Political writers can easily recognise the 'reluctant candidate' syndrome in which a politician protests that he does not want a particular office so long and loud that it is clear that he wants to tell people that he is actually in the running. Estate agents can recognise the syndrome of the house buyer who looks at house after house but is actually unable to buy any of the houses he looks at. Pathological lying is another syndrome in which a person becomes addicted to telling lies even when there is nothing to be gained. Anorexia nervosa is a very serious syndrome affecting young women and involving a refusal to eat. These young women often start by dieting and then acquire a distaste for food. They lose weight and can easily starve themselves to death.

Whenever a pattern of events or features starts to be recognisable as something in itself we can talk of a syndrome. There is a danger in regarding all behaviour in terms of syndromes: the spoiled child, the lazy child, the hyperactive child, the deprived child and so on. It is better to be slow to recognise syndromes than too fast.

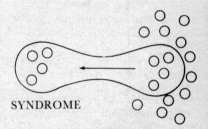

SYNDROME

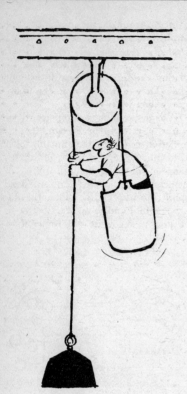

It is only in the last few decades that we have begun to understand the nature of systems. We have a very long way to go. The major advances in our understanding of science, society and ourselves will depend on our ability to cope with systems. We are used to dealing with things and with concepts as if they were packets of frozen vegetables awaiting our interest and our cooking. Systems, however, are quite oblivious of our attention and carry on according to their own nature.

The main purpose of most systems is to survive. This is because most systems have come about through a process of evolution which has depended on chance, self-organisation and success. Systems can have subsystems which have the purpose of contributing to the survival of the major system.

A system is more than a structure. A system is more than an accumulation of the parts that go into it. The diagram shows how A affects B which in turn affects C. For its part, C affects D but also affects the way A affects B. Through D, C also affects A again. It is the combination of all these interactions that make up the system.

A system is the total of all the parts and the way they affect each other. Traditionally, in our thinking and in our culture we have shied away from systems and done our best to destroy any understanding of them. This habit arose from the concern of the Greek philosophers with analysis. If you break a system down into its separate parts you destroy the system as surely as if you were to chop a person into pieces in order to see how he works. As soon as the parts are separated their interaction ceases.

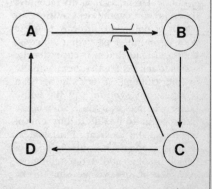

When Napoleon invaded Russia, various battles, big and small, were fought. There were also skirmishes and local advances and retreats. All these were part of the tactics of the war. The overall strategy of the Russian general was, however, to draw Napoleon into Russia so that his lines of supply would be over-extended and the war could be prolonged into winter. For that reason he refused to commit his forces in a major battle or to regard the occupation of Moscow as a defeat.

Moment to moment tactics are important. They are not just a matter of occupying time until the strategy takes effect. The strategy is carried out by means of the tactics. The tactics have two purposes: to carry forward the overall strategy and to respond to the situation of the moment.

A government may have an overall strategy of inactivity. It may do nothing about a devaluation of its currency because it knows that such a devaluation will help exports and that a devaluation imposed upon it will not be followed by reciprocal devaluations elsewhere (as would a deliberate devaluation). Nevertheless, from day to day there may be speeches, conferences, commissions and the like which carry out the tactics of the operation.

A company may have an overall marketing strategy. The implementation of this strategy will involve day to day tactics as regards personnel, incentives, product price changes, advertising.

In a long distance race the strategy of one runner might be to tire his major rival. To do this he may use different tactics: setting a fast pace; varying the pace; sticking close to the rival and

making him run faster and faster.

In war it is easy: generals have strategies and colonels use tactics. In ordinary life a person may himself have to set the strategy and also devise the tactics for carrying it out.

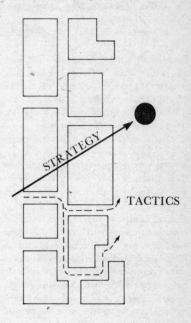

An athlete doing the high jump and an aircraft have in common the fact that they both leave the ground. But there is a crucial difference. The athlete leaves the ground when he wants to. The aircraft leaves the ground when its speed is such that it becomes airborne. In the athlete's case it is an intention whereas in the aircraft's case the situation has reached a point where the aircraft has to leave the ground.

A clothing manufacturer is trying to launch a new fashion. He spends more and more on advertising and public relations. Suddenly the fashion takes off: everyone wants the garments and he cannot keep up with the supply. He does not need to spend any more money on advertising since the people buying and wearing the clothes have themselves become walking advertisements. The take-off point has been reached and the project is off the ground. On another occasion the take-off point may never be reached and the project may stay on the ground in spite of any amount of investment.

Every now and again a group of people try to start a new political party or a new religion. They are usually unsuccessful. The take-off point is seldom reached. The take-off point occurs when a project is self-fuelling. It no longer needs to be pushed; as it proceeds it generates the fuel for it to proceed further. A new product reaches the take-off point when the revenue coming in from sales is enough to fuel the advertising and provide a profit (and to pay for expanding production).

A motor car engine will not start on a cold morning. The driver gets out and pushes the car towards a down-hill slope. It is hard work. Suddenly the work starts to get easier and the car starts to roll down the slope. The driver quickly gets in. In practice the take-off point is as real and as tangible as the sensation felt by the driver when the car started rolling of its own accord.

The problem is to decide how much more effort and investment is necessary to reach the take-off point, or whether to cut one's losses instead.

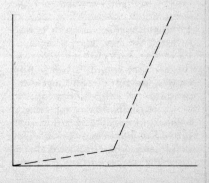

Technology is landing men on the moon; developing a telephone system that will allow a person in England to dial a person in Australia; developing strains of wheat and rice that are more resistant to diseases and yield several times as much per acre as the older strains. The luxuries and standard of living of developed society depend very largely on the huge increases in productivity in agriculture brought about by technology. Over the last two hundred years there has been an almost thousandfold increase in agricultural productivity (the amount that can be produced by one man) brought about by the use of machinery, fertilisers and new strains of crop.

Science is the pursuit of knowledge: an attempt to understand the basic laws of nature. Technology is an attempt to put this knowledge to good use. The traditional view that technology is the application of science is misleading. Very often it is technology that takes the initiative. The development of the petrol engine and subsequently of the motor car did not await a thorough understanding of the physics of exploding petrol–air mixtures. The development went ahead, step by step, from the finding that an exploding gas–air mixture could drive a gas engine. The development of special materials for springs and engines in cars was usually a combination of science and technological experimentation. In contrast the development of nuclear energy depended entirely on the impetus given by science in the first place.

Technology is directed towards problem solving. In the course of solving specific problems general principles may be derived. For example Norbert Wiener's development of cybernetics arose from solving the problem of accuracy of anti-aircraft fire. Today it is no longer so certain that the route of pure scientific investigation is the best route for the advancement of science. It may have been so in the days when technology was primitive.

Technology has its own momentum: once something is found possible then the next stage is also possible (bigger or faster). In their attack on the desirability of such momentum many people attack the notion of technology itself, forgetting that even a horse and plough is technology. Technology is only a direction; it should not be difficult to redefine this direction for social ends.

A child is cutting little figures of men out of newspaper. There are at least four ways he can proceed. He can go ahead and create an outline of a new man each time with his scissors. He can draw the outlines of men on the paper first: either free-hand or by careful measurement. Using a piece of carbon paper he can follow the outline of a master man and so transfer this to the paper. Finally he can use as a template the figure of a man cut out of cardboard. He holds this on the paper and cuts around it.

In the construction of a boat, either model or full scale, a builder may make use of a template which is held against the side of the hull at certain places to indicate the curvature which the hull should achieve.

A template is like an external mould. Normally material is poured into a mould so that when the mould is removed the material has taken the form of the mould. A template carries the form that is to be achieved but it is held against the object to be shaped and the shape is adjusted until it matches the template.

This moulding activity of a template is shown by the remarkable DNA process in the human body. Proteins are produced by means of a DNA template which consists of a number of different positions which can hold different amino-acids. Held in these positions the amino-acids link together to form a protein which then floats free of the template. This process can be repeated again and again, producing an endless number of identical proteins.

The purpose of a template is to produce repetition. It is a guide to the repeating of some shape or form that is regarded as useful. Even in itself the template is useful (whatever the shape) because it removes the need for decision at each stage. The template sets the pattern: it is then easier to follow the pattern than to create a new one. Our habits, ideas, experiences and perceptions become templates to shape the way we interact with the world around us.

Something which was never intended as a template can become a template or model for behaviour if there is no other available. Imitation is the easiest of the learning processes.

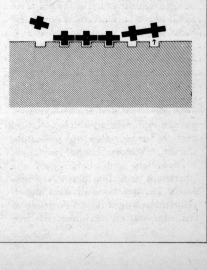

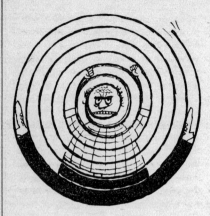

There is tension in the office following a public argument between two of the executives. There is racial tension in a city following the stabbing of a black student. There is tension in a prison following a break-out. Tension suggests energy coiled like a watch spring but likely to explode into violence. Where energy cannot follow through into immediate action it tends to pile up pending the opportunity for action. The energy has usually been created by events but has not yet been dissipated by a follow-through to such events.

Both teams in a tug-of-war may be so evenly matched that the rope is stationary and to a distant observer nothing seems to be happening. And yet the tension in the rope is totally different from that in a stationary guard-rope hanging between supports. In the tug-of-war any change in the fine balance leads quickly to violent action.

Tension is the best preparation for action. Human muscles have a special system that keeps the tension in them right for immediate action. In be-tween action the muscles are not floppy or relaxed but in a state of ready tension. An actor is tense before going on stage. An athlete is tense before running a race.

Up to a point tension is helpful but beyond that point it interferes because the amount of energy released when action becomes possible is excessive. An over-tense person is stiff and awkward and performs badly.

Tension and stress in daily life are said to be responsible for such illnesses as high blood pressure, heart disease, thyroid disease and headaches. If the reaction to events such as a quarrel or frustration cannot be dissipated in action then tension builds up. Because this results in the body being permanently ready for flight or fight a strain is put on the system.

Tension is a reservoir of energy. It is a pity that the human body does not have a more effective way of storing psychic energy.

A doctor can sometimes cure a disease with as much finality as a mathematician can solve a problem. A child has a throat infection caused by the streptococcus germ. The doctor treats this with penicillin which kills the germ and the condition is cured. At other times the doctor's treatment does not actually cure the condition but simply makes things better: a person suffering from hay fever takes an anti-histamine which reduces the unpleasant symptoms; a person with osteo-arthritis takes some pain-killers which relieve the pain but do not cure the arthritis.

Every now and again a psychiatrist writes a book about the therapeutic value of quarrels in a marriage. The expression of emotion and feeling is supposed to prevent the marriage getting worse and help to improve it.

Economists are more naturally inclined to diagnosis than to therapy. The basis of much of our thinking is that if we can understand something thoroughly then the cure for a problem will be obvious. We put the emphasis on understanding, analysis and description. What we forget is that often the need for treatment can be urgent and cannot await a fuller understanding of the disease. For years doctors used the drug digitalis, which comes from the foxglove, in the treatment of heart disease. They found the drug to be effective even though the doctors had no idea what heart disease really was or how the drug worked. Even today, after an immense amount of research, we do not quite understand why a failing heart leads to retention of fluid with oedema of the legs. But from the beginning the effect of the foxglove on reducing this 'dropsy' (as the oedema was called)

was noticed. Tons of aspirin are used every year and yet we do not know exactly why aspirin works. There are times when action is called for and therapy is needed. Trial and error and chance observation are not very satisfactory as a means of deciding therapy but they may be all we have available in some situations.

Are your inclinations diagnostic or therapeutic? This question might well be asked of anyone who had to deal with a situation. Are you going to describe it or do something to put it right?

DISEASE

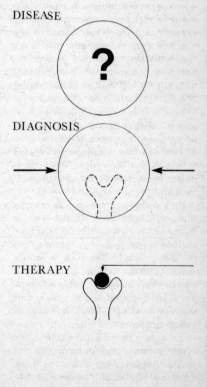

DIAGNOSIS

THERAPY

We think of the threshold as the doorstep of the house and over this threshold the bridegroom carries his bride. Once the threshold has been crossed then it becomes a different scene: the bride was supposed to become docile and helpful but often became a tyrant; the husband was supposed to become a good provider but could become a brute. Writers are always talking about the world being on the threshold of a new era (whether the symptom be computers, atomic energy or the plural family). Threshold is more than just a boundary it is a boundary which, if crossed, leads to a different state of affairs.

Greyhounds are surprisingly docile and tolerant. A young child can crawl all over a greyhound and pull its tail. Suddenly the greyhound will make a mock snap at the child as a warning that the accumulated irritation has reached a threshold and if the irritation continues the dog will take action. There is a build-up to a threshold for action. Complaints pour in about a certain employee. At first nothing happens but then the threshold of tolerance is passed and he gets fired. A government department does nothing until public opinion builds up and the threshold is reached when suddenly all is action (or at least pretended action).

The diagram shows a doorstep again. The river has flooded and the road is full of water. The level of water rises. The house is still perfectly dry. Then the threshold is reached and the water pours over the step and the house is flooded.

The nerves in our brain and in our body work on a threshold basis. Electrical stimulation builds up at the point where one nerve impinges on another. When the stimulation exceeds the threshold the second nerve fires and so carries the message on to another nerve.

Resentment may quietly build up until the threshold is reached and action or revolution follows. Because nothing is happening does not mean that nothing is happening.

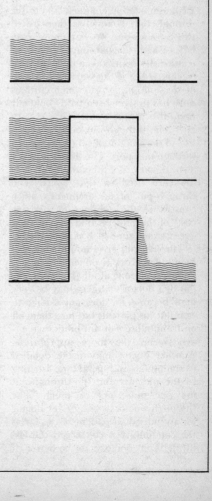

Through-put is similar to turn-over and traffic: it refers to the quantity that is put through a certain process. In a magazine office the through-put of feature ideas may be enormous. The same may be true of an advertising agency. In contrast the through-put of new ideas in a government department may be small while the through-put of work may be large.

Through-put treats any situation as a communication channel. The traffic through that channel is then called the through-put. A warehouse may have a high through-put if goods are continually being taken out and then replaced. But if the warehouse is full of alcoholic liquor on which customs duty has not yet been paid (bonded) then the through-put may be very low. The through-put of a port consists of the amount of cargo that passes through that port. The through-put of a court consists of the number of cases that are tried in that court. The through-put of an architect's office consists of the volume (or perhaps cost) of the projects that are handled over a stated time such as a year.

Through-put gives no indication of how much work is done, or whether any work is done at all. The through-put of a doctor's surgery may be very high because he does not bother to examine his patients but puts them all on tranquillisers or antibiotics whichever seems the more appropriate. Another doctor may make detailed examinations and spend time listening to the patients and his through-put may be only half as much. The thorough doctor is the better doctor for an individual patient but as far as the community is concerned the fast through-put doctor may be better (if

there is a shortage of doctors).

It is possible to talk of a through-put of decisions. One person in a position to make decisions may never make any. He is replaced by another person whose through-put of decisions is very high, both in clearing the backlog and in moving ahead.

A high through-put is the opposite of a bottleneck. And yet a high through-put at one stage may show up as a bottleneck further downstream. If the right side of the heart achieves a slightly higher through-put than the left side there is congestion in the lungs and what is called heart failure.

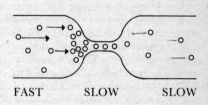

FAST   SLOW   SLOW

Suppose you lived in a country where you had to get a special permit to travel from one town to another; where you could not decide to go and look for work in that town without specific permission which was unlikely to be granted. In this country wages would be controlled centrally and so would prices. The type and quality of goods in the shops would also be controlled. Literature and the press would also be controlled. A writer would have to belong to a writer's club and there would be restrictions on what he wrote. Scientists would be told what to work on. In fact almost everything would be controlled by the state in a totalitarian country.

Just as a human body is made up of individual cells each of which carries out its appointed task for the good of the body as a whole so in a totalitarian state each member carries out the task that is going to benefit the total body of the state. In return the efficient functioning of the state will ensure stability and security in his own life just as the cells in a healthy body are fed with nutrients by the blood stream.

The totalitarian state would regard individuals who wished to pursue their own ambitions much as the body would regard cells that started to go their own way: as potential sources of cancer.

We all drive on a certain side of the road (even though this differs from country to country) so that traffic will flow smoothly. For the same reason we obey traffic signs and traffic lights. We give up some freedoms in order to enjoy the freedom to move about safety in a car. In Switzerland there are no conductors on the trams to check that the correct fare is paid. It is left to people's honesty to pay the fare. By obeying this rule the cost of running the trams is lowered and so presumably the fare is lowered. Most people accept the payment of taxes because they realise that some things such as police and defence have to be catered for centrally. The problem is to decide how much control and how much freedom are allowable. What is the right balance between the efficient functioning of the state and personal happiness? Is it possible that in some cases a little inefficiency is allowable because to remove it would mean much loss in personal happiness and the enjoyment of life? If there would be fewer accidents if all cars were painted yellow should the state insist on that colour for all cars? Does the state or do people come first?

The management of an insurance company is worried about the efficiency of the organisation. They feel that they are not giving the public a good enough service. There are several ways in which they could test the efficiency of the organisation. They could ask for complaints from the public; they could check the work at each level; or they could use tracers. The management could arrange to send in their own applications and claims forms using fictitious names. These would be the tracers. By seeing how these tracers were handled the management could obtain a good idea of what was happening.

Gunners shooting at night find it difficult to tell where their fire is going, so tracer bullets were invented. These glowed as they flew through the air and so the gunner or his observer could see a stream of 'fire' moving towards the target.

A tracer is something that is put into the system to show up what is happening. The major use of tracers is probably in the medical world. It is very difficult to look inside the body and see what is happening. This is especially so of its chemistry. But if you put in a chemical of your own which is almost identical to the one used in the body and can follow this about then you can trace what is happening. Usually this chemical is identical to the one normally used by the body with the difference that it is very slightly radioactive. This radioactivity makes it possible to follow the chemical around and to measure it. For example radioactive iodine is given to a patient with suspected thyroid disease in a very small dose. This may become concentrated in small areas in the thyroid gland. This gives an indication of the activity of the gland and also whether there are any 'hot nodules'.

The principle of a tracer is that it is treated by the system in a completely normal way but can nevertheless be detected by the user. Birds and fish such as salmon are often tagged with small metal tags. Such tagged creatures become tracers insofar as a later recovery of a tag can tell something of their movement and migration.

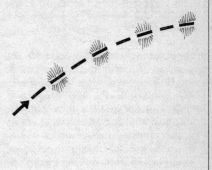

Trade-off is a very important word even though we rarely use it. The world runs on a trade-off principle though we always pretend it does not. Trade-off suggests a bargaining procedure as in a Turkish bazaar. The carpet seller gradually comes down in price and the customer gradually goes up in price until a level is reached at which the customer is prepared to give up something (his money) in exchange for something else (the carpet). A trade, deal or bargain has been reached.

Everyone believes that the maximum effort is made to reduce road accident deaths which form the major cause of death in most industrialised countries up to the age of forty-five. But the maximum effort is not made. We know that if all traffic crawled at five miles an hour there would be very few accident deaths so a maximum effort would involve a speed limit of five miles per hour. But such a speed limit would obstruct communication and production and make life in a complex society almost impossible. So we give up the extra safety of the low speed limit for the necessary convenience of a much higher speed limit. In fact we operate a trade-off between speed and safety.

In the diagram a tall and somewhat unstable tower of bricks is shown. This is then changed to a more stable structure. The more stable structure is not so tall. There has been a trade-off between height and stability. All business and all government runs on a trade-off principle though we dare not admit it. A toy manufacturer may want to go on improving the quality of a toy. But the cost would go up and the price would go up until he had the perfect toy that was so expensive that no one could buy it. So there is a trade-off between quality and price and the most successful toy manufacturer is one who can provide the highest quality at a reasonable price. By spending much more on education, hospitals and the police any government could provide a greatly enhanced public service but people would be unwilling or unable to pay the requisite high taxes. So there is a trade-off between cost and effectiveness.

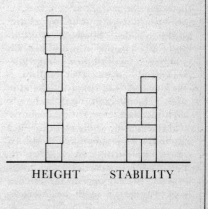

HEIGHT   STABILITY

There may never be any traffic along a particular stretch of road that links an isolated cottage to the hospital. The communicating channel is there but there is no traffic through it. On the other hand there is a great deal of traffic flowing over the harbour bridges in Sydney and San Francisco. The existence of a communication channel and the use that is made of it are two different things. There is a potential communicating channel between members of the public and their representative in Congress or in Parliament. Everyone can send a letter as often as they like. But there may not be much traffic flowing along the communication channel. Some telephone lines carry a lot of traffic, others carry very little.

A road may be built to cope with the traffic in an area. Experience has also shown that once a road is widened this not only copes with existing traffic but actually generates more traffic since drivers abandon other roads in order to use the one that has been newly widened.

The type of traffic flowing along a road may vary. At some time of day there may be mainly private cars, at other times there may be trucks and goods vehicles. Similarly a communication channel in an organisation may have a lot of traffic flowing along it although no one ever bothers to check on the type. It may be found to consist chiefly of 'orders' and only rarely of ideas.

Traffic is a convenient way of referring to the actual use that is made of a communication link. A 'message' or 'signal' refers to a particular use just as a car or a truck is a particular user of a road. Traffic is a more general term and refers to the general use. Traffic bears the same relationship to message that people bears to person.

When dealing with roads we rightly pay attention to traffic more than roads. But in almost all other fields we pay more attention to the communication channel itself than to the traffic using it.

CHANNEL OR ROAD

TRAFFIC

Transcendental philosophies or religions seek to go beyond or to transcend ordinary human experience. They seek to discover in the mind experiences and ecstasies that are not based on ordinary experience but on an innate communion with the supernatural. The purpose of training in meditation or in yoga is to free the mind from the intrusions of the world so that it can contemplate these higher things. The process tends to be one of discovery and release. There is the urge to discover experience beyond that of ordinary life. There is an urge to release the human spirit from the humdrum demands of daily life.

Transcendental beauty is beauty that surpasses ordinary experience. A transcendental truth is one that surpasses ordinary logic and expression and is likely to be unintelligible if expressed in the language of ordinary experience. This does, unfortunately, leave the way open for gibberish which is equally unintelligible but not necessarily transcendental.

It is possible to have experiences that are out of this world – through meditation, training, drugs or starvation. What is not certain is whether these are discoveries or creations. If you are unaware that you are looking through a piece of distorting glass you will see strange shapes that are not comparable to anything in your experience. To that extent they are transcendental. You may be inclined to regard these shapes as particularly beautiful or as ugly, but whatever their nature they are likely to be powerful. Anything which is real but unfamiliar tends to have a powerful effect. Similarly the distortion of emotion or feeling produced by drugs can seem to reveal transcendental truths.

Opposed to this interpretation is the view that the various methods are required to liberate pure feeling and pure experience from within an individual. This might be similar to what would happen if an electrode were placed in such a position in the brain as to produce a pure feeling of pleasure (this has been done already with rats). The claim, however, goes beyond this and maintains that after sufficient training the mind can perceive a higher form of being that transcends ordinary existence. This is not a creation of the conditioned mind but a perception of the de-conditioned mind which has been freed of its petty habits.

The most accurate measurement of blood pressure is made by inserting a needle into an artery in the arm. The needle is attached by a fine, liquid-filled tube to a transducer. The transducer is a device for changing the pressure of the blood into an electrical current. The electrical current can then be made to drive a pen across a recording roll and so give the pressure produced by each heartbeat.

A transducer is a device that changes something which cannot be observed into something which can. All scientific instruments are transducers. A compass is a transducer which changes the magnetic attraction of the North Pole into the visible deflection of a needle. An ordinary mouth thermometer is a transducer that changes the body temperature into the length of a column of mercury against a scale. A barometer is a device that changes an imperceptible fall in air pressure into the swing of a needle on a dial. A speedometer in a car is a transducer that changes the speed of the wheels into a movement on a dial.

A translator is a transducer. When a communication gap exists because the listener cannot understand the language of the talker, the translator changes the spoken language into the understood language. With a good translator the meaning of what is translated is not altered. A transducer acts in exactly the same way. Communication is effected between one thing and another by means of the translation carried out by the transducer.

In science we have a variety of transducers that make it possible for us to follow the track of an atomic particle (in a Wilson cloud chamber or on a photographic plate); listen to the radio transmissions from stars thousands of light years away; measure the amounts of different salts in the blood and compare the take-off noises of one aeroplane and another. Unfortunately the methods of science are not yet available for us to compare emotion and mood and pleasure and pain. Governments are asked to act upon the most inadequate information regarding the feelings of the people. Writers and journalists and pollsters are the only available transducers.

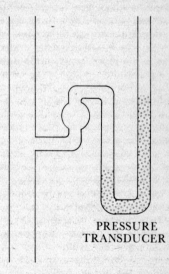

PRESSURE
TRANSDUCER

When something turns into something else there is a brief transition stage. The transition stage between schoolboy and working adult may last weeks or months. The transition stage between a caterpillar and a butterfly may be a chrysalis.

One of the great strengths of Communism as an ideology arises from the emphasis which Karl Marx put on the transition stage between capitalism and Communism. This transition stage was to be a stage of struggle and it is this concern with struggle that has given a sense of purpose and mission to the movement. Instead of concentrating on the utopia that was to be provided by the Communist world, Marx focused clearly on this all-important transition stage.

The problem with learning a foreign language lies in the transition stage when the new language is not yet adequate to express one's needs and so there is a retreat to the native language. Once the transition stage is passed and basic needs can be conveyed in the new language then there is no longer any need to use the native language and practice rapidly improves the new one.

Changing over from one type of medical treatment to another can be tricky because there may be an interaction between the two drugs and yet the patient must be covered in the transition stage.

Fear of change is most often fear of the transition stage rather than fear of the end result. A proposal to ban cars from cities in favour of improved public transport would be unpopular with car owners who fear the transition stage in which they would lose the convenience of their own car and not immediately gain the benefit of better public transport. Many couples would like to get divorced but fear the transition stage.

The transition stage from a dictatorship to a democracy is always a difficult one since opportunists see this as an occasion to assume power and it takes time for democratic parties to become established. In evolution the transition from the original species to a new one may involve several short-lived stages.

A water-polo player treads water while he waits for the ball to be thrown. He has to tread water in order to stay afloat but there is no definite direction yet for him to swim in. He waits for the game to develop and a direction to emerge.

Inactivity or a pause in activity is different from treading water. In treading water there is a great deal of activity going on, but it is not aimed in a particular direction. The activity may be needed for the organisation to survive and keep going. Alternatively there may be a great flurry of activity which is intended to show observers that much energy is being expended but at the same time this energy is not being directed towards any aim.

In treading water the lack of direction, purpose or aim is deliberate. There is an 'active waiting'. This may be because doing nothing is the best course of action under the circumstances. For example if there is a flurry on the currency markets there may be pressure for the government to do something. And yet it may be best to do nothing and allow the market to sort itself out. At the same time there may have to be an appearance of activity in order to avoid the accusation of passivity or feebleness. At other times the intension is to keep the system highly active but to await the development of a definite direction instead of taking any direction that may suggest itself. This is rather like having a car with the engine running: ready to move swiftly in a direction but with the direction not yet decided.

Treading water is not the same as 'churning the air'. That description arises from a mental picture of a ship high on the crest of a wave whose propeller is consequently churning round in the air and not serving to propel the vessel. So 'churning the air' implies a great deal of activity which is not serving to achieve any purpose. With treading water the lack of direction is a matter of deliberate waiting rather than of ineffective activity.

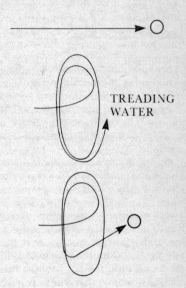

TREADING WATER

There is a trend towards shorter hair. There is a trend towards more compact cars. There is a trend towards students taking more vocational degrees. There is a trend away from violence in the cinema.

If something is noticeable and someone believes that it is becoming more noticeable then a trend is claimed. A trend is an unformalised movement in behaviour or style. A trend may only involve a few people. A trend may occur right at the beginning of a new fashion swing. A trend is more a tendency than an outright movement.

A two per cent increase in the sales of adult games when other items experienced a two per cent fall in sales would be hailed as a trend towards 'home entertainment'. Population statistics may show a trend towards the two-child family but this may really be a trend towards smaller families.

A trend may involve a swing away from something: for example a trend against getting married at a young age. A trend may also involve a swing back to something: for example a trend towards living in city centres.

There is a considerable advantage in noticing a trend before other people do. If you notice a trend towards Victorian furniture you quickly buy up some choice pieces, either because you like them or because you want to resell at a profit. A manufacturer who notices a trend towards multi-purpose cars can get his models on the market before other people. Since cars take a few years from design to production the trend has to be spotted very early.

There are fashion-setting people who claim to create trends. In some cases this is true but in others it seems that they spot the trend before anyone

else and take it over by creating a fashion around it. It could also be that in spite of the great number of people trying to create fashions those who turn out to be riding a trend succeed.

It also happens that a 'noticed' trend accelerates into a real trend since each example is now given more significance.

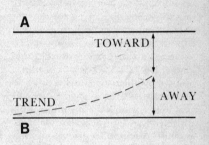

Pressure on a trigger can fire a pop gun, a shot gun or a field gun. The pressure on the trigger is not at all related to the effect of that pressure. The same trigger could be used whether a blasting charge consisted of half a pound or two tonnes of dynamite. An electrical trigger could start the turbines of a vast dam working, open a bank vault or just deliver coffee in an office vending machine.

It is characteristic of a trigger that what is set off is ready to function and explode and the trigger unlocks that happening. Just as a key can open a tool box or the door into a secret garden so the effect of a trigger is important but unrelated to the nature of the trigger. In setting traps for wild animals considerable ingenuity has to be used to obtain a trigger that can be easily set off and a trapping effect that will resist the struggles of the captured animal. With electronic amplification a slight pressure on a button can be arranged to trigger off anything from a space rocket to a world war. In a rifle or shot gun there is really a double triggering effect for the trigger releases a pin that hits and explodes the percussion cap at the end of the cartridge and it is the explosion of this that sets off the main propelling charge in the cartridge.

In a gun there is a trigger, a charge, a bullet, an aim and the gun itself. Nothing happens unless the trigger is pulled and what happens takes place immediately after this. Pulling the trigger is quite ineffective unless there is a charge in the gun. The charge itself is ineffective unless the energy of the explosion can be converted by the bullet itself into a destructive device. The gun provides the structure for all

this. Finally the effect has to be aimed at something.

It is said that the First World War was triggered off by the murder of an Austrian archduke in Sarajevo. This seems to have been the case but the situation was one in which the build-up of tensions on both sides was likely to result in a war at some time or other. Quite often patients attribute the onset of arthritis or cancer to some blow they have received. It seems obvious to them that there must have been a cause or triggering factor and so they choose any incident that seems to fit. There is a difference between a situation where any trigger will set things off and one which requires a specific trigger.

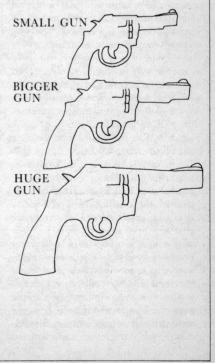

SMALL GUN

BIGGER GUN

HUGE GUN

A shop in New York is selling clothes. The shop always seems to be full of people buying things, perhaps because the prices are somewhat lower than at any other shop. The accounts show that hundreds of thousands of dollars worth of goods are passing through the shop. Then suddenly the shop goes bankrupt. This seems astonishing because the turnover has been so high. But even though the turnover has been so high the profit margins have been insufficient to keep the shop going. The high turnover was achieved by low pricing and heavy advertising and both of these were made at the expense of profits.

A nearby antiques shop is always empty and seems to have the same piece of furniture in its window for months on end. But the shop keeps going. The turnover is very low but the profit on each item sold is huge because of the rarity value of the pieces.

Imagine you are holding a basket and one person is putting goods into the basket but another person is taking them out. If both people are working very fast the actual volume of goods that have gone through the basket – the turnover – may be very high, but this may not be of much benefit to you. But if you get a commission on everything that passes through the basket you would be better off with the high turnover. If, however, the commission you get is inversely related to the turnover then there is a certain point above which an increase in turnover will not be worthwhile. For instance if added turnover in a shop means you have to take on another assistant then the cost of her wages may mean a smaller profit on a higher turnover.

At a school in a depressed part of a town the turnover of schoolteachers runs at about forty-five per cent a year. This is because no one really wants the job and only takes it after having failed to get a job elsewhere. As soon as a job turns up elsewhere the teacher leaves. The similar situation occurs in advertising agencies – though for opposite reasons – where the turnover in copy-writers may approach fifty per cent in their first year. A copy-writer who has been full of promise turns out to be no good and has to be replaced by another one full of promise.

Turnover is like the flow of water through a pipe. What does in comes out, no matter what the speed of flow might be.

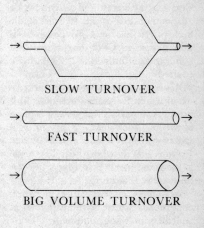

SLOW TURNOVER

FAST TURNOVER

BIG VOLUME TURNOVER

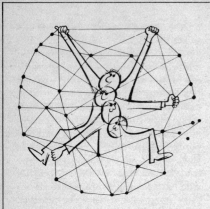

universe changes and the balls roll off. The background conditions have changed. When you are playing tennis you play the rules of tennis and not the rules of volley-ball.

It is only when we do not realise that the universe is different that we wonder why actions which used to be successful are no longer so. When the universe changes the rules of the game have changed too.

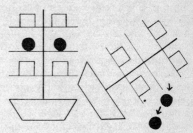

Jesus Christ spent a lot of time talking about the 'kingdom of God' which was going to be so different from the society his listeners knew. This 'kingdom of God' was a different universe in which all people were equal. Instead of the high priests having a privileged position nearer to God the proud were going to be humbled and the humble exalted.

A deep-sea diver lets go a piece of wood which floats upwards out of his grasp. A man on shore lets go a piece of wood which falls on his toes. A spaceman lets go a piece of wood which remains exactly where it is. The wood is the same in all three cases but the universe is different.

A universe is the situation, rules, conditions, world, circumstances in which something happens. These background rules affect whatever happens in the universe. The universe of a small village is different from the universe of a large city. A world without gravity would be different from the world we know.

The diagram shows a shelf-like structure which holds both balls and cubes. When the structure is tilted the

Uptight is the opposite of 'hanging loose'. Uptight is the opposite of a 'shrug'. Uptight is tenseness and over-reaction and anxiety and clenched fists. Uptight is not anger or rage or dynamism. Nor is it sensitivity in the true sense of the word. It is an over-reaction to some situation: a neurotic reaction of fear and tension. One person may be uptight about women's lib. Another person may be uptight about ecology or pollution or life in New York. It is easy to be uptight about a mother-in-law or a boss. The image is that of the person's mind being coiled up like a spring which is ready to fly apart at the slightest provocation.

In practical terms being uptight is a cause of stress, of anxiety and pre-sumably of all those ailments which are thought to arise from stress. An uptight person is brittle and frenzied. A person who is uptight about some-thing is unable to give the matter its proper perspective. Japanese philo-sophy is full of allusions to the sapling that is strong because it bends with the wind and when the wind is past springs upright again. This is the opposite of uptight. The uptight meta-phor would refer to a brittle pole that was set into resonance by the slightest breeze and then shook itself to pieces.

The besetting problem is always that of assessing the level of reaction a situation demands. At one end of the scale there is inertia, apathy, detach-ment and lack of interest. At the other end there is over-reaction and uptight-ness. Somewhere in between there is a reaction which is appropriate to the situation and capable of dealing with it. The expression 'cool' is supposed to describe the state of reaction that is confident but not emotional, out of control or uptight.

A person tends to be uptight about something because he is seeing a different 'something' to someone else. A visitor who sees a secretary being given a very normal order by her boss is not to know that in her mind this is yet another example of the boss's in-difference to her as a person. An up-tight person may bring to a new and innocent situation the reactions that he acquired in a totally different situa-tion in the past: for instance in a bad marriage.

A valve is a device which affects flow in one way or another. It is possible to pump up a motor car tyre because the valve allows air to enter the tyre but not to leave it. An ordinary reciprocating (as distinct from centrifugal) pump only works because it has two valves: one allows the piston to suck fluid into the cylinder of the pump and the other allows the piston to expel the fluid in the desired direction. If there were no valves the fluid would slop in and out without moving in any specific direction. The valves in a car engine allow the explosive petrol and air mixture to be sucked into the cylinder at the appropriate moment and then allow the exhaust gases to be expelled after the explosion has taken place.

A reducing valve on a cylinder of highly compressed oxygen allows the gas to reach the patient at a normal pressure. The escape valve on a steam boilder allows the steam to escape if the pressure reaches a dangerous level.

A valve is a device which interferes with flow according to pre-set instructions. These instructions may be concerned with the direction of flow, the pressure, the velocity, the volume or any other aspect. Such instructions could be given by an outside instructor at every moment or they could be given by a feedback system. Instead they may be built into the mechanical structure of the valve just as the valve tube of thin rubber acts in a bicycle tyre to allow air to move in one direction only.

Many of the economic troubles of society are possibly due to a failure to build in suitable valve mechanisms. For example if it becomes fashionable to invest in property then property prices rise and it makes good sense to invest in property. Industrial investment is neglected meanwhile. Finally the property boom reaches its peak and starts to collapse. Because of the insistence on a free market economy there are no inbuilt valves to reduce an excess flow on funds in any one direction. Valves are not the same as feedback systems (checks and balances) and are not likely to cause the violent upswings and downswings associated with any system that has a positive feedback element. Planning is a type of valve except that its results are unpredictable.

A fat lady is depressed so she eats more. This makes her fatter and she gets more depressed. So she eats more.

The Post Office increases the charges for the mail service. Because of the increased charges fewer people send letters so the revenue actually falls. This means a further increase in charges. Even fewer people use the service.

The local authority build a brand new road into town. Because the road is so good many more people start to drive into town so they have to widen the road. This encourages more people to use the roads.

To quieten fears about the strength of a particular currency the government of that country announce cuts in government spending. Speculators interpret this as a sign of serious trouble and increase their depreciation of the currency.

All these are examples of positive feedback situations in which the result of an action feeds back to make things worse. The term 'vicious circle' is used for those positive feedbacks where the trend is towards disaster. It may not be possible to avoid them by doing nothing. The more you struggle in a quicksand the more quickly will you sink. But if you do not struggle you will still sink. Similarly in the example above if the Post Office does not put up its charges it will still lose money.

There is a second type of circularity which can be just as vicious:

Groucho Marx once declared that he would not want to join a club which would have him as a member.

You cannot get an Equity card unless you have an acting job but you cannot get such a job unless you have the card.

In Joseph Heller's book *Catch 22* a fighter pilot asked to be excused from flying on grounds of insanity only to be told that to refuse to fly showed a strong streak of sanity and therefore he could not be excused from flying.

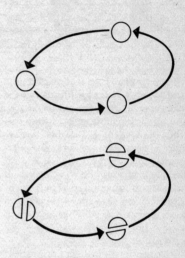

There is obstruction. There is friction. And there is viscosity. Obstruction is when some obstacle stands in the way and prevents movement. Friction is when movement is possible but requires a great deal of effort and generates a lot of heat. Viscosity is different. Treacle is viscous and so is heavy oil. Neither treacle nor oil resist movement – you can move a spoon slowly in a bowl of treacle or oil – but movement is slowed down by the viscosity of the medium.

Viscosity seems to do nothing except slow down movement. Shock-absorbers in motor cars often use movement through a viscous medium to slow down the bounce of the springs. In some organisations trying to get anything done is not unlike dancing in treacle. There is no actual opposition nor are there any real obstacles. It is just that everything needs a sustained effort. Nothing runs freely with its own momentum: the push has to be there all the time. Communication is very slow.

In a situation where viscosity can be said to be high it is almost as if the passage of time had been altered so that what had taken a short time now needs a long time. Certain communication channels are much more viscous than others. If a message has to pass through a chain of command it is likely to take much longer especially if each link has to explain the message to the next. In fact it could be said that the purpose of communication is to set up paths or channels which have a much lower viscosity than the surrounding medium.

Viscosity arises in fluids from the friction between the different molecules as they pass over one another. In practical terms the difference between friction and viscosity is that friction implies a difficulty or deliberate 'roughness'. Viscosity means that everything is very slow-moving without any ill-will on anyone's part.

Viscosity does have a purpose: to damp down excessive swings and oscillations and to reduce the rate of change so that it can be coped with. Unfortunately the viscosity in most systems is not there for this specific purpose but because of the nature of the system.

In traditional warfare a general sought always to protect his flanks. He knew that if he attacked down the centre this would expose his flanks and make him vulnerable. A boxer knows that he is most vulnerable when he abandons defence in order to hit his opponent. Both generals and boxers spend a lot of time circling around each other trying to find the vulnerable spots.

In the event of a war a country may find itself vulnerable as regards its energy supplies. Many officials have proved vulnerable to blackmail because of their private lives. A person who gets himself into debt is vulnerable to temptations to sell secrets for money and turn himself into a spy. A public figure is vulnerable to a smear campaign that sets out with innuendo and allegation to suggest something which is reinforcing the more it is denied.

A hedgehog rolled up into a prickly ball is not vulnerable. A tortoise withdrawn into its shell is not vulnerable. A government department withdrawn into its shell of inactivity is not vulnerable. But as soon as the hedge-hog or the tortoise or the government department wants to move it becomes more vulnerable. The only way to be truly invulnerable is to be unnoticed and invisible. The next best way is to be defensive the whole time and never to take risks. The third way is to be all-powerful but this way is the most dangerous because power itself can make a person vulnerable. The art of judo and ju-jitsu is to use a person's power and aggression against himself.

A vulnerable point is not necessarily the same as a weak point. A system may have a weak point that is not functioning very well: it is weak in the sense of not making its proper contribution to the system. A vulnerable point is a point where the system can be attacked and destroyed.

It has been suggested by a politician in Denmark that money spent on defence and the armed services could be better spent on social services. All that would be required for defence would be a tape-recorder broadcasting in Russian: 'We surrender, we surrender.'

One of the greatest intellectual feats in man's history was performed by a Scotsman, James Clerk Maxwell. Using his brain and without help from experimental evidence he showed that light, heat and magnetism were all due to electromagnetic waves which simply differed in wavelength. He even predicted radio waves and X-ray waves, neither of which had then been discovered. All these radiations which seemed so different were really based on the same wave energy: all that differed was the wavelength.

Even within radio waves themselves there are different wavelengths just as there are within light waves. The colours of the spectrum arise from differences in wavelength between the different colours. Finding a particular radio station depends on tuning the receiver to pick up the wavelength that is emitted from that station. When the station has been found the receiver is 'in tune' with the station.

This general idea of tuning and wavelength has come to apply to communication systems that do not actually depend on electromagnetic waves. You may know a person very well and may hear the words that he is saying to you but it is clear to you that he is not on the same 'wavelength'. The channel of communication is open and messages are being sent out but nevertheless little real communication is taking place. This idea of being unable to tune into a communication is a useful one because we tend to feel that if a communication channel is set up then communication must flow along it. When one person is on a different wavelength the words, concepts, values, emotions, experiences, sensitivity all seem to be different and yet taken separately each is understandable. The opposite to being on a different wavelength is to be so finely tuned to another person that you can tell what he feels or is going to say even before he says it.

A radio receiver is tuned by adjusting its structure so that it resonates to the incoming signal. The wavelength concept is one of resonance: the nature of the receiver must be such that it resonates with the sender. With people this is a matter of personality rather than the clarity of the communication. Powerful public speakers are able to hit the right wavelength and so set up a resonance with their audiences.

We talk of a strong-willed person as someone who is determined and who knows how to get what he wants. A strong-willed woman is usually associated, in literature, with a weak hen-pecked husband. In practice having a strong will usually goes with rigidity, ruthlessness, callousness and lack of sensitivity. A strong-willed person shapes circumstances to his intentions whereas a weaker willed person shapes his intentions to the circumstances. It must be clear that a change in circumstances will have no effect on the intentions of the strong-willed person but may completely alter the intentions of the weaker willed one. The performance of a strong-willed person is likely to have peaks and troughs. Whatever he does will be effective: the successes will be effective and so will the mistakes. The weak-willed person follows a path of evolution being as much shaped by circumstances as trying to shape them. The real disadvantage of the weak-willed person is that fear and timidity can obstruct what would otherwise be a sensible course of action.

The strong-willed people who are successful are noted for their success which is attributed to their strong wills. The equally strong-willed people who are failures are ignored and regarded as stubborn. As a result of this selective attention we come to give too high a credit to 'strong wills'.

Philosophers have much favoured the concept of will because it has seemed the essence of a human being. When everything else is in order (motivation, circumstance, ability) then it must seem that the final cause of action is the will. It is somewhat like a model electric train being arranged on the track. Everything is in order but motionless until the switch is operated, whereupon the train bursts into action. The will is likened to this switch. A clear distinction exists between wish and will. A wish implies a desire that something 'should happen' but a will implies an intention to 'make it happen'. Lying in a comfortable hot bath one may wish to get out and go to bed but the actual 'effort of will' seems unusually difficult.

Existentialist philosophers feel that man is only human at the moment he uses his will to rebel against the flow of circumstances which engulf, include and carry him along as part of the environment.

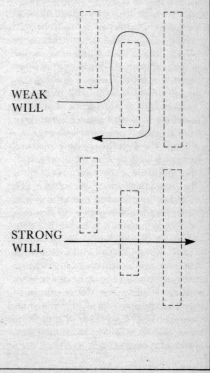

WEAK WILL

STRONG WILL

When you are launching a space rocket which is going to land men on the moon you cannot shoot it off at any time you choose. There is a relatively short time when the moon is in the right position. You have to wait for this time and if you miss the opportunity you have to wait until another opportunity comes round. A physical window is a gap in a wall through which you can look out in order to see something. If the window is in the wrong place you will not be able to see what you want. Imagine you are trying to shoot an arrow at a tree in the garden. The wall in front of you is a movable wall with a small window in it. You have to wait until you can see the tree through the window and then you shoot off the arrow. If you miss the opportunity you have to wait until the window comes by again. The 'window' exists when everything is in order for the action you want to take.

Toy manufacturers know that they have to have their new products ready for the series of toy fairs in January and February. This is when buyers from the big stores place their orders. If they miss this opportunity they have to wait a whole year and miss the Christmas trade of that year. The launch window for a new toy product is quite small.

The time gap between Europe and the United States is five to six hours. Since people on each side of the Atlantic work roughly the same office hours the communication window might be quite small. When an American financier gets to his office it is already two o'clock in the afternoon in Europe. If the European leaves his office at five o'clock there is only a three-hour communication window.

Governments are often conscious that a decision may only be possible at a certain stage in the economic cycle. There is a window. If the same decision is made earlier it will be ineffective. If it is made later it may be dangerous. For the same reason there are investment windows when the conditions are right. A window is an opportunity when the conditions are suitable for the intended action. This opportunity lasts for only a limited time.

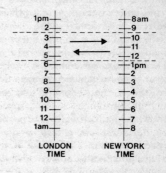

A child of three learns how to push a button and switch on the television. Her mother knows which button to push to start the washing machine. Her father knows which buttons to push to drive off to work in the morning. None of them may know much about what happens inside the television set, the washing machine and the car. None of them know anything about the 'wiring' of the system.

A sophisticated computer programmer works out an elegant system for handling insurance premiums. But if something goes wrong with the computer he has to call in the engineer who knows all about the wiring.

The wiring is what actually makes something work. It matters where the wires go and what they do. Wires are communication channels which carry messages and effects. All systems are assemblies of such communication channels. The overall effect can, however, be appreciated and used without any understanding of the wiring. Very few car drivers have any idea of how an internal combustion engine works. Very few telephone users understand the wiring of the telephone system.

So long as a system is functioning well it is not necessary to know the wiring. But when it breaks down then the user is helpless unless he can get hold of someone who does understand the wiring. Even so this wiring expert may not need to know everything about the wiring. Nowadays he is more likely to try plugging in one new part after another rather than trace and put right the fault. Eventually this will mean that the only person who needs to know the wiring is the person who designed the system in the first place.

Of course when a person wants to make a system work for his own purposes he may have to find out about the 'wiring'. A lobbyist in Washington may spend a great deal of time finding out about the wiring: the communication channels, the people who matter, the amplification points, the breakdown points, the effector points, the power source and so on.

WORDLIST